ADOBE®
PHOTOSHOP® CS2

THE
ART OF
PHOTOGRAPHING
WOMEN

KEVIN AMES

WILEY

Wiley Publishing, Inc.

Photoshop® CS2: The Art of Photographing Women

Published by
Wiley Publishing, Inc.
111 River Street
Hoboken, NJ 07030-5774
www.wiley.com

ISBN-10: 0-470-04825-5
ISBN-13: 978-0-470-04825-2

Manufactured in the United States of America

10 9 8 7 6 5 4 3 2 1

1K/SR/QY/QW/IN

Published by Wiley Publishing, Inc., Indianapolis, Indiana

Published simultaneously in Canada

For general information on our other products and services or to obtain technical support, please contact our Customer Care Department within the U.S. at (800) 762-2974, outside the U.S. at (317) 572-3993 or fax (317) 572-4002.

Wiley also publishes its books in a variety of electronic formats. Some content that appears in print may not be available in electronic books.

Library of Congress Control Number: 2006925891

Credits

Acquisitions Editor
Tom Heine

Project Editor
Katharine Dvorak

Technical Editor
Joan Sherwood

Copy Editor
Paula Lowell

Editorial Manager
Robyn B. Siesky

Business Manager
Amy Knies

Vice President & Executive Group Publisher
Richard Swadley

Vice President and Publisher
Barry Pruett

Project Coordinator
Adrienne Martinez

Graphics and Production Specialists
Jennifer Mayberry
LeAndra Hosier
Lynsey Osborn

Quality Control Technicians
John Greenough
Christine Pingleton
Charles Spencer

Book Designer
Daniela Richardson and
Marie Kristine Parial-Leonardo

Proofreader
Laura L. Bowman

Indexer
Steve Rath

Cover Image
© 2006 Kevin Ames

Cover Designer
Douglas Broward

Foreword

Back in 1984, Aldus PageMaker (the first postscript page-layout application) was introduced and, although it did a lot to astound people, it also did a lot to anger people. Well, one group in particular—typographers (people who set type for a living). They mocked PageMaker. They laughed at it. Most totally dismissed it and continued to do so until PageMaker, and another page-layout application, QuarkXPress, put them right out of a job. Getting these people to change—to give up the way they had been setting type for years (which was tedious, inefficient, and costly)—and join the desktop publishing revolution wasn't easy. Even though it could be proven that desktop publishing was faster, easier, and a whole lot more fun, getting people to give up their "comfortable old way" and try a revolutionary new way was one tough battle.

Now it's 2004 and we're right smack dab in the middle of another technological revolution—the digital photography revolution. Even if you're not yet shooting with a digital camera, you're working with Adobe Photoshop, a digital darkroom that does for photography what PageMaker did for page layout—it makes the process faster, easier, and a whole lot more fun. When Photoshop was first introduced, photographers mocked it. They laughed at it. Most totally dismissed it. But they don't any more.

Today you can watch similar battles brewing between photographers shooting traditional film and photographers who now strictly shoot digitally. Stop by your local camera store and it'll take you all of about 30 seconds to get into a "film is better/digital is better" debate. Even though the revolution is well underway, not everybody has come aboard. For example, Photoshop is more than 12 years old, yet you'll still find a few photographers with traditional darkrooms. Digital photography isn't quite that old yet, and you'll find photographers, even some professionals, still shooting with traditional film. But every day, more and more of these film photographers are going digital, and they aren't looking back. It's a one-way trip. Just like using Photoshop. Once you start really using it, it's hard to go back to mixing chemicals in the dark.

This digital photography revolution didn't happen overnight. The Photoshop revolution took 12 years and counting. And the digital photography revolution that asks professional photographers to give up their darkroom for Photoshop, and their Nikon F-5 for a Nikon D1x digital SLR, has been one tough battle.

That's why revolutions need strong leaders. Evangelists. Trainers. Educators. People who care so passionately about what they've found, and how it's changed their lives for the better, that they're driven with a burning desire to share those ideas with others. And that's why you and I are so lucky. We both found Kevin Ames, the author of the book you're holding in your hands right now.

Kevin is a digital revolutionary in every sense of the word. He's an artist, educator, a craftsman, a passionate evangelist and most important—a leader. He's exactly the person you want to be learning Photoshop techniques from. I should know. I'm one of his students. And every time I hear him speak, read his articles, or spend time with him one-on-one, I learn something new, despite the fact that I'm fairly handy with Photoshop and not a total hack of a photographer.

I was first introduced to Kevin through a mutual friend, digital photography guru Jim DiVitale. As conference technical chair for the PhotoshopWorld Conference and Expo, I was putting together an after-hours session called "The Creative Side of Digital Photography," and I had asked Jim to moderate the session. Jim told me "You've got to get Kevin Ames on this panel. This guy is doing cutting-edge stuff, he's a great public speaker, and a hell of a photographer." Jim is one of the most respected names in digital imaging and photography, and if Jim says you're good—you're good. So I contacted Kevin, he agreed to be on the panel, and as you might expect, he was a huge hit. So the next year, I asked Kevin to not only be a part of the late night session, but to do a regular conference session. He rocked the house. Now Kevin is a fixture at PhotoshopWorld, doing live fashion shoots, panels, retouching sessions, and basically doing what he does best—educating and evangelizing. Kevin gets you excited about Photoshop. Excited about digital photography. Excited about what the two can do together, and he always gives you a look into what's coming down the road. He knows, because he's out there blazing the trail.

I've been encouraging Kevin to do a book for some time for two reasons: First, Kevin is doing things with digital photography and Photoshop that no one else out there is doing; and second, he's a gifted trainer who's willing to share everything. If he knows it—he shares it. He doesn't hold anything back.

That's why I'm so excited about *Photoshop CS2: The Art of Photographing Women*. Very few books have the power to change the way you work, impact your career, and suddenly change everything. This is one of those books. It opens doors. It challenges old ideas and introduces new ones. And perhaps best of all it introduces you to a truly talented, gifted, and giving educator who really just wants one thing. To show you the way and share with you how it's done.

You're going to love learning from Kevin. Welcome to the club.

Scott Kelby
Editor, *Photoshop User* magazine
President, National Association of Photoshop Professionals

Preface

Author's Note: *Photoshop CS2: The Art of Photographing Women* is a thorough update to its predecessor, *Photoshop CS: The Art of Photographing Women*. Part 1 has been rewritten to further help any photographer overcome the greatest challenge digital capture offers—that of becoming one's own photo lab. Part 2 reprises the projects in the original book with additions covering CS2's new features—Smart Objects, RAW files in layers, and the changes to the Layers palette to name a few. At first glance, the projects in Part 2 look like the originals. Take the time to work through them. You'll learn solid techniques and be well on your way to being a well-versed user of Photoshop CS2!

Photoshop CS2: The Art of Photographing Women is about passion—passion for photography and passion for photographing women. There is an art to photographing women. And the art has changed. Those changes and how to master them are what the book you hold in your hands is all about.

Digital photography has revolutionized the act of recording light with a camera. Moments after releasing the shutter, the image appears, and for now the photographer has instant feedback. A client once asked me, "When can I see the final shot?" I pointed at the monitor and replied, "Right now." Seeing the actual photograph instead of a Polaroid of what it might be on film has revolutionized photography. The instant feedback comes with a price. You, the photographer, are now the photo lab.

The first part of *Photoshop CS2: The Art of Photographing Women* is about the processes of digital photography. Chapter 1 focuses on lighting. *Photo* means light. It is the first word of both photography and Photoshop. Understanding some basics of how light works makes working postproduction in Photoshop much more rewarding.

The next four chapters are all about how to be your own lab. I give you the background on RAW and JPEG capture. I show step-by-step how to set up a workflow to archive and manage your digital negatives. I explain the distribution of photographs on the Web, by e-mail, and on traditional printed and—thanks to Photoshop and Bridge—custom contact sheets. Finally, I introduce the principles of non-destructive image editing in Photoshop that allow a file saved in layers to have literally, unlimited undos forever. By the way, the techniques in the first part work on any digital photographic subject. If you shoot buildings, products, portraits, proms, weddings, or whatever, this book is for you. Work through the projects to build your workflow using my photographs of women as a metaphor. Then substitute the images produced by your passion. It's an easy-on-the-eye way to learn to be your own lab.

Adobe Photoshop CS2 is as integral to modern photography as the darkroom was at the turn of the last century. Back then a photographer had to develop film or glass plates and make a print to view the work. Now photographers must have a working, although not necessarily an in-depth, knowledge of Photoshop. The days of handing film to a client and getting paid are just about gone. Clients want digital files for their brochures, advertisements, catalogs, and Web sites. Clients often don't (and some will not) deal with multiple vendors to prepare files for output. They look to the photographer for these services. This makes the photographer who embraces the promise of digital post production more valuable to clients than in the days of film.

Photography is now very similar to making a movie. As in movie production, there is shooting and postproduction work. I approach postproduction as part of the planning of a photograph. Every shot begins with the questions, "What is best done in the camera?" and "How will Photoshop improve the resulting photography?" It is not ever about "fixing things in Photoshop." I share my thinking in realizing each process so you will understand how to find that point of diminishing returns where making it prefect in the camera (if possible) is the most effective method.

The second part of this book is all about photographing women and the work in Photoshop CS2 that makes the finished photographs of them beautiful. Here, too, I take a step-by-step approach to each project. My goal for this book is to help you understand how similar techniques are applied to achieve results in differing situations. The old saying, "Give a man a fish and he'll eat for a day, teach him to fish and he'll eat for a lifetime," seems the best way to describe how I wrote this book. It is not a tips and tricks book. Now don't get me wrong, I love tips and tricks. They are fun, interesting, and often contain gems that are cool and very useful. This book is project- and process-oriented. Each project builds skills for the ones that follow.

By the time you have worked through all of the exercises you will have a working knowledge of Photoshop CS2, how camera work relates to postproduction, and how to do it for yourself. More important, you will understand the reasoning behind the postproduction from the photographer's point of view. In my mind, the greatest gift of digital capture is that it got photographers talking to each other. In the "good old days" of shooting film, photographers kept secrets, terrified that if they spoke to one another they would lose what made them unique and lose clients as well. Now we realize that there is such an abundance of possibilities that even when I tell you exactly what I did and lay it out step-by-step as I do in this book, you and I have different visions. Your results will be uniquely yours. How cool is that? I am so glad to live in a time that film is now what you find on your teeth in the morning before brushing.

I shot every photograph in this book. Okay, I didn't shoot the photo of me in the pool (Chapter 14) or my portrait by my good friend and amazing digital photographer, Jim DiVitale. This is important because I can share what I was thinking at the time of the shoot and the decisions that I made either on set or location and how I planned to finish the images in the editing suite. Then I take you through the steps of post-producing the photographs in Photoshop CS2.

I am hopeful that after you've read and worked through the projects in this book you'll come away with a feel for how photography and Photoshop are intertwined. And that you'll develop a strong understanding of how to use Photoshop on your own photographs and know when to move from behind the camera to in front of the computer. Remember, great Photoshop begins with great photography.

Kevin Ames
Atlanta, Georgia

Acknowledgments

These are all of the wonderful and amazing friends, teachers, writers, and photographers who have made a contribution either directly or otherwise to the writing of *Photoshop CS2: The Art of Photographing Women*. What you are about to read is my list of credits that roll at the end of a movie that so few in the audience stay to watch. Please don't leave this theater early; take a couple of minutes to acknowledge them with me.

For support and understanding above and beyond the call, I extend my heartfelt thanks and love to Starr Moore. I truly could not have written this book without you.

To David Chapman, manager of Professional Photo Resources in Atlanta, who has counseled me and countless others about digital cameras, lenses, equipment, and life, and who kept those early Macs running with selfless caring and love, thank you.

Thanks and love to Jim DiVitale, my brother in digital photography, teaching, concerts, long walks in Dublin, Ireland, and in Piedmont Park discussing everything and solving some of it. The way of the fast retreat and much artistic inspiration are his.

Special appreciation of the heartfelt kind to Linda Adams, stylist and art director extraordinaire; to Lois Thigpen, Kitty Bundy, Victoria Duruh, and Rodney Harris of Elite Models/Atlanta for booking so many fabulous models; and to Justin Larose, the best digital and photographic assistant any photographer could dream of working with.

Thank you, thank you, thank you to my editor from Wiley, Katharine Dvorak, for encouragement, advice, good grammar, and humor; and to my technical editor, Joan Sherwood, who's secret identity is that of technology editor for *Professional Photographer* magazine. To Barry Pruett, my publisher, and Tom Heine, my acquisitions editor, for the courage to go to bat for the important things.

For the art directing and designing the front and back cover of this book, my heartfelt thanks to Douglas Broward, creative director extraordinaire at Grizzard Performance Group.

Deep and everlasting gratitude goes to my friend from way before computers, Eddie Tapp, who was my first Photoshop guru and studio mate in the early years of this digital craziness.

Thanks and kudos, too, go to everyone affiliated with Photoshop World and *Photoshop User* magazine. Especially to Scott Kelby, president of NAPP, Editor in Chief of *Photoshop User*, and all around good guy and friend. I offer heartfelt thanks and admiration to Jim Workman, Dave Moser, Jeff Kelby, Felix Nelson, Dave Cross, Kathy Siler, Chris Main, Larry Becker, Julie Stephenson, Barbie Taylor and my editors at *Photoshop User*,

Barbara Thompson, Michael Mackenzie, and all of the wonderful folks at KW Computer Training. The members of the Photoshop World Dream Team, who have shared tips, ideas, encouragement, and insight into the book-writing process, also deserve high praise and commendation, especially Ben Willmore, Burt Monroy, Julianne Kost, Jack Davis, Peter Bauer, Russell Brown, Joe Glyda, Taz Talley, Deke McClelland, Daniel Brown, Terry White, and Vincent Versace, and to those who have contributed graciously to my knowledge, which I humbly offer here.

For always asking, "How's your book coming along?" and not to mention great meals, thanks to all at Everybody's Pizza in Virginia Highlands and Java Jive on Ponce de Leon Avenue in Atlanta. Aurora Coffee is my official purveyor of extraordinary coffee to start the day and add that extra kick to afternoons.

To Rob Carr, master retoucher, Katrin Eismann, Photoshop Diva, Jeff Schewe, Bruce Fraser, Andrew Rodney, and Greg Gorman for their special insights and kindnesses.

To Douglas Broward, Dave Cruickshanks, and Joe Gottlieb of Cohen, Goldstein, Port & Gottlieb.

To my dear friend and fabulous fashion photographer, Lisa Sciascia, for sharing her ideas and the passionate discussions on concepts, light, and style.

To the photographers who have left us recently including my mother Janette Guthmann Ames, Dean Collins, Richard Avedon, Helmut Newton, and Eddie Adams.

Dean Collins taught me lighting, the importance of giving back by teaching others, and gave me the opportunity to become one of Software Cinema's authors. Thanks, Dean. You are missed by so many.

Thanks to Gary Burns, Linda Collins, Chris Lang, and David Burns of Software Cinema, Scott Shepard host of Inside Mac Radio, Kevin Gilbert, Reed Hoffman, Alan Comport, Sara Morrel, and Michelle Ruegg of Blue Pixel for furthering education in photography.

Last and certainly not least, thanks to you for spending your time to read the credits. I truly appreciate you. It is my sincere hope you'll have a lot of fun working through *Photoshop CS2: The Art of Photographing Women* and that it will help you get the ideas that may have been stuck in your head on to a photographic print.

About the Author

Kevin Ames began his photographic career at the age of 12, when he sold pictures of a class field trip to his schoolmates for a tidy profit. From this entrepreneurial and creative beginning, Kevin has become a recognized leader in the fast-evolving world of commercial digital photography. His full-time job and joy is Ames Photographic Illustration, Inc., where he provides commercial photography, retouching, and still post-production services to corporate and advertising clients. His passion is light and recording it to share with others. "I've always wanted to be a photographer," Kevin will tell you. "Everyday I'm making photographs is a perfect day. Being able to see it right now and tweak it later is the icing on a pretty amazing cake!"

Photograph copyright © 2004
by Jim DiVitale.

Kevin is much in demand as a workshop leader and speaker teaching both demonstration and hands-on classes. He is a Photoshop World Dream Team instructor and presents Blue Pixel's The Pro Digital Workflow with Kevin Ames tour. He has written three books on digital photography, including *Digital SLR Photography with Photoshop CS2 For Dummies*. His fourth book, *The Digital Photographers' Notebook*, will be published in 2006. He is also a Software Cinema author and presenter. He has taught classes at art schools and conferences around the world, including Fotographia Orvieto in Orvieto, Italy; Arthouse in Dublin, Ireland; Professional Photographers of Canada National Convention; and at the Commercial and Industrial Photographers of New England conference in Boston as well as at the Palm Beach Photographic Center, the Digital Technology Center, FotoFusion, and Photo Plus East in New York.

"I want to share the new way of thinking that digital photography offers," Kevin says. "When I'm helping people learn the possibilities of digital, my main concern is to show the problem-solving abilities that are the underlying power of the tips and tricks. I want to help others learn how to apply techniques creatively to get the visions in their heads out on a print for others to see."

Kevin also writes the "Digital Photographer's Notebook" column for *Photoshop User* magazine. His articles and reviews have appeared in *Studio Photography & Design*, *Photo>Electronic Imaging*, and *Digital Output* magazines. He is the digital photography correspondent for Inside Mac Radio.

His credentials include being a Certified Professional Photographer, Certified Electronic Imager, Photographic Craftsman, and an Approved Photographic Instructor. He has served as Co-Chairman of the Digital Imaging and Advanced Imaging Technology Committee and as Chairman of the Commercial Advertising Group for the Professional Photographers of America. He is a member of PPA, ASMP, and CPI.

Kevin can be reached at kevin@amesphoto.com.

Contents

For Little Bear, again

part 1

Workflow: From Capture to Digital Postproduction

Chapter One

Illuminating Light: How Light Works in Photography

After changes upon changes we are more or less the same.
Lyric from "the Boxer" by Simon & Garfunkel

Once upon a time, photographers concentrated on which lens offered the most lines of resolution and the best contrast. They debated which film had the tightest grain with the highest speed. There were discussions of the developer that produced the greatest number of zones and the paper/chemistry combination that reproduced the most tones. Which format was superior? Was it 8 x 10, 5 x 7, or 4 x 5? When portability was the issue, did you pack the medium format or the 35mm? What camera system had the best optics? Which one was the most durable? Whose shutter was more accurate? And what about films?

Fujichrome, Kodachrome, Ektachrome, Vericolor, Fujicolor, Agfa, GAF, Ilford, Fuji, Kodak, 3M, Konica . . . (the list goes on and on) were all hot topics of conversation on Saturday mornings at the local professional camera store.

A very short time ago (or a long time ago in computer years) the digital imaging thunderstorm burst through; lightning flashed and rained down upon photographers. Some of us got wet. Some saw the light, and the topics shifted. Tips and techniques for using Adobe Photoshop were shared. New acronyms and terminology popped into the language of photography—RAM, ROM, CCD, LCD, RGB, HSB, LAB, DPI, PPI, PSD, JPG, CMOS, Macs, PCs, megapixels, megabytes, gigabytes, dye-sub printers, ink sets, inkjet printers, substrates . . . (as you can imagine or have already experienced, this list, too, goes on and on)—and became subjects for heated debates in coffee houses and Internet chat rooms around the world. Everyone was now so concerned with recording and reproducing light that lighting itself had been left in the dark.

Light, Writing, Vision

The word photography means *light writing*. That makes *light* literally the first word in photography. It is also the first word in Photoshop. Doesn't it seem slightly odd that most photographers concentrate on the *writing* part and pay little, if any, attention at all to the light? It's important for a book on photography (Photoshop and postproduction aside) to pay the appropriate homage to photography's first word and in the process shed some light on *light*.

Okay, I know you are thinking, "I already know all of this stuff." That's fine. Let me ask you one question and if you get it right, you can skip this chapter.

"Do you feel lucky?"

Oops. Wrong movie.

The question is, "As you get closer to a light, does it become harsher or softer?"

Figure 1.1 is a close-up of Laura without any makeup (1.1). The "Sunny" image is lit with harsh light as indicated by the very sharp-edged cast by her nose. Skin texture is revealed. Note the two beauty marks above her left eyebrow, the pores, and the very fine hairs on her forehead. Also notice the specular high-lights (mirror images of the light source) on the left side, tip, and bridge of her nose caused by naturally occurring skin oils. Compare these light quality clues with the "Overcast" photograph. The only difference is the light source has

Desperately Seeking Soft Light

been diffused (spread out into two dimensions) so that it is huge when compared to the size of the sub-ject. The soft light quality minimizes the skin textures and oils by spreading out the shadow edge. Soft light makes textures almost disappear. Add makeup, and the retouching becomes a whole lot easier.

Sunny Overcast

1.1

No, I'm not going to tell you now. If you're curious, read on. . . .

Defined by the *Merriam-Webster Unabridged Dictionary,* light is *something that makes vision possible.* How cool is that? Light makes vision *and photography* possible. Let's explore those possibilities. This chapter begins by looking at some of the properties of light and how to use them. Then it moves into how to measure light in a way that can be used to accurately render a subject digi-tally. (Deep-Dark-Never-Before-Revealed-Secret—this stuff works great with film, too, even though film is now officially an alternative process.)

> **Note**
> *Soft* light makes skin creamy, eyes liquid, and fabrics flowing. Women *love* soft light.

Understanding Quality Versus Quantity

First, let's talk quality. One of the most difficult concepts to understand about lighting is the difference between quantities and qualities of light. Much of this confusion comes from thinking that bright light is harsh light. Bright light isn't necessarily harsh. And yet it can be. One of the most important principles of how light behaves is that *the larger the light source is in relation to the subject, the softer the quality of light.* That means that the closer the subject gets to the light source, the softer the quality of the light on the subject. (In other words, the source of light becomes larger in relation to the size of the subject as the subject gets *closer* to the light.)

At first this concept seems to make absolutely no sense at all. The light gets harsher, not softer, we say to ourselves. ("Look at how bright the light is!") Ah-hah!

What really happens is that as the subject moves closer to the light source, the light becomes both *brighter* and softer simultaneously. The actual problem is that almost every description of the quality of light is confused with the quantity instead. The harsher/softer description is really a quantity/quality issue. As the subject moves closer to the light source, the light in fact becomes brighter (quantity), while becoming softer (quality). The key to the harsher/softer question is the edge of the shadow cast by the subject.

Here is an everyday way to think of this concept. On a bright, clear, and cloudless sunny day the light source is the sun. The sun is 864,000 miles in diameter, give or take a mile or two. It is also 8.32 light minutes away from the camera and our subject. The sun is a high-intensity light source about the size of a thumbnail held arm's length from the eye. In relationship to the subject, the sun is a very small light source indeed. It's bright, too. For example, in this figure our model, Laura, is lit by the sun (1.2). A shadow is cast on the wall behind her. Is it harsh or soft? Well of course we know it's harsh. Bright sunlight is harsh light. That is a true statement. We've heard this all of our photographic lives. So how do we know it's true? The answer lies in the distinct, hard edge that demarks the dark shadow from the rest of the wall. The sharp edge of this transition is the visual clue that the light is harsh. This demarcation is called the *shadow edge transition*. A very short transition from highlight to shadow denotes harsh light.

The cause of confusion is the word *bright*. The more accurate statement is *"On a clear day sunlight is harsh light."* Bright is a quantity term. Harsh is a quality term. During an eclipse the sunlight becomes very dim. Yet the shadows don't change. The contrast does. You find out more on contrast later in this chapter.

Continuing the example, look at Laura after clouds roll in front of the sun, making the sky overcast (1.3). Two things happen: The light source becomes larger in relationship to the subject, and the clouds diffuse (spread over a larger area) the light, so the quality of light becomes much softer. The quantity of light is reduced two ways: by the density of the cloud cover and by the spreading of light over a larger area dimensionally (the whole sky). Check it out. The shadow edge transition of the cast shadow on the wall widens over a much greater distance indicating a softer quality of light. Shadows cast on a very overcast day can be nonexistent because the light source is so incredibly large when compared to the size of the subject.

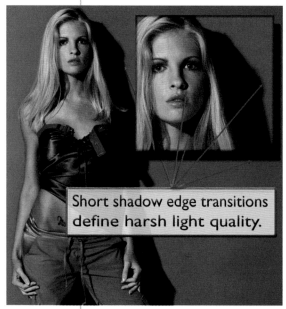

Short shadow edge transitions define harsh light quality.

1.2

Most women, even those who choose not to wear makeup on a daily basis, understand that it is a great help if not a necessity when being photographed. They welcome the makeup artist with open arms and often hugs. Men on the other hand, especially those who are not used to being photographed, might feel intimidated by the prospect of wearing it. It helps to assure them that unless they tell someone they have makeup on, no one will notice. They might hear comments of how good they look that day. And no one will ever say "(insert man's name here), I just love your makeup!"

I have found that the soft brushes used to apply a light amount of powder knock down the shine on male skin by dulling its surface efficiency (shininess caused by oily skin). There is a great added benefit. It also calms them down quite a bit. Most men have *never* had a makeup brush run over their face! After making the first series of exposures, bring your male clients to the makeup counter and powder them down. They really have no clue about how good a makeup brush feels. (If you are a male and reading this, put this book down right now and have someone—women usually have these things—run one of these brushes over your face; close your eyes first. You'll know immediately what I'm referring to. And ladies, if you haven't powdered your guy, what are you waiting for? You don't even have to add powder. Just brush lightly over his face. You know the drill!) Now you know why this is great for those uptight "real-men-don't-wear-makeup-types" before shooting, er . . . photographing them.

Make Up!

Long shadow edge transitions define soft light quality.

Note

Harsh light is ideal for revealing textures because of the sharp shadow edge transition that defines it visually. It is good for revealing weaves of fabric, strands of hair, and the makeup of a surface. Skin is a surface, too. Seeing texture in a woman's skin is not a good thing. (Texture in skin means wrinkles, lines, and pores.) Women *really* don't love harsh light.

1.3

The sun is the *origin of light* in each example. On clear days it is both the origin and the source of light. On overcast days the cloud cover becomes the source of light. The sun remains the *origin* of light. A sharp shadow edge transition defines the light quality as *harsh*. A wide shadow edge transition defines the light quality as *soft*.

Shedding Some Light on Light

Another concept that confuses what we think light is doing and what it actually is doing is *contrast*. Contrast is the difference between a highlight and a shadow measured in f/stops. Contrast is concerned with the quantities of light and its relative brightness and not its quality. High-contrast situations are often considered to have harsh light even when the shadow edge transitions are wide, indicating soft light. In order to lower the contrast of a scene, light is added to the shadows. Lowering the contrast does not change the quality (harshness/softness) of light, only the relative brightness within the image.

Compare these two images of Laura (1.4). The left image is sunlit with no fill. The right image is the same exposure with a reflector positioned to bounce some of the sunlight back into the right side of the photograph. The added light brightens the shadow (and the highlights) *lowering* the contrast of the shadow in comparison to her skin. Look at the shadow edge. It is the same in both photographs. It's still a short transition. The quality of light is still harsh; the only difference is lower contrast. More detail is visible in the shadow. Compare the backgrounds. The one on the right that has light reflecting into it has a lighter background. The fill is not enough to change the exposure; it is enough to add a bit more life to the image. Controlling contrast is important especially when photographs are reproduced on web printing presses where shadows can load up with ink (dot gain) and lose detail.

Note

Harsh light that is low in contrast is a compromise that reveals textures in fabrics without revealing too many flaws in skin, especially when a makeup artist is involved in enhancing the skin's natural beauty.

Note

Today's incident meters are all handheld. They come in two varieties: ambient and flashmeters. My advice is always buy the flashmeter even though it costs more. At some point you will want to meter electronic flash. Flashmeters read both the light in an environment (ambient or existing) and electronic flash. An investment in a high-quality incident meter that can also read flash will last for many years. I have switched to Sekonic flashmeters. I have a Minolta Flashmeter IV that is fifteen years old. That's a great service life and return on investment!

1.4

One more concept to go: Light either hits a subject or bounces off of it. It is considered to be either incident or reflective depending on where it is in relation to eye, capture device (sensor chip), or film. *Incident* light falls onto the subject. *Reflective* light bounces off of the subject and is on its way to the camera or the eye.

INCIDENT LIGHT METERS

Incident light meters measure the light before it gets to the subject. An incident meter measures light that has not been influenced by the qualities of a subject. These qualities can include color, shape, and tonal efficiency of the surface. Because incident meters see only the quantity of light hitting the subject, they report an exposure that represents the true tone of the subject in a photograph. This is called the *diffused value*. The diffused value is the proper exposure for a photograph. The diffused value is the aperture (f/stop) and shutter speed set on the camera.

REFLECTIVE METERS

Reflective meters, like the ones built into cameras, measure the light after it has bounced off of the subject. Reflective meters measure the relative brightness in f/stops (contrast) between the highlights and the shadows. These readings determine contrast within a photograph. Contrast is subjective. It is one of the creative controls a photographer can use to establish mood or drama. Harsh and soft light qualities can be represented in situations of high, medium, or relatively low contrast.

Photoshop's Eyedropper and Color Sampler measuring tools display reflective data in the Info palette. You can use them to measure the relative brightness between areas in an image. The advantage of using these tools is that they are much more accurate than a light meter. They read the actual reflectivity of objects in the captured image. In the traditional capture world it would be like using a densitometer to read reflectivity from developed photographs as they are made in the field—impossible with film, simple with a digital camera, laptop, and, of course, Photoshop! Remember that in photography, accuracy rules!

Lighting: "Great Photoshop Starts with Great Photography"

Three things are of concern when lighting a subject for photography: the quality of the light, the exposure for the diffused value, and the relative brightness between the highlight and shadow areas. These considerations are important because their interplay defines the quality of the image artistically and how well the image will reproduce on the printed page, on a photographic or inkjet print, or on the Web. Paying attention to these considerations can greatly reduce time-intensive postproduction services.

Photographs can have many quantities and qualities of light at the same time. Quantities of light are relative to each other. They are measured in relationship to the chosen exposure for the image. For the following fashion shot, I discuss how I set up the lighting and which incident controls I chose and why. I then discuss setting the diffused value—the exposure—with both an incident meter and a GretagMacbeth ColorChecker chart. One thing that might surprise you is how little time is actually spent working with the camera.

Origin of Light

Laura Phillips from Elite Model Management/Atlanta is the model for this shoot. I start the session with one light on Laura. The origin of light in this case is a 22-inch "beauty dish" placed at a 45-degree angle above and to the right of the camera. This figure shows the effect of a single light (1.5). An incident meter in the scene reads the light falling on the subject (1.6). The diffused value is f/16. Examine the shadow edge transitions—they are short. The light on Laura is harsh. The aperture setting on the camera's lens for this image is f/16. The shutter speed for all the photographs in this section is 1/125 of a second.

1.5

As with light meters, lighting controls are either reflective or incident. *Reflective controls* deal with light after it has hit the subject and is on its way to the imager. Filters for color correction or soft focus and vignetters are reflective controls. They are mostly used with film.

Incident controls are devices that come between the origin of light and the subject. They do their work on the light before it strikes the subject. Diffusion panels, scrims, flags, and cookies are examples of incident lighting controls. I use each one of these controls in the shoot.

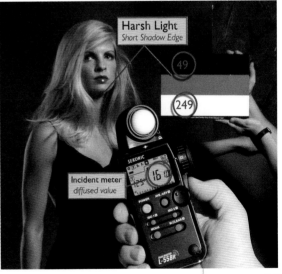

Harsh Light
Short Shadow Edge

Incident meter
diffused value

I place a *diffusion panel* made of translucent sailcloth fabric stretched on a Chimera 42 x 72-inch frame in front of the origin of light and move it closer to Laura. The shadow edge becomes wider and the light quality softens (1.7). The panel spreads the light two-dimensionally over a 21-square-foot area making the source much, much larger in relation to the size of her face (about half of a square foot). The panel is now the *source* of light and the beauty dish on the flash head is the *origin* of light.

1.6

Diffusion Panel

1.7

Note

The aperture controls the light made with flash in photographs. A burst of light from an electronic flash travels at the speed of light. Shutters are not fast enough to control the amount of flash recorded at the camera.

The diffusion panel also lowers the amount of light reaching Laura. Whenever I modify the origin of light, I take a new incident reading. The diffused value is now f/8.0.4, or almost one and a half stops darker than the harsh light exposure. I set the new exposure on the camera, allowing an additional stop and a half of light to reach the sensor. The light panel reduces the amount of light reaching Laura by one and a half f/stops. The exposure doesn't change even if I move the panel closer to or farther away from the model.

The background areas become brighter because the exposure is now one and a half stops more than before. Laura remains the same in both examples because I adjusted the exposure to compensate for the diffusion panel. The ColorChecker in both images shows the same reflected brightness. These Photoshop readings are considered reflected because they show the relative brightness of the black and white patches on the card.

The exposure as read from the ColorChecker shows that Laura will record with detail in her skin and hair (R, G, B: 249) and in her black dress (R, G, B: 49) (1.8). The shadows under the wrinkles around her waist read in the low 20s.

The names and placement of the lights and incident controls used in this lesson are shown in this figure (1.9). I've labeled the effect of each one on the corresponding photograph illustrating the building of the lighting. The flag in front of the strip light blocks its light from hitting the lens and causing flare.

Decimals and Thirds

Modern incident and reflective light meters provide readings that are accurate to one-tenth of a stop. This causes confusion because some f/stops have decimal points in their names. By popular convention, a light meter reading of 5.6.3 means f/5.6 and three-tenths (roughly 1/3) of an f/stop, which is equivalent to f/6.3 (f/5.6 plus 1/3 of an f/stop) on your camera. The reading on the soft light image (Figure 1.8) reads f/8.4, telling the photographer that the correct exposure is f/8.0 and between a third and a half. Depending on personal preference, photographers round the tenth of a stop in this instance either up to a half f/9.5 (very slightly underexposed) or down to a third f/9.0 (very slightly overexposed). It is important to use tonal references such as a GretagMacbeth ColorChecker Chart or a ColorChecker Gray Scale card used in the examples in this chapter.

Soft Light
Wide Shadow Edge

49

249

Incident meter
diffused value

1.8

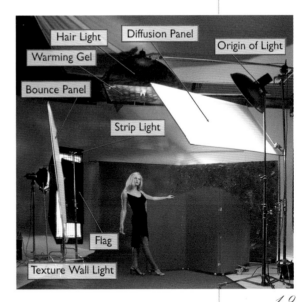

Hair Light
Diffusion Panel
Warming Gel
Origin of Light
Bounce Panel
Strip Light
Flag
Texture Wall Light

1.9

I use an incident control to lower the contrast by adding light to Laura's shadows. The bounce panel is a Chimera 42 x 72-inch frame covered with a white reflector panel, which I place to the side opposite the source of light (the diffusion panel). Light bounces into the shadows on her hair and arm (1.10). Now details in these areas open up becoming more visible. Notice that her back is beginning to separate from the background. Notice, too, that even though the contrast is lower, the shadow edge transition did not change. The brightness or darkness of shadow areas is subjective. You can raise contrast for a moody and dramatic look or lower it for a more open feeling.

Bounce Panel

1.10

Densitometry is the science of charting how much light causes an increase of the amount of silver retained on a negative after the film is developed. An f/stop of density measured from a black-and-white film negative has a logarithmic value of .3. A density change of .1 is the equivalent of one-third of an f/stop. In Photoshop, an opacity change of 13 points is, by general rule, a third of a stop (above 25) and is subject to what amounts to reciprocity in bright highlights (above 249) where more and more light is needed to drive the numbers up to 255.

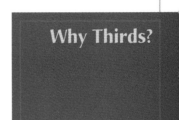

Why Thirds?

Hair Light w/grid

1.11

Laura's blond hair has very little life and it merges with the background. I add a Chimera medium soft box fitted with a fabric grid and a warming gel directly overhead. This separates her hair, shoulders, and arms from the background. The grid minimizes spill on the background. The warming gel (Rosco 3407) puts a golden glow in her hair and warms the color on her arms (1.11).

After firing this light independently of the other lights and measuring it with a reflective meter pointing at her hair, I then adjust the power of the light until it is about half a stop brighter than the diffused value.

Laura's back and dress still get lost in the background. A large Chimera strip light with a grid adds a beautiful highlight that separates them nicely. A reflective reading of the highlight is again about a half stop brighter than the diffused value (1.12).

Contrast and Seeing

Controlling the quality of light and constraining it to a range that the camera can record and, even more important, to one a printer can reproduce is what lighting is all about. One of the biggest problems with recording images is that digital chips (CCD, CMOS) and film have limited contrast ranges they can capture. Our eyes are limited to about the same range except that we have brains. When we look at a high-contrast situation, our eyes "see" an image. What really happens is that first we view the bright areas, and the brain remembers the details in the highlights. Then the iris of the eye instantly opens wider to see into the dark areas while the brain remembers the bright ones and integrates them into a single picture we refer to as *sight* or *vision*. Capture media has no brain. It can record a limited contrast range. Contrast must be controlled to allow the subject to be photographed with recordable detail in the highlights and shadows.

The last goal of the lighting scheme is to bring up the illumination on the background elements. They consist of a texture wall on the right and red background paper that runs from above the set down to and then along the floor. I aim a light with a 16-inch reflector with a red Rosco #25 gel at the wall. Barndoors keep the light from spilling anywhere but the wall (1.13). The red background paper is still very dark so I place a bare bulb head behind the texture wall. It shines through a four-foot square panel with leaf-shaped holes cut in it. This incident control is called a *cucoloris* or *cookie*. It breaks up the light into the pattern on the background paper (1.14).

Lighting the background is very important especially when the fashions to be photographed are sheer and flowing. The background must have enough brightness to silhouette her shape through the fabric. If it doesn't,

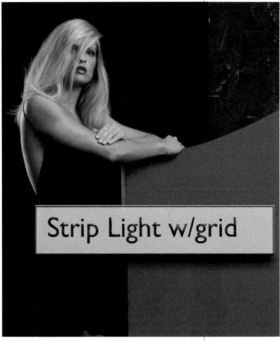

1.12

1.13

1.14

the garment will appear to be opaque even though it's sheer (1.15).

After the scene is lit, the photography starts. Shoot until you are sure you have the image you want. Then experiment. Exploring your photographic creativity takes nothing but some time. This is the time to play, experiment, and explore. Put on music, turn on a fan, invite your model to participate and contribute to the session. The results will more often than not exceed your original ideas. When the session is working there is an energy that flows through everyone involved. When the photographer feels this energy it is a rush. The excitement shows in the final images.

In the next chapter I introduce digital photography's back story—bit depth, image quality, color correction by the numbers, and more.

1.15

Tip

When a diffusion panel is introduced to a lighting set, it affects the color of the light. Be sure to shoot a ColorChecker again so that you can neutralize the color shift from the panel as I did in these examples.

Ambience: Light existing in the surrounding or pervading environment.

Contrast: The difference in f/stops between the highlights and the shadows. Contrast that is too high produces a photograph that has loss of detail in the highlights and/or the shadows. Adding light to the shadows reduces contrast.

Diffused value (or highlight): Represents the true brightness or tone of an object. You use the diffused value to set the exposure for a photograph on the camera.

Diffusion: A method of making an origin of light larger by spreading light two-dimensionally (height and width).

Gobo: An incident lighting control that goes between the light source and the subject used to block light.

Incident control: Modifies the origins of light before light strikes a subject to be recorded. This includes the choice of light, tungsten or electronic flash, the number of lights and their output, as well as diffusion panels, gobos, and so on.

Incident metering: Determines the amount of light striking an object. The reading of an incident meter aimed at the predominant light source indicates proper exposure for the diffused value.

Origin of light: The point from which light energy begins (such as electronic flash, flood light, sun, and so on).

Reflective metering: Determines the amount of the light reflecting off of an object. This type of metering is used to establish the difference in contrast (brightness) between two objects or areas in a photograph (such as the subject and background).

Shadow edge transition: The area of transition between a diffused value (highlight) and a shadow. A transition that covers a small area results in a hard shadow edge. A harsh quality (from a small light source) of light is defined by a short shadow edge transition. One that covers a large area indicates a soft shadow edge. The quality of light from a large shadow edge transition is described as soft. This indicates a large light source.

Source of light: A two-dimensional surface that illuminates an object.

Chapter Two

Bit Depth, Image Quality, and Color by the Numbers

A beautiful photograph begins in a photographer's mind. The journey to capture an image and turn it into a work of art for the wall, book, or client hinges on careful planning and execution of the details—casting, props, wardrobe, hair, makeup, and sets—either in the studio or on location.

One step in planning a photograph is determining what tasks you can accomplish in the camera and what you will finish in digital postproduction. Learning to see what is happening at the camera and whether to change it on the set or refine it in postproduction is a skill that comes only with practice and lots of it. It is also a skill that is critical to learn in a world where a photograph is not finished with the click of the shutter and a trip to the lab.

1-bit = 2 tones

2.1

Lighting and capturing the image are the underpinnings of a successful photograph. Recognizing, understanding, and deconstructing the photograph into its components for editing in Adobe Photoshop CS2 prior to shooting are also important steps in the process. The work that comes after the image is recorded on film or digital media contributes to the ultimate success of the image.

Sometimes circumstances prevent perfection at the camera. A working knowledge of the capabilities of Photoshop and how to apply them is invaluable when work at the camera falls short of fulfilling the concept.

Let's begin at the beginning, which is always a good place to start. This chapter explains what *bit depth* is and presents the important differences between 16- and 8-bit images. An exercise in this chapter demonstrates these differences and why they are important to the success of a final print. This chapter also illustrates a technique for seamlessly burning in highlights using 16-bit files. This technique is useful for producing an optimum file for digital output. It also helps build a foundation for working in 16-bit, especially from RAW files—one of the keystone features of Photoshop CS2. This chapter also shows how to tweak exposures and perform color corrections to JPEG files. Chapter 3 covers how to make the same corrections on RAW captures.

Bit Depth In Depth

2-bits = 4 tones

2.2

Bit depth is the number of tones represented by each pixel in an image. A 1-bit image is black and white with no grays at all (2.1). A 2-bit image has four tones: black, white, and two gray tones (2.2). A 4-bit image has 14 gray tones, black, and white (2.3). No matter what bit depth is involved, two of the tones are always black and white. Notice that the 4-bit photograph has distinct bands between each gray tone. The higher the bit depth becomes, the smoother the representation of these tones. An image that is 8-bit, or that contains 256 steps, is considered continuous tone. Continuous tone photographs have so many shades of gray that the transitions between them appear smooth (2.4). The progression doubles the number of tones for every single increment of bit depth. The higher the number of bits a camera or scanner is able to record, the more tones available.

Black-and-white digital photographs are most often 8-bit files: black, white, and 254 grays for a total of 256 tones. The value 0 always equals black. The value 255 always equals white. Color digital photographs have three 8-bit channels—red, green, and blue (RGB)—making what is sometimes referred to as 24-bit color (that is, 3 channels of color times 8 bits per channel equals 24-bit color). An 8-bit RGB file carries the possibility of over 16 million colors. (For the math whizzes in the audience: 256 red tones times 256 green tones times 256 blue tones equals 16,777,212 colors. Yes, I know that the multiplication really equals 16,777,216, but black and white only count once, so you have to subtract 4.) This number provides more than enough information because the finest digital printers and printing presses can only reproduce a few thousand distinct colors. The 8-bit format is also the standard for the vast majority of output devices, including inkjet, dye-sublimation, LED, four-color printing presses, and the Internet. Also, because 8-bit files are easily damaged in postproduction, a high bit depth workflow is desirable.

4-bits = 16 tones

2.3

Photoshop CS2 enables the user to work in the very high quality 16-bit mode. Layers, layer masks, vector masks, adjustment layers, and gradients are now fully supported in 16-bit mode. Photoshop now also supports PSD files and TIFs up to 4 gigabytes (GB) and PSB files up to 100GB in size.

Certain creative filters are still reserved for the 8-bit mode although Photoshop CS2 has much improved 16-bit functionality. In a typical Photoshop editing session, you would work in 16-bit mode non-destructively for the highest quality. (Chapter 6 discusses non-destructive Photoshop in detail.) To apply the Artistic, Brush Strokes, Pixelate, Sketch, and Texture filter suites now available in the *Filter Gallery,* you would convert a duplicate of the file to 8-bit. The special filter tools—Extract, Pattern Maker, and some third-party plug-ins are also 8-bit only. Filters that work only in 8-bit are grayed out in the menu when you're editing a 16-bit document (2.5).

8-bits = 256 tones

2.4

Editing a digital file degrades its quality. File degradation is cumulative. Working in 16-bit up to the point of extracting a subject from a photograph or applying a creative filter ensures that the highest quality file is available for output.

You make 16-bit files from film by setting the scanner's software to 16-bit and dragging the Highlight and Shadow sliders all the way to the left and right, respectively. The preview will look very flat. This technique ensures that the resulting file has all the information the scanner can capture. From digital captures, 16-bit files result by converting RAW camera files in either Photoshop or Bridge using Adobe Camera Raw 3. You can use the software that comes with the camera or use a third-party conversion package. Unless the image is only going on a Web site, I strongly recommend that you only build out RAW files to 16-bit TIFs. Most camera manufacturers' software will make 16-bit TIFs from their version of RAW files. Remember, JPEG only supports 8-bit files. The linear nature of a RAW file also provides a superior method of increasing the resolution of a file created from the linear RAW data. For more on Camera Raw, see Chapter 3.

2.5

Understanding Digital Negatives

So what's the big deal about 16-bit anyway? The sensors in digital cameras and scanners capture in bit depths that are significantly higher than 8-bit. The current crop of digital single-lens reflex (DSLR) cameras capture 12 bits or 4,096 steps for each of the three channels—Red, Green, and Blue—that make up a digital photograph. Some new digital camera backs already capture actual 16-bit files.

Cameras set to save images in JPEG or TIF formats throw away data that isn't needed to make an 8-bit file. In the case of a sensor that records 12 bits of data, fully 7/8 of the information is thrown away. That data is gone. Forever.

Back in the day, no photographer would consider having her or his precious film processed and printed at a less than top-grade lab! (And every frame we shoot is potentially precious, isn't it?) Sometimes this choice had to be made, especially when traveling overseas with the difficulties of getting unprocessed film through airport security without damage from overzealous x-ray machines. No matter how bad the drugstore print, the negatives could always be reprinted at a great lab. No one ever knowingly threw them away, especially without even looking at the prints.

Now think about it like this: Imagine dropping off a roll of film at a drugstore. When it is finished, you pick up the prints and before you even see the prints you run the negatives through a shredder. Even though you would never do that to film negatives, that is exactly what happens to digital negatives when a

Digital single-lens reflex cameras and some point-and-shoot digital cameras can capture photographs in the RAW format. This is the format of choice for producing files that will be output with the highest-quality reproduction. Some professional digital cameras only save in RAW format. Some offer the choice of RAW, RAW and JPEG, or (and this is where, in my opinion, the camera becomes rank amateur) JPEG and TIF. Files saved in RAW have all the information that the image sensor saw, every bit of it (pun intended).

A couple of RAW file traits exist that might seem to be drawbacks to this option. First, RAW files have more data so they take up more space on the storage device in the camera. Second, because RAW files are bigger, they limit the *burst rate*, or number of frames the camera can save without pausing. I like to think of this pause as when I would be changing the film in my camera back in the bad old, er, I mean film days. After the shoot is over, the next step is to download the CompactFlash card, Microdrive, or whatever media is in vogue at the moment to the computer and back it up onto a CD or DVD. This process is the preproduction workflow, which I cover thoroughly in Chapter 5.

What Are RAW Files Anyway and Why Are They Complicating My Life?

photographer chooses camera-based conversions to 8-bit JPEG files or TIFs over saving as a RAW file.

A photograph saved as a RAW file contains all the information that the camera's sensor is able to capture. A lot more data exists than even the monitor can show. The data is available to bring back blown-out backgrounds (Chapter 14), control contrast (Chapter 13), and to correct any other tonal and color problems that would severely challenge (damage) an 8-bit capture. As mentioned earlier, you can generate much higher resolutions than were originally captured from the linear RAW file with no discernable quality loss. Additionally, you can build out a RAW file to a 16-bit file, giving Photoshop the data with which to make changes so great they would ruin an 8-bit file, resulting in banding or posterization in the final output. These adjustments include correcting over- and underexposure, correcting color shifts, and interpolating the file to a much larger size beyond the larger sizes available in Camera Raw. You can make all of these changes without degrading the resulting 8-bit files. Here's why it works and how to do it yourself.

A 16-bit file has 65,534 tones of gray plus black and white for a total of 65,536 tones per channel. This is an incredible amount of information to sample down to the 256 tones per channel of an 8-bit file. The following exercise demonstrates the effects of tonal (exposure) changes in 16- and 8-bit files.

It includes a technique for combining different versions of the same image to bring down an overexposed highlight.

You can download the sample 16-bit file used in this exercise from www. amesphoto.com/learning. Click the Photoshop CS2: The Art of Photographing Women link, which takes you to a registration page. Enter your e-mail address as the user name, then fill out the rest of the information. Enter the book code **PW48255**. (The reason for registering to download the photographs is to protect my copyright and the usage rights the models have granted for you to use photographs of them for practice. More information about registration is on my Web site. If you have further questions, feel free to send an e-mail message to me at learning@amesphoto.com. I'll get back to you as soon as I can.)

The photograph you will download is a digital image captured in black and white with a Leaf DCB II digital back on a Fuji GX-680 II without the filter wheel. At the beginning of digital photography, black and white was the only way we could capture people in high resolution.

2.6

Step 1: **In Photoshop CS2, open Bridge by clicking its icon in the Options bar or by pressing ⌘/Ctrl+Shift+O (2.6). Navigate to the folder for Chapter 2 and double-click the 16-bit.tif thumbnail to open it.** Information about the image appears either at the bottom of the document window (Mac) or application window (Windows) or in the Info palette.

Step 2: **Set the display to Document Sizes by selecting it in the fly-out menu (2.7). You can also set up the Info palette to display document sizes by clicking on its fly-out menu, choosing Palette Options, and then selecting Document Sizes (2.8).** The file size appears below the readouts in the Info palette. The file size is 8MB because it was captured in 16-bit grayscale. In order to learn how Red, Green, and Blue work "by the numbers," you must first convert the file to RGB. I discuss color and tone corrections later in this chapter.

Step 3: **Choose Image ⇨ Mode ⇨ RGB Color to convert the file to RGB.** Notice the check mark next to 16 Bits/Channel. The file size is now 24MB. Three 8MB channels—one for Red, plus one for

2.7

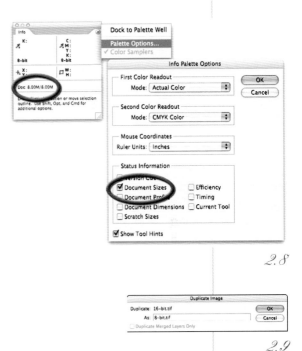

2.8

2.9

Green, plus one more for Blue—equal 24MB. The document size now reads "Doc: 24M/24M."

Step 4: **Make a copy of the file by choosing Image ➪ Duplicate.**

Rename the file **8-bit.tif** (2.9). You use this file in the final composite of this exercise and to see what happens to an 8-bit file when it undergoes exposure changes in Photoshop.

Step 5: **Convert 8-bit.tif to an 8-bit file by choosing Image ➪ Mode ➪ 8 Bits/Channel.**

Notice that the file size is now 12MB, half the size of 16-bit.tif (2.10). A 16-bit file has 256 times more tones per channel as an 8-bit file (256 x 256 = 65,536 tones per channel). It is also twice the size in megabytes.

2.10

Document Size

The document size of an image in Photoshop appears in the bottom of the document window and, if you choose, in the Info palette. In this example the document size displays as Doc: 62.6M/190.4M (2.11). The first number is the size of the flattened image. The second is the size of the image with layers. If the size isn't displayed, use the fly-out menu that appears there to get the size and other information about the image. Another way to see the file size and dimensions is to choose Image ⇨ Canvas Size. The Canvas Size dialog box not only displays the file size and shows the dimensions, but it also enables you to resize the image canvas.

2.11

After you convert the file to 8-bit, the photograph still has good overall exposure, yet the model's shirt is overexposed. It has lost some detail and is bright enough to draw the eye away from the model's face. It is difficult to see the water droplets on her arm. Let's set up the files needed to fix this problem while learning the advantage of working in 16-bit. The numbers tell the story.

Step *6*: **Display the Info palette by choosing Window ⇨ Info.**
A check mark indicates whether it is already visible.

Step *7*: **Make 16-bit.tif active by clicking inside the image or on its header bar. Press ⌘/Ctrl+L or choose Image ⇨ Adjustments ⇨ Levels to open the Levels dialog box.**

Step 8: Hold down the Option/Alt key and then click and hold the Highlight slider (the white triangle on the right). The image displayed goes black. Move the Highlight slider to the left.

The areas that appear first are the brightest highlights. Make a mental note of the area displayed, in this case, the model's shoulder.

Step 9: Release the Option/Alt key; the screen returns to normal. Hold down the Shift key and click where the highlights were brightest in Step 8. This action places a color sampler (#1) on the photograph. Click Cancel in the Levels dialog box (or press Esc on the keyboard) to close it without applying changes.

Look at the Info palette. It has increased in size, adding an area for Sampler #1. It shows the values as R: 251, G: 251, and B: 251. Because 255 is pure white, we know from the numbers that probably no printable detail exists there (2.12). (For more on what the numbers mean, check out the sidebar, "Steps, Tones, and the Meaning of Life.") Onwards. . . .

2.12

Step 10: Choose the Color Sampler tool from the fly-out menu of the Eyedropper tool (2.14) and set the Sample Size to 3 by 3 Average in the Color Sampler tool Options bar.

Samplers appear when you select the Color Sampler tool or when a Curves or Levels dialog box is open.

Step 11: Open the Levels dialog box by pressing ⌘/Ctrl+L and move the Gamma (Midtone) slider to the right to darken the highlights. Continue moving the slider until the middle Input Levels box reads 0.45 (2.15).

The overall photograph is very dark.

Tip
The keyboard shortcut for the Color Sampler tool is i+Shift+i.

Steps, Tones, and the Meaning of Life

The top section in this figure is a gradient of the continuous tones of black to white—0 to 255 (2.13). These are the steps that make up a photograph on the monitor, on an inkjet or photographic print, or even on the printed page. Below that gradient is a 21-step chart showing blocks of values. The steps are helpful when visualizing the values between groups of tones. Shadow detail starts at around 25. 18% gray is right where you would expect it at 127. And yes, I know what you are thinking: "128 is the middle of 256." Yes, it is. When you run the cursor over middle gray in Photoshop, it reads 127. Why? It's because 127 is the middle value for the 254 tones of gray in a 256-step, 8-bit image that includes a step each for pure black and pure white. About the highest number where white with detail will reproduce is 242. When a reading moves into the high 240s and the 250s, highlight detail is lost rapidly. At these readings some detail might appear on the monitor. It will not reproduce on a print or on the printed page. Depending on the output device (printer and so on), values less than 25–29 will have no detail in the shadows.

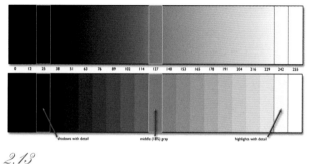

2.13

2.14

Step 12: Look at Sampler #1 in the Info palette. It shows 251/247, indicating a move from 251 to 247, which brings those highlights back into a printable range. Click OK in the Levels dialog box.

Sampler #1 now reads 247, per the changes made by the Levels adjustment. All the work has been done in 16-bit. The following steps show you why.

Step 13: Click 8-bit.tif to activate it, and then press ⌘/Ctrl+Option/Alt+L on the keyboard.

Adding the Option/Alt key tells Photoshop to apply the settings used last for Levels. The Levels dialog box appears, displaying the exact adjustments in the midtone Input Levels box (0.45) as in Step 11. Click OK to accept the settings. The 8-bit.tif file has received the same adjustment as 16-bit.tif. Now it gets interesting.

Step 14: **Press ⌘/Ctrl+L to open the Levels dialog box again and look at the histogram.**

The "dropouts" in the histogram are areas where data has been lost (2.16). This effect is called *combing* because the remapping of pixels creates gaps, making the histogram resemble a comb. The lost data in this 8-bit file can result in banding or posterization when it is printed.

Step 15: **Click Cancel or press Esc on the keyboard to close the Levels dialog box.**

Because you use 8-bit.tif later in another step without the Levels adjustment, press ⌘/Ctrl+Z to undo Levels. The image reverts to the brighter version.

Step 16: **Click 16-bit.tif to make it active, and then open the Levels dialog box.**

Notice that this histogram, which represents exactly the same changes made to 8-bit.tif, is solid and shows no evidence of combing (2.17). It works because a huge number of additional tones are available (65,536 per channel in 16 bit and only 256 in 8 bit) to use in making the tonal adjustment. This means that you can make fairly massive changes in a 16-bit file without data loss when you convert it to 8 bit. When you've finished checking out the histogram, click Cancel or press the escape (Esc) key to close the Levels dialog box.

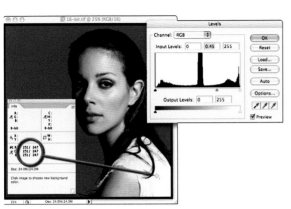

2.15

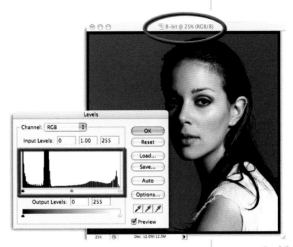

2.16

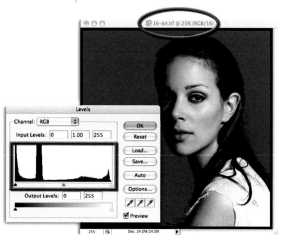

2.17

Now, I know what you're thinking: "Okay. If I have an 8-bit file that really, really needs a big exposure adjustment, I can convert it to 16 bit, fix it, and convert it back to 8 bit." Good try. This is one of these something-from-nothing scenarios that look great in theory and even seem to work in Photoshop and wind up looking not quite as good as complete and total garbage when printed. This method won't work, so don't even bother. And remember: To achieve the highest quality, always begin post-production in 16 bit.

Step 17: Duplicate the darker version of 16-bit.tif by choosing Image ⇨ Duplicate and naming the new file 8-bit burn.tif.

Step 18: Convert the new file to an 8-bit image by choosing Mode ⇨ 8 Bits/Channel, and then close 16-bit.tif without saving it.

Step 19: Activate 8-bit burn.tif by clicking it, and then select the Move tool by pressing V on the keyboard. Hold down the Shift key and drag 8-bit burn.tif onto 8-bit.tif. The Shift key centers an image in the file you drag it to using the Move tool. If the files are exactly the same size, they will be in perfect pixel-to-pixel registration with each other. Look at the Layers palette. 8-bit burn.tif has become Layer 1. The whole image is dark. Close 8-bit burn.tif without saving.

Step 20: In the 8-bit.tif file, double-click the words "Layer 1" in the Layers palette and rename the layer "Burn." Go to the bottom of the Layers palette. Hold down the Option/Alt key and click the Add Layer Mask icon (2.18). The dark image disappears. A black layer mask is added to the Burn layer. A Layer Mask icon appears to the right of the thumbnail and a light border appears around the mask indicating that it is ready to edit. (Black layer masks are called "Hide All" masks because they conceal everything that is on their layer.)

2.18

Step 21: **Press ⌘/Ctrl+Option/Alt+0 to zoom to 100% and press B on the keyboard (or click the Brush icon on the Tool palette) to select the paint brush.**

In the Brush Options bar, choose a 125-pixel soft-edged brush from the Brush Preset Picker and set the Opacity to 100% or press 0 on the keyboard (2.19).

2.19

Step 22: **With the foreground color set to white and the Burn layer active, click the layer mask to activate it. Brush over the model's shirt and arm.**

You are burning in the washed-out highlights by revealing darker areas from the Burn layer when you paint white on the layer mask.

Step 23: **Look at the Layer Mask icon (2.20).**
The area just painted appears white, allowing the darkened shirt and arm to blend with the brighter version below. If an unwanted dark area appears where your brush moved onto the background around her arm or back, switch the foreground color to black (X on the keyboard) and paint it out.

2.20

Step 24: **Change the opacity of the layer to fine-tune the effect (2.21), and then save the image to your hard drive.**
This image will be useful for practicing retouching flyaway hair and skin smoothing later in the book.

2.21

2.22

Understanding Colorcast

Colorcast is the appearance of one or more colors dominating the highlights, midtones, and/or shadows within an image. Let's use another image to look at a pure example of how colorcast works and what a neutral color balance is.

Step *1*: **Open the 8-bit file Christina.tif.**

Step *2*: **Display the Info palette by choosing Window ⇨ Info.**

A check mark by the word *Info* indicates the Info palette is visible. If you don't see it, look for the Info tab. It is docked with the Navigator tab by default. Click on the Info tab to activate the palette.

Step *3*: **Choose the Color Sampler tool from the Tool palette or press Shift+I on the keyboard.**

Step *4*: **In the Color Sampler tool's Options bar, set the Sample Size to 3 by 3 Average and then click on the model's cheek to set Sampler #1. Set Sampler #2 on her jacket and Sampler #3 on a midtone on her jeans (2.22).**

Step *5*: **Look at the Info palette. Notice the additional readouts numbered 1, 2, and 3.**

These correspond to the color samplers you just placed. Make sure your placements read as close as possible to the values in the sample Info palette shown here (2.23). To move a sample, hold down the ⌘/Ctrl key and click and drag it to a new location. The Color Sampler tool allows you to place up to four sample pickers on an image.

Step *6*: **Look at the numbers. Your samples may be slightly different than those shown here.**

The number in each sample is the tonal value of that color on a scale of 0 to 255. Sampler #1 in the Info palette shows equal tonal values for the Red, Green, and Blue channels, which in this case is 250. This means that the value of that sample is a highlight with very little detail. Remember that 255 is pure white. Sampler #2 samples the shadow area of her jacket and reads 24 for each of the color channels. The last sampler, #3, shows an almost perfect middle gray with an RGB reading of 126.

2.23

Step *7*: **Press ⌘/Ctrl+L to open the Levels dialog box.**

At the top of the display is a drop-down menu labeled Channel. By default, the composite of all three channels—RGB—is displayed. Click the drop-down arrow. The four choices are composite RGB, Red channel, Green channel, and Blue channel. The keyboard shortcuts are displayed, too.

Step *8*: **Choose the Green channel and then click the Gamma (Midtone) slider (the gray triangle in the middle) and move it to the right until the middle box of the Input Levels is 0.65.**

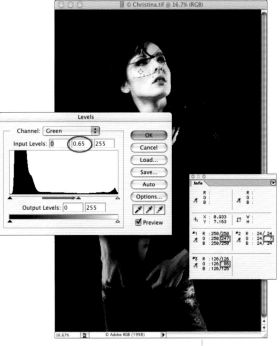

Look at the image on the screen. It has a magenta cast (2.24). Green is the complement of magenta. By reducing the amount of green, magenta becomes dominant. In the Info palette, a second set of numbers has generated. The readings to the left of the slash are the original readings, and the

2.24

2.25

right-hand numbers show the changes. The green channel now reads 247, 7, and 86. The Red and Blue channels remain at 250, 24, and 126. The sampler numbers indicate more red and blue and less green. Red and blue in equal amounts make magenta.

Step 9: Press ⌘/Ctrl+3 to make the Blue channel active and move the Gamma (Midtone) slider to the right until the middle box of Input Levels reads 0.65. Take a look at the Info palette. Now the Green and Blue channels read 247, 7, and 86, while the Red channel stays at 250, 24, and 126. The image has taken on a red colorcast. There is more red (3 points in the highlights, 40 points in the midtones, and 17 points in the shadows) than green and blue, hence the overall red color (2.25). Click OK in the Levels dialog box to accept the changes.

Step 10: Reopen the Levels dialog box by pressing ⌘/Ctrl+L. Notice the combing in the histogram. There isn't much damage. (Remember, the effects are cumulative.) This concept is also useful to know when toning black-and-white images in Photoshop. More effective and less damaging ways of toning exist, which I explore later in this book in Chapter 11.

Step 11: Click Cancel to close Levels without applying any changes. Close the file without saving it.

You have experienced the quality of 16-bit files and have an understanding of colorcast. In the next section of this chapter you learn how to use Levels on a 16-bit file to neutralize the color and Curves to remove colorcast.

JPEG: Exposure Tweaks and Color Correction by the Numbers

Tungsten white balance   Daylight white balance

2.26

This section demonstrates how to color correct a JPEG photograph or a photograph scanned from film by neutralizing the highlights and shadows. I also demonstrate a technique for removing colorcast from the midtones. These techniques are useful to tweak the colors and exposure of a photograph in post-production and can be useful for fine-tuning files generated in Adobe Camera Raw 3, which I discuss in more detail in Chapter 3. After you make the corrections, applying them to other images from the shoot is easy. They are not meant to cure problems caused by having the wrong white balance set on your camera. Unless you are already shooting RAW files (see Chapter 3), correction of mismatched white balance in the camera can be a big problem (2.26). Great Photoshop begins with great photography. Great photography happens in the camera. Digital post-production's job is to add the icing to an already tasty cake.

CORRECTING COLOR

In the last exercise, finding highlight, midtone, and shadow values to sample in our image wasn't hard because the black-and-white photograph was composed of nothing but neutral tones. Finding highlights, midtones, and shadows in color photography is much more difficult. Unless the image has highlight and shadow values that you know are neutral, accurately color balancing an image is difficult. Often, finding neutral values in a color photograph is nothing more than a SWAG (also known as a Scientific Wild A** Guess). Therefore, having a neutral reference in the first frame of each lighting setup is important.

"Why the first frame?" you might ask. Because doing so is more likely to become a habit if you always do it first. Otherwise you can easily get caught up in the heat of the shoot and completely forget to make one. A photograph with the GretagMacbeth ColorChecker Chart or their ColorChecker Gray Scale card is an essential tool for good color.

A photograph made during magic hour—that incredible time shortly before the sun sets when the light is golden and the sun is low in the sky—will often be too warm. It has too much orange in it. I know what you're thinking . . .

Note

The placement of the color samplers is somewhat arbitrary. Your numbers might not exactly match the ones in the book. It is all right to use the ones you choose. The techniques are the same.

"Orange! What combination of RGB makes um, well, 'O'? And how in the world do I fix that?" That is exactly the question this section answers.

This exercise uses one of the tools (Levels) discussed earlier to correct the color and fine-tune the exposure at the same time. The first exercise gets the color accurate to about 90% most of the time. The next one is for color fanatics who want to work on the midtones as well as the highlights and shadows. The last exercises show you how to apply the corrections in the first two to multiple files as easily as dragging and dropping layers.

Step 1: **In the Folders pane of Bridge, double-click the folder containing the files for Chapter 2 that you downloaded earlier. Thumbnails with the filename underneath appear in the lightbox. Double-click the file, colorchecker.jpg to open it in Photoshop CS2.**

At first glance the model's skin tones look great (2.27). A closer look reveals a colorcast so orange that it looks as if Elizabeth might have had a very bad out-of-the-bottle-bronzing kind of day. Look closely at the gray swatch. Notice it is very orange in its overall colorcast.

Step 2: **Display the Info palette by choosing Window ⇨ Info.**

Step 3: **Select the Color Sampler tool by pressing i + Shift + i. Check the Options bar to be sure the Sample Size is set to 3 by 3 Average. Place Sampler #1 on the white patch, Sampler #2 on the black patch, and Sampler #3 on the gray patch (2.28). This is not the order in which the swatches appear on ColorCheckers. It is the order in which you'll make the corrections: highlights, then shadows, and then midtones. The Info palette expands to display the readings for Samplers #1, #2, and #3. The readings show the color bias for each of the three tones. Sampler #1 shows**

2.27

highlights with detail—R: 239, G: 223, and B: 210. Red and then green are the dominant colors because of their higher values. The image has an orange colorcast in the highlights (red + less green + even less blue = orange). Sampler #2 displays shadow values of R: 29, G: 24, and B: 20. This time red and green dominate again with the highest value indicating that the colorcast in the shadow is orange. Remember that a neutral tone is one whose RGB numbers are equal. Driving the lower values up to the brightest one, in this case red, neutralizes highlights. It works the opposite way in the shadows—you drive the brighter values down to the lowest one.

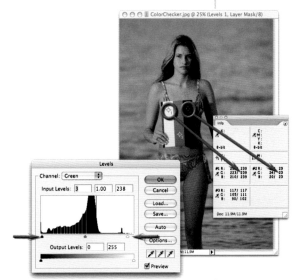

2.28

Step 4: Create a new Levels adjustment layer by clicking the half black/half white circle at the bottom of the Layers palette (2.29). Choose the Green channel from the Channels drop-down menu or press ⌘/Ctrl+2 on the keyboard.

Step 5: Click the Highlight slider and drag it to the left while watching the numbers in the Info palette.
Notice that the Info palette now displays two sets of numbers separated by a slash. The numbers on the left represent the starting point. The numbers to the right are the changes that have been made with the adjustment. When the Green channel reading to the right of the slash on Sampler #1 reaches 239, release the mouse.

Step 6: Press ⌘/Ctrl+3 to select the Blue channel, and then click and drag the Highlight slider to the left until Sampler #1 (the highlight) reads 239.
Use the up and down arrows on the keyboard to make fine adjustments. Going from 210 to 239 is a big change. Notice that this adjustment has changed the shadow reading in the Blue channel from 20 to 23. Because 23 is still the lowest shadow number, it gets no adjustment here.

2.29

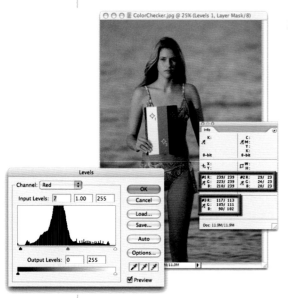

2.30

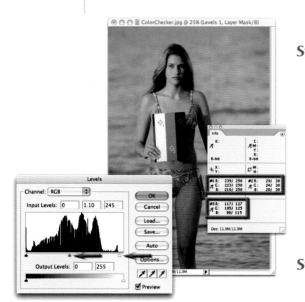

2.31

Step 7: **Press ⌘/Ctrl+2 to go back to the Green channel. Click the channel's Shadow slider and drag it to the right until the Info palette reads 23, the same as in the Blue channel. Now press ⌘/Ctrl+1 to return to the Red channel. Drag the Shadow slider to the right until Sampler #2 again reads Red 23.**

The highlights read R: 239, G: 239, and B: 239, and are neutral because they are equal. The shadows are neutral, too, reading R: 23, G: 23, and B: 23. Color balancing of the highlights and shadows is complete (2.30). Notice that the midtones are not neutral with readings of R: 113, G: 111, B: 102. I show you how to use another tool in a later step to balance the midtones. While the Levels dialog box is still open, we'll fine-tune the exposure.

Step 8: **Press ⌘/Ctrl+~ to activate the composite RGB channel and then click the Highlight slider and drag it to the left until the highlights (#1 Info field) read R: 249, G: 249, and B: 249.**

The white tile on the ColorChecker chart has no detail. Boosting it into the very high 240s or even 250–252 is all right for the upper exposure (tonal) values. The shadow values, while still neutral, are brighter by a point and now read R: 24, G: 24, and B: 24.

Step 9: **Now click and move the Gamma (Midtone) slider to the left until the shadows (#2 Info field) read R: 30, G: 30, and B: 30 (2.31).**

Again, no detail exists in the black tile. Increasing the shadow numbers into the mid-30s reduces the overall contrast by adding light to the shadows. (Sound familiar? If not, check out Chapter 1.) These changes may result in one channel being a point off. You can correct this problem by going into the channel that is not equal to the other two and either boosting it in the highlights or dropping it in the shadows. Sometimes the values fall in between and getting the numbers exactly the same is not possible. If they are within a point or two, the image will still be very close to being neutral. Two and a half points represent less than a 1% difference.

Note
The tilde (~) key is under the Esc key on both Macintosh and Windows keyboards.

Step *10*: **Click OK in the Levels adjustment layer dialog box.**
The highlights and shadows are now neutral and have had their exposures tweaked. The settings have been saved so you can use them to correct files shot under the same light without the ColorChecker chart.

Here's the part of the process that needs finesse. Look at Sampler #3 in Figure 2.30. The midtones (#3 Info field) read R: 127, G: 125, and B: 115. These colors are not neutral—not even close. Midtone colorcast happens when the camera itself is not white balanced for the lighting situation that exists at the time of making the exposure. You might think that you could fix highlights and shadows by moving the Gamma (Midtone) slider and balancing to the middle value. Unfortunately, using the Levels dialog box causes changes across the entire tonal range, which means that a shift of a color in the midtones also affects the shadows and highlights. Try neutralizing the midtones (Sampler #3) with the Gamma slider in the Levels dialog box and see what happens. Afterwards, press Esc to cancel the change.

CORRECTING THE MIDTONES

Correcting the midtones is not difficult when using different adjustment tools: Curves and a calculator. Here's how the process works:

Step *1*: **Click the New Adjustment Layer icon at the bottom of the Layers palette and choose Curves.**
A new Curves adjustment layer appears in the layers stack labeled Curves 1, and its dialog box opens.

Step *2*: **Set the grid to Fine in the Curves window by pressing Option/Alt and clicking in the window.**
The diagonal line that cuts the box in half from lower left to upper right affects the histogram as the individual sliders do in the Levels dialog box. The lower-left portion represents shadows; the middle, midtones; and the upper right, highlights.

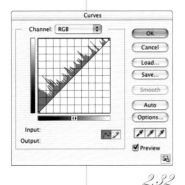

2.32

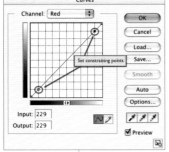

2.33

I superimposed a histogram to give you the idea (2.32). (Don't look for it in the Curves window because it isn't there. Photoshop CS2 now offers a floating Histogram window that you can watch as you make changes.) Levels is a linear correction across the entire range of tones in a channel. Curves is more selective and a truly versatile and elegant tool. You can set a point to move the whole curve or sections of it. In the case of the midtones, you are going to isolate then change the middle part of the curve. Because the colorcast is in the midtones, you make the neutral-ization to the average of those RGB values (R: 127 + G: 125 + B: 115 = 367 divided by 3 channels = 122.3. Round down to 122).

Step 3: **Press ⌘/Ctrl+1 to choose the Red channel.**
Count one box up and over from the lower-left corner along the line and click to set a point. Count one box down and one box over on the line from the upper-right corner and click to set a second point (2.33). These points isolate the midsection that controls the midtones we want to neutralize.

Step 4: **Click in the middle of the curve and enter the Red value,** 127, **in the Input box.**
The line changes into a curve and the color turns very cyan. Don't panic.

Step 5: **n the Output box, enter the average of the RGB values:** 122.
The curve softens and the colors become more balanced.

Step 6: **Now press ⌘/Ctrl+2 to bring up the Green channel and set the constraining points the same way you did in the Red channel.**
Click in the middle of the line to set a point. Enter the green value, **125**, in the Input box. Press the Tab key to highlight the output value and enter the first two digits of the RGB average, **12**. The image is very magenta (2.34) and the green value in the Info palette is 12. Add the second **2**, which makes the output 122. The image looks better now.

Step 7: **Finally, press ⌘/Ctrl+3 for the Blue channel and again set the restraining points on the curve.**

Click the middle of the curve to set the point for the adjustment. Enter **115** in the Input box and the RGB average of **122** in the Output window. Look at the Info palette (2.35). The midtones are neutral and so are the highlights and shadows.

Step 8: Click OK. Press ⌘/Ctrl+Shift+S to open the Save As dialog box.
Save the file as **ColorChecker.psd**. Leave it open.

COLOR CORRECTING ADDITIONAL FILES

Color correcting a group of JPEG files is really easy once you have the Curves and Levels adjustment layers you created in the last section. Here's the inside dish on how:

Step 1: Click the Go to Bridge icon in Photoshop CS2's Options bar or use the shortcut ⌘/Ctrl+Option/Alt+O. Hold down the ⌘/Ctrl key and click the two photographs of Elizabeth wearing the two-piece swimsuit named 2062-Q-1125.jpg and 2062-Q-1127.jpg.
Both are now highlighted in the content area. Double-click one of the photographs to open them both in Photoshop. You'll learn how to use it as you work through the rest of the book.

Step 2: Hold down the ⌘/Ctrl key and click Levels 1 and Curves 1 in the file ColorChecker.psd.
You did leave it open when you finished the last section, didn't you? If not, open it now by double-clicking its thumbnail in Bridge. Select the Move tool from the toolbox or press its keyboard shortcut V (2.36).

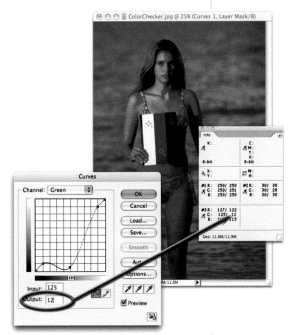

2.34

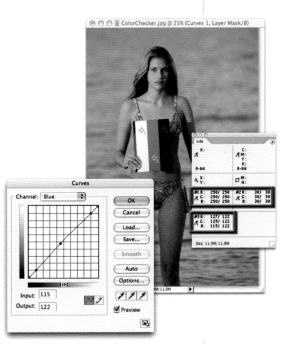

2.35

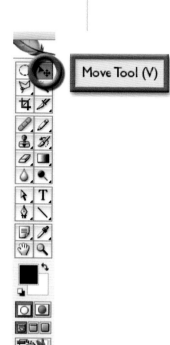

Move Tool (V)

Step 3: **Drag the Levels 1 and Curves 1 adjustment layers onto 2062-Q-1125.jpg.**

The color corrections and exposure tweaks carried in the layers are instantly applied to the photograph (2.37).

Step 4: **The 2062-Q-1125.jpg image is now active and the two adjustment layers in it are selected. Drag them onto 2062-Q-1127.jpg to correct it, too (2.38).**

Step 5: **Press ⌘/Ctrl+Shift+S to open the Save As dialog box. Save all three files as Photoshop documents (.psd).**

This format preserves the layers so you can make changes later if you want to.

Compare the starting point of each of the photographs of Elizabeth to the final versions (2.39). This chapter has taken you through a lot of digital territory. Color and exposure correction and learning how adjustment layers work and

2.36

2.37

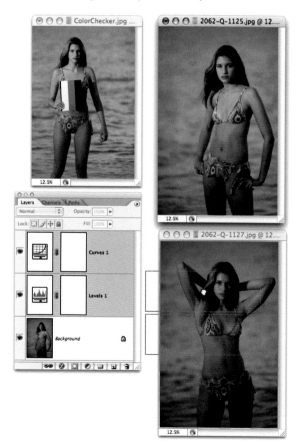

2.38

how to apply them to other files are the high points for working with JPEG. Bit depth provides the background information that will make working with RAW files easier to understand in terms of their quality. In the next chapter, I show you how Adobe Camera Raw 3 (ACR3) will make your photographic life easier, faster, and much, much better.

Before expsoure and color correction

After expsoure and color correction

2.39

Chapter Three

Adobe Camera Raw 3

Fundamental differences exist between JPEG and RAW file captures. A digital camera set to shoot in JPEG mode still captures a lot more data than it delivers to the final file. As a matter of fact, the camera records into memory all the information the sensor sees and then discards about seven-eighths of it. A gamma curve is applied to distribute the pixels to mimic the way our eyes perceive tonality. Finally, the camera compresses the information into a JPEG file. The JPEG spec also limits the density of the pixels to 8 bits, or 256 steps per pixel (3.1). The grayscale file shows the even, continuous progression from black through gray into white.

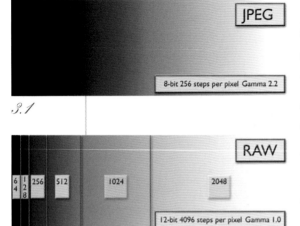

3.1

JPEG

8-bit 256 steps per pixel Gamma 2.2

RAW

6 1 256 512 1024 2048
4 2
8

12-bit 4096 steps per pixel Gamma 1.0

3.2

Digital cameras on the market today, particularly digital single-lens reflex cameras (DSLRs), can capture high bit depths usually in the neighborhood of 12 bits (4,096 steps) per pixel. A DSLR shooting a RAW file records every bit of data the sensor delivers. These linear files are extraordinarily rich with image information. Linear means that the distribution of tones is as the sensor records them. Sensors capture more data in the highlights than in the shadows. A RAW file holds 50% of the image data in the brightest f/stop of exposure. A 12-bit RAW file has 2,048 tones in that brightest stop. The next brightest f/stop, has 1,024 tones, and so on. By the sixth f/stop, the exposure is deep in the shadows with only 64 shades of darkest gray (one of them is black) being stored (3.2).

Bit Depth Chart

Bits	Tones
1	2
2	4
3	8
4	16
5	32
6	64
7	128
8	256
9	512
10	1024
11	2048
12	4096
13	8192
14	16384
15	32768
16	65536

3.3

RAW converters, including Adobe Camera Raw 3 (ACR3), read the linear data and produce a preview of the image with a normal gamma curve applied. Adjustment tools allow the photographer to control exposure, white balance, brightness, contrast, and saturation, and to fix issues like chromatic aberration (where one or more colors don't quite focus on the sensor causing a colored fringe). The converter then outputs a digital file in either 8 bit for lower quality purposes (such as the Internet, e-mail, or printing) or in 16 bit for the highest quality editing in Photoshop CS2. In the interest of accuracy, the 16-bit editing space in Photoshop is really 15 bits plus 1. This makes the math work faster with less demand on our computer's processor(s). The image quality is outstanding in 16 bit, and 16-bit editing offers a lot of headroom to accommodate drastic changes to a file but with very little degradation to the histogram, as you saw when you did the bit depth exercise in Chapter 1. Compare the number of tones in 8-, 12-, and 16-bit files (3.3).

A non-destructive note: RAW files aren't affected by any change you make to them in ACR3. You can't alter or destroy RAW files short of deleting them from your hard drive or microwaving the DVD they're saved on. (This smells bad and is not good for the microwave oven either.) Editing a RAW file is truly non-destructive. No matter what you do to one, you can always go back to the original file, which is good to know especially if you fail to dial in the appropriate white balance on the camera. You can set it right after the fact in ACR3. This feature is not only useful, it's also totally cool!

Introducing Adobe Camera Raw 3

ACR3 is a complete color and black-and-white processing lab in a single dialog box. Commercial photographer and Photoshop guru, Jeff Schewe, says that Photoshop is a plug-in for Camera Raw. After you read this chapter, I think you'll agree with him.

Camera Raw was born during an Italian vacation being enjoyed by Photoshop's author, Thomas Knoll, who was shooting with a Canon EOS D-60. Thomas loved the camera but didn't enjoy the software for making Photoshop editable files. So he wrote his own. Camera Raw version 1 debuted as a $99 plug-in for Photoshop 7. Version 2 was included for free with Photoshop CS. ACR3 has matured as a sophisticated production tool, and it, too, is included with Photoshop CS2 (3.4). It also works in Adobe Bridge, the replacement for File Browser. I cover Bridge thoroughly during the rest of this section.

GETTING TO KNOW THE TOOLBAR

ACR3 is a very powerful part of both Adobe Bridge and Photoshop CS2. Let's start with the toolbar located at the top of the dialog box (3.5). The tools from left to right along with their timesaving keyboard shortcuts are as follows:

Adobe Camera Raw 3.0 Dialog

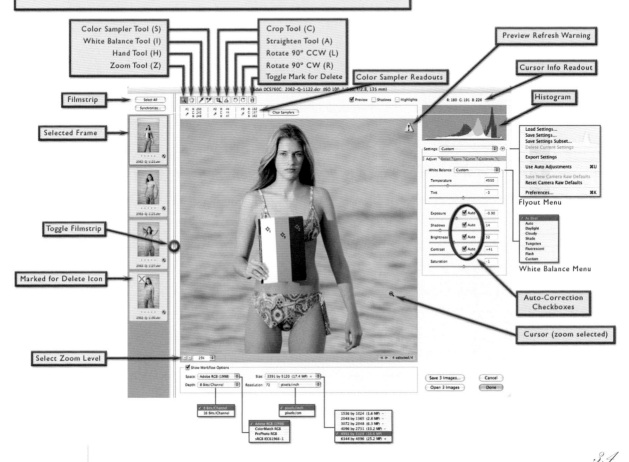

Color Sampler Tool (S)
White Balance Tool (I)
Hand Tool (H)
Zoom Tool (Z)

Crop Tool (C)
Straighten Tool (A)
Rotate 90° CCW (L)
Rotate 90° CW (R)
Toggle Mark for Delete

Color Sampler Readouts

Preview Refresh Warning

Cursor Info Readout

Filmstrip

Selected Frame

Toggle Filmstrip

Marked for Delete Icon

Select Zoom Level

Histogram

Flyout Menu

White Balance Menu

Auto-Correction Checkboxes

Cursor (zoom selected)

3.4

→ The **Zoom tool (Z)** is selected by default when the ACR3 dialog box opens. Click to zoom in or click and drag to zoom to a specific area of the image. Hold down the Option/Alt key and click to zoom out. You can change the preview size by clicking the + and – boxes or choosing a percentage from the menu under the lower-left edge of the preview.

→ The **Hand tool (H or spacebar)** allows scrolling of the preview window by dragging. Hold down the spacebar to toggle into the Hand tool for quick scrolling. Release the spacebar to return to the previously selected tool.

→ The **White Balance tool (I)** corrects color shifts. Click a neutral color (white, gray, or black) to automatically white balance an image. The tool moves the Color Temperature and Tint sliders to make the clicked RGB values equal. The Color Temperature slider controls the warm/cool colors, while the Tint slider handles magenta/green colorcasts.

→ The **Color Sampler tool (S)** places a color sampler wherever you click it in the preview. You can place up to nine color samplers in an image. To move a sample point, hover the cursor over it until the icon changes, and then click and drag it to the new position. The color samplers display their RGB values right below the toolbar. Remove the samplers from the preview by clicking Clear Samplers. Use this tool to sample highlight and shadow values for exposure and color correction.

→ The **Crop tool (C)** is also new to ACR3. Click and hold the Crop tool icon to display the Crop menu.

→ The **Straighten tool (A)** draws a line when you click and drag over either a known vertical or horizontal reference in the preview. Crop marks that show the rotation the Crop tool will use to make the image level appear when you release the mouse button.

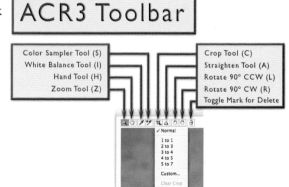

→ The **Rotation tools CCW (L)** and **CW (R)** rotate the preview in ACR3 and Bridge 90 degrees. This tool is great if the camera does not record orientation data in the RAW file's EXIF metadata, which I cover in Chapters 4 and 5.

3.5

→ The **Toggle Mark for Delete** icon appears in the toolbar only when more than one RAW file is open in ACR3. Select a RAW file you want to delete by clicking on it in the filmstrip. (Shouldn't that be called a thumbstrip? Credit the Photoshop Diva herself, Katrin Eismann [www.photoshopdiva.com], for asking this question first!) A red X appears on the thumbnail telling you that the file will be moved to the Trash/Recycle Bin when you click Done, Save, or Open. The file is deleted from the hard drive the next time you empty the Trash/Recycle Bin. Personally, I believe this tool is very, very dangerous and recommend that you never, ever use it. Photographers of old who shot film didn't cut out bad negatives. Don't delete bad RAW files. They might come in handy one day. You never know. . . .

Okay. That's a rundown of the toolbar. The Zoom and Hand tools are self-explanatory. Experiment with them as you do the next exercises. Use the Rotation tools by selecting and rotating thumbnails to their proper orientation if necessary. Let's jump right in and put 'em to work, beginning with the Color Sampler tool (S) and the White Balance tool (I).

Correcting color and white balance

The color correction section of the last chapter took you through the somewhat arduous process of fixing minor color shifts in the JPEG workflow. The versatility of the linear data in the RAW workflow streamlines the process in a major way.

To get started, download the Chapter 3 exercise photographs from www.amesphoto.com/learning. Click the thumbnail of the cover of this book and either create an account or, if you already have one, enter the e-mail address you registered and your password. Then enter the code **PW48255** to go to the downloads section. (More information is on the Web site concerning how you may use the photographs.)

Tip

Launch Bridge and Photoshop together. Press ⌘/Ctrl+K to open the Photoshop preferences. Select the Automatically Launch Bridge box.

Step *1*: **Open Adobe Bridge by clicking the Go to Bridge icon in Photoshop's Options bar (3.6).**
The keyboard shortcut is ⌘/Ctrl+Shift+O.

Step *2*: **Click the first thumbnail of Adelina standing in the water. Hold down the Shift key and click the last thumbnail in the series.**
This selects the entire series of Adelina (3.7). Press ⌘/Ctrl+R to open the series in ACR3 (3.8).

ACR3 has automatic exposure, shadow, brightness, and contrast settings turned on by default to help the previews look good when RAW files first appear in Bridge. They are fine for a quick look or to get a feel for what Camera Raw thinks are good settings. They are not particularly useful for fine-tuning digital photographs.

3.6

3.7

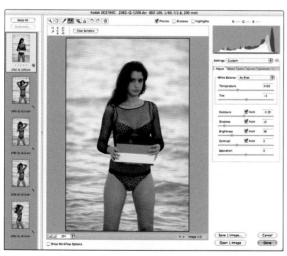

3.8

Note

Double-clicking selected thumbnails in Bridge opens them in ACR3 inside of Photoshop. Pressing ⌘/Ctrl+R opens them in ACR3 in Bridge. This latter option is where you want to work because Photoshop can process RAW files independently while you work on others in Bridge. You can find more on this topic in Chapter 5.

3.9

3.10

Note

A channel is said to clip when it reaches its brightest possible point (255) or its darkest (0).

Step 3: Turn the Auto settings off by pressing ⌘/Ctrl+U.

Step 4: Now make the change permanent. Click the triangle to the right of the Settings drop-down menu box. Choose Save New Camera Raw Defaults from the fly-out menu that appears.

This menu also has the Use Auto Adjustments selection if you don't remember the keyboard shortcut (3.9).

Step 5: Press S to choose the Color Sampler tool. Adelina is holding a GretagMacbeth Gray Balance Card that has colorimetrically neutral white, gray, and black swatches. Click the white swatch to place Sampler #1. Put Sampler #2 on the black swatch by clicking it.

The preview shrinks to provide space for the RGB readouts to appear below the toolbar. The photographs have a blue color-cast, attested to by the color samplers—R: 236, G: 242, and B: 252. The Blue channel is the highest number in each (3.10).

Step 6: Click the Select All button to select all the images in the filmstrip.

Step 7: Select the White Balance tool by pressing I, and then click the white swatch in the preview next to Sampler #1. Look at the readouts for the samplers. The highlights now read R:242, G:242, and B:242, and the shadows are R:54, G:55, and B:55. The White Balance tool has eliminated the blue cast, neutralized the white swatch, and made the shadows all but neutral as well. Notice that all the previews in the filmstrip have updated with the new Temperature (7,050) and Tint (–4) in the White Balance portion of the Settings section (3.11). Any change made to the image in the Preview pane also happens to the selected images in the filmstrip. This feature is not only very handy, but it is also a huge timesaver.

Tweaking exposure

After you balance the color, the next part of processing RAW files is tweaking exposure. You use the same color samplers, this time with the addition of modifier keys to show exactly where the channels clip.

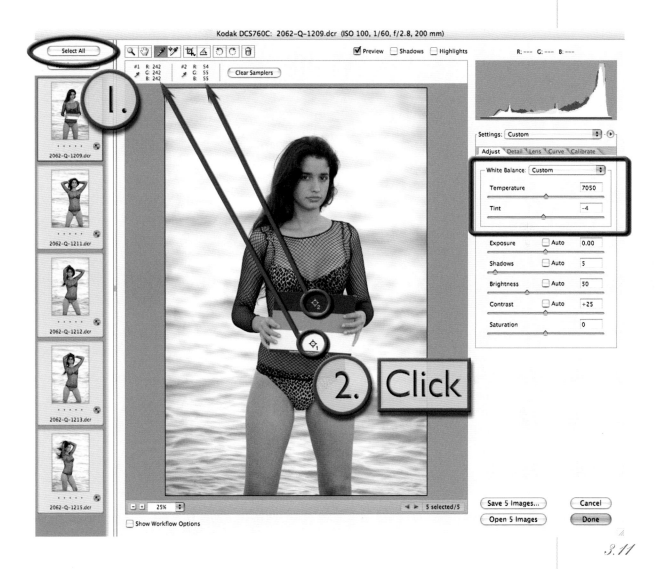

3.11

Tip

Hold down the Shift key to switch to the White Balance tool from the Zoom, Hand, Color Sampler, or Straighten tools.

Note

A highlight or shadow is considered neutral when a known white (very light gray really) area (highlight) or a black (very dark gray) displays RGB numbers that are equal. The same amount of all three channels makes a tone with no color bias.

Step 1: **Hold down the Option/Alt key and click the Exposure slider in the Adjust tab.**

The screen goes black. Start dragging the slider to the right until it reads +1.00 (3.12). The readout for Sampler #1 is R:255, G:255, and B:255, indicating that the white swatch of the Gray Scale Balance Card is at its brightest. Look at the areas of white around Adelina's silhouette. The white areas mean all three channels are at 255. Where blue appears, the Blue channel is at 255. Cyan indicates the Blue and Green channels are clipped at 255.

Step 2: **While still holding down the Option/Alt key, drag the Exposure slider to the left and back into reality.**

Watch Sampler #1's numbers. When they read R:249, G:249, and B:249, the detail has returned to most of the file (3.13). Minor amounts of clipping are fine, especially with a specular highlight. The Red areas indicate R:255. Yellow is R:255 and G:255. The reading for Sampler #1 indicates that the printed file will have barely perceptible detail in the white swatch. Release the Option/Alt key. The full color preview returns. The overall exposure of the highlights is now good.

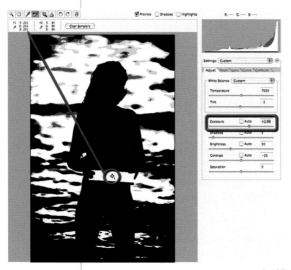

3.12

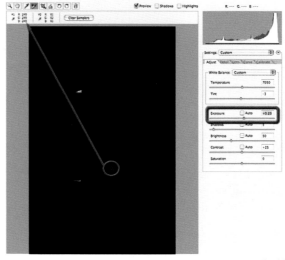

3.13

Step 3: **Once again hold down the Option/Alt key. Click the Shadows slider and move it to the right, stopping when the Shadows window reads 8.**

Look at the readout for Sampler #2. The Shadows have darkened from the low 60s to the low 50s. Where black appears in the preview, all three channels are 0. Where Cyan shows, Blue and Green are 0, and so forth (3.14).

Step 4: **Let go of the Option/Alt key.**

The preview returns to normal color.

Step 5: **Click the Clear Samplers button to the right of the Sampler readouts.**

The preview gets larger as the samplers on the ColorChecker and their readouts disappear.

The Brightness slider affects values between the shadows and the highlights while leaving the brightest highlights and deepest shadows alone. Use it to increase or decrease the lightness of the middle tones. Moving the Contrast slider below the default of 25 darkens the brighter values and lightens the darker ones. Moving it above 25 brightens the lighter values and darkens the lower ones. The Saturation slider has a similar effect to those of the Saturation controls in Hue/Saturation adjustment layers.

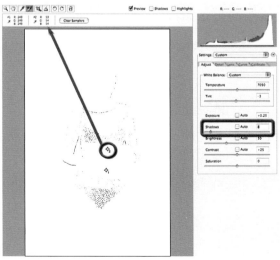

Note

A *specular* highlight is the reflection of either the source or origin of light. The sun glinting on a chrome bumper is a specular highlight. Specular highlights have no detail and usually read 255 in all three channels.

Tip

A quick way to see a RAW file in black and white is to drag the Saturation slider to −100.

3.14

On Shadows: Pleasing the Eye and Making Prints

The temptation is to really boost the Shadows setting because it provides a nice contrasty result. Resist this temptation. On a good day, going downhill with the wind to its back, a high-quality printer can only hold detail in the shadows on readings around 25. You can always intensify shadows later in Photoshop. If they are too dark coming out of ACR3, you can do little to bring them back in Photoshop. I rarely boost the shadows in Camera Raw. If anything, I usually flatten them out a bit because my goal is to make a great print, not to make a great-looking image on the screen.

Tip

Click a slider then use the up and down arrow keys to change the values one step. Add the Shift key to move 10 steps.

Tip

⌘/Ctrl+clicking a thumbnail adds it to or, if it is already selected, subtracts it from the selected thumbnails.

The thumbnails in the filmstrip update to reflect the changes made to the exposure. If you choose not to select all the images in the filmstrip before adjusting the ColorChecker image, click Select All and then click Synchronize. The Settings dialog box appears. Click OK to apply the setting to the rest of the images in the filmstrip.

Cropping

ACR3's Crop tool (C) is completely non-destructive. You can always change the crop later. The Crop tool tells ACR3 which pixels to make into a Photoshop editable file. You can even change the crop on a set of images while the previous set is still saving. Here's how:

Step *1*: **All the thumbnails in the filmstrip are still selected from the previous exercise. Hold down the ⌘/Ctrl key and click the photograph that has Adelina holding the ColorChecker to deselect it.**
The preview shows the next thumbnail below in the filmstrip; it has a blue border indicating it is the preview shown.

Step *2*: **Click and hold the Crop tool's icon in the toolbar.**
The Crop tool menu appears under the icon.

Step *3*: **Choose Custom to open the Custom Crop dialog box. Choose Inches from the Crop drop-down menu. Enter 4 and 6 in the entry windows (3.15).**
These numbers set the crop for a 4 x 6-inch size.

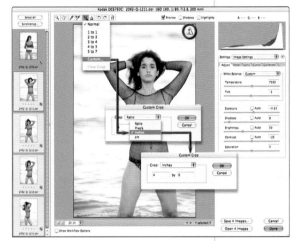

3.15

The yellow triangle with an exclamation point in it that sometimes appears in the upper-right corner of an image warns that the preview has not completely updated. Thumbnails of selected RAW files in the filmstrip display this symbol while changes made to them in ACR3 update. If a preview is zoomed in closer than the Fit in Window view, it will look out of focus until the update completes. This process usually takes just a few seconds.

Step 4: **Drag a crop across Adelina including both of her elbows (3.16).**

Watch the thumbnails in the filmstrip. They update with the same size crop. This feature is a huge timesaver.

The resulting crop is for a horizontal image. Obviously, Adelina is much more vertical. In Photoshop, you would have to undo the crop, change the width and height, and recrop. Not so in ACR3.

3.16

Step 5: **Click the lower-right corner of the crop box and drag it down toward the water.**

Boom! The crop box jumps from horizontal to vertical (3.17). The selected thumbnails in the filmstrip also update to show the change! Now that's handy.

Step 6: **Notice that the last thumbnail of Adelina (2062-Q-1215.dcr) cuts off her blowing hair on the left. Click that thumbnail in the filmstrip.**

It displays in the preview window. The other files are deselected.

Step 7: **Click inside the crop box and reposition and/or resize it.**

The size is still 4 x 6 inches. The crop has been adjusted to fit this image (3.18).

3.17

3.18

3.19

Tip

Move between multiple selected thumbnails in the filmstrip by using the up or down arrows on the keyboard. The preview and the blue border move by one thumbnail for each key press. The thumbnails remain selected. Clicking a thumbnail in the filmstrip selects and displays it in the preview. The rest of the thumbnails will be deselected. Hold down the Option/Alt key and click a thumbnail to choose it without deselecting others in the filmstrip. If you hit the arrow keys and the preview doesn't change, check the entry windows in the tab open in the Settings section. One of them will be highlighted. The arrow keys are changing the number in the highlighted field instead of moving from thumbnail to thumbnail. Option/Alt+click a thumbnail to return the focus to the filmstrip.

Look at the thumbnails in the filmstrip. They display two icons, one in each of the lower corners (3.19). The one on the left indicates that the image has been cropped. The one on the right indicates that adjustments (exposure, white balance, and so on) have been made in ACR3.

Step 8: Click Done in the lower-right corner of ACR3's dialog box. Click into Bridge.

The preview thumbnails of Adelina show all the adjustments, including the crop to 4 x 6 inches done in the previous steps. The adjustment and crop symbols appear in each frame (3.20).

Straightening

Sometimes the camera just isn't level and things that you know have to be level don't come out that way in the photograph. The shot of Elizabeth in the ocean is a good example. The ocean's horizon line is one of those it's-really-gotta-be-level things. Slightly off doesn't cut it. If it's not level, all the water will run out of the photo! This is a job for the Straighten tool (A). The Straighten tool is really the Crop tool rotating to a known horizontal or vertical line. Here's how to use it:

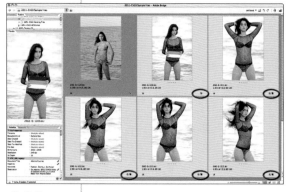

3.20

Step *1*: Go to Bridge. Select the RAW file of Elizabeth, 2062-Q-1124.dcr, and open it in ACR3.

Step *2*: Select the Straighten tool by pressing the keyboard shortcut A or clicking the tool in the toolbar. Click the left side of the horizon line and drag out to the right.

Step *3*: Move the cursor up or down until the dotted selection line is parallel with the horizon. Release the mouse button; a rotated cropping box appears.

The top and bottom of the crop are now parallel to the horizon line (3.21).

Step *4*: Click Done.

All's well with the world and the water will remain in the photo and not on the floor (3.22). (Yes, I'm kidding about the water running out of the photo. You *knew* that!)

That wraps up our discussion of the toolbar and an introduction to the filmstrip and most of the settings in the Adjustments tab. The remaining part of the Adjustments tab consists of the White Balance menu.

USING THE WHITE BALANCE MENU

The White Balance menu is analogous to the white balance settings in digital cameras. For example, open the RAW file of Elizabeth and select the Tungsten setting. Everything turns blue as it would when shooting with a digital camera outdoors with the white balance set to Tungsten (3.23).

Remember that anything done to a RAW file isn't permanent. Color balance can be changed after the fact. Very cool! Just don't put your camera on Auto White Balance. That causes extra work in this part of the Adjustments tab. The Tint slider controls the magenta/green values. It is used for handling the sickly institutional greens that happen when shooting under fluorescent light.

The Detail tab controls include Sharpness, which alters the amount of sharpening for previews only. Luminance Smoothing lowers noise that results from shooting at higher ISO settings as well as long exposures. Color Noise Reduction lowers noise that appears as green and magenta specks in deeper shadows or (in some cameras) in the lighter highlights.

3.21

3.22

3.23

The Lens tab fixes a problem that high-resolution sensors reveal, especially with zoom lenses. The effect is called *chromatic aberration*, which means that certain wavelengths of light focus either behind or in front of the sensor. Chromatic aberration shows up as color fringing. Use the Fix sliders to reduce the Red/Cyan or Blue/Yellow glows around areas of high contrast. The Vignetting slider compensates for a property some wide-angle lenses have of being darker at the edges of the sensor. It is also a useful creative tool.

Play with the effect by opening the RAW file of Elizabeth again. Click on the Lens tab. Move the Vignetting Amount slider to –75. The edges of the image become darker. Move the Midpoint slider to 35. The effect subtly spotlights Elizabeth and brings her forward in the photograph (3.24).

The Curve tab is new to ACR3. This tab enables you to apply custom curves to RAW files. It comes with three preset Tone Curves—Linear, Medium Contrast, and Strong Contrast—and a Custom option. The Linear curve delivers a flat-looking file. The Medium and Strong Contrast curves do exactly what their names say they do. Choose the one that delivers the result that works best for you. I use the Medium Contrast curve most of the time.

The Calibrate tab holds a lot of potential for creativity and just plain fun. The power of ACR3 runs much deeper than tweaking exposure and neutralizing colors. The high bit depth linear file lends itself to achieving extraordinary special effects. The processing possibilities go from amazing black-and-white conversions, to toning, and even to false colors. The following exercise uses false colors to create . . . well, you'll see. First, let me offer some background.

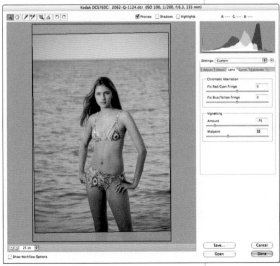

In black-and-white photography, the color of the filter lightens that color and darkens its complement. A red filter darkens cyan and lightens red. A green filter lightens green while darkening magenta. A quick look at Photoshop's Info palette tells the tale (3.25). Digital photographs comprise three black-and-white channels— Red, Green, and Blue. Because the sliders under the Calibrate tab control the color of these channels, you can use them to mix black-and-white values.

3.24

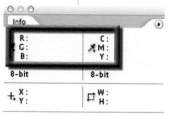

3.25

Now, armed with this knowledge, start slidin' those sliders to your advantage. The photograph used in this example is part of a magazine editorial showing current fashion influenced by past decades, which in this case is the 1980s. For this exercise, I want the skin tones to go whiter than normal. The technique described makes skin tones whiter and with more contrast to minimize skin flaws.

Step 1: Highlight the file Joanna.dcr in Bridge, and then open it in ACR3 by pressing ⌘/Ctrl+R.
The basic exposure and color fine-tuning has already been done.

Step 2: Move the Saturation slider all the way to the left. It reads –100 (3.26).

The Calibrate tab has seven sliders: one for the shadow tint and two for each of the color channels—one for hue and one for saturation. The labels are for the most part self-explanatory. There is a catch. These sliders don't adjust the color of their label. They control the other two. So the Red sliders affect the Green and Blue channels, the Green sliders work with the Red and Blue channels, and the Blue sliders move the Red and Green channels. If this setup seems counterintuitive, remember you're dealing with photography. If it seems kind of backwards, it's probably right. Think back to the camera, for example. The big number (f/22) is for the smallest aperture while the smallest number (f/2.0) represents the widest aperture. If that isn't backwards. . . .

3.26

Step 3: Click the Calibrate tab in the Settings section. Move the Green Hue, Green Saturation, Blue Hue, and Blue Saturation sliders all the way to the left until they each read +100 (3.27).
The skin tones have lightened.

Step 4: Select and clear the Preview box to see the difference and then click the Adjust tab.

Step 5: Click the Tint slider and begin dragging it to the left until it reads –94. Again check the preview to see the difference.

Yes, it is subtle, and there's more. . . .

Step 6: Fine-tune the conversion by going to the Adjust tab and increasing the Brightness to +70. The photograph looks flat. Move the Shadows slider to 11 and decrease the exposure to +0.60. Finally, increase the Contrast to +95.

What have these adjustments done to the color image? Here's where the false color part comes in.

Step 7: Drag the Saturation slider in the Adjust tab back to 0 to reveal the underlying color.

She's, well, really green (3.28). What the settings have done is force the data in the Green channel to dominate the photograph. Making the Saturation –100 uses this Green channel information in black and white with the added benefit of being able to adjust the Shadows, Exposure, Brightness, and Contrast values to taste something that's impossible to do in Channel Mixer alone. You can save the settings just made to Joanna.dcr right in ACR3.

Step 8: Drag the Saturation slider back to –100. Click the fly-out triangle to the right of the Settings field.

Step 9: Choose Save Settings from the drop-down menu. Name the file Joanna b-w.xmp and click Save.

Photoshop automatically saves it to the Settings folder.

Step 10: Spin down the disclosure triangle in the Save Raw Conversion Settings dialog box to find the path for the Settings folder.

You can apply the setting to other files by opening the group of them in ACR3 and choosing the Joanna b-w setting from the drop-down menu (3.29).

3.27

This figure shows the progression of the steps in this project (3.30). The image on the left is the exposure and color-corrected version. Next is the –100 Saturation, then the modified Joanna b-w, and finally, her underlying greenness (Saturation slider at 0).

3.28

3.29

3.30

I encourage you to play with combinations of the sliders in the Adjust tab and with those in the Calibrate tab. Remember that any changes you make to any of the sliders in ACR3 are completely non-destructive. You can return to any setting at any time without degrading the file at all! Amazing creations are lurking for you to discover in the powers and possibilities of ACR3. Go forth and explore!

Setting Up Workflow Options in Adobe Camera Raw

Workflow refers to all the things that you have to do to prepare a file for delivery to a client. The whole point of ACR3 is to convert RAW images into editable files for Photoshop to prepare for output to the Internet, digital printer, printing press, or video. Shooting RAW images has huge benefits when it comes to optimizing the file before conversion to TIF, JPEG, or PSD. ACR3 offers automation within itself for saving files and in conjunction with Bridge and Photoshop.

This section shows how to set up the Workflow Options section for Bridge and how to use ACR3's own file-saving features. In this exercise, you output RAW files to a set of JPEGs to make 4 x 6-inch and 5 x 7-inch prints.

Step *1*: **Open the four RAW files of Adelina you cropped in an earlier exercise in ACR3 by selecting them in Bridge and pressing ⌘/Ctrl+R . Press ⌘/Ctrl+A or click the Select All button at the top of the filmstrip.**

Step *2*: **Select the Show Workflow Options check box to reveal them (3.31).**

Step *3*: **Set up the options as follows:**

Space: sRGB IEC36966-1
Depth: 8 Bits/Channel
Crop Size: 4 by 6 inches
Resolution: 300 pixels/inch

Step *4*: **Click the Save 4 Images button in the lower-right corner of the dialog box (3.32).**
The Save Options dialog box opens. The number of images to be saved button (or open button below it) is determined by how many images are selected in the filmstrip.

Tip
Hiding the Workflow Options makes the preview window larger.

Note
Most minilabs are calibrated to output prints from files in the sRGB colorspace.

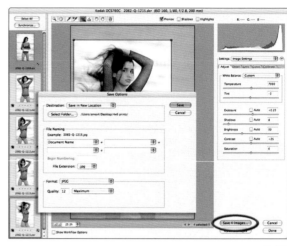

3.31

3.32

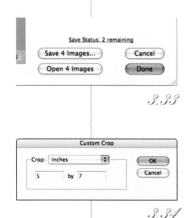

3.33

Step *5*: **Click the Select Folder button.**

Step *6*: **Click the New Folder button to make a new folder on the desktop. Name it** 4x6 prints.

Step *7*: **Select the new folder. Choose JPEG as the Format and keep the Quality at Maximum (12).**

Step *8*: **Click Save.**

ACR3 begins converting and saving the files in the background. The status is displayed above the Save, Open, Cancel, and Done buttons (3.33). ACR3 keeps saving the 4 x 6 files while you are cropping the images to another size.

Step *9*: **The four thumbnails of Adelina are still selected in the filmstrip. Click and hold the Crop tool to open the Custom Crop menu. Enter 5 and 7 into the text boxes, and then choose Inches from the Crop menu (3.34).**

The size of the crop in the Workflow Options changes to 5 x 7 inches.

3.34

Step *10*: **Adjust the position of the crop on each thumbnail by clicking it in the filmstrip and moving and/or sizing the crop box as desired.**

Step 11: **Click the Save 4 Images button and then make a
new folder called** 5 x 7 prints. **Click Save.**

ACR3 finishes saving the 4 x 6 files (if it hasn't already) and
starts saving the 5 x 7s. After you tell ACR3 to save the files,
click Done to return to Bridge.

The ACR3 settings in effect when you click Done remain active the next time
you open Camera Raw. Here is a closer look at the four menus in the
Workflow Options area (3.35):

→ **Space:** ACR3 supports four color workspaces for the RGB files it outputs. Match the setting in this menu to the working color space set in
Photoshop's Color Settings dialog box (⌘/Ctrl+Shift+K).

→ **Depth:** This menu sets the bit depth of the output to either 8- or 16-
bit. Set Depth to 8-bit when going directly to JPEG files. The JPEG
specification does not support 16-bit. Use 16-bit when you are going to
make the highest quality edits in Photoshop.

→ **Size:** Choose from these standard pixel dimensions for output. A size of
1536 by 1024 pixels is much easier to downsize for the Web than one
built to the full size of the camera's sensor, for example. When doing your
highest quality editing work in Photoshop, choose a larger size than what
you will output to edit. When you reduce the file, it will look great! The
minus signs indicate ACR3 will produce a file smaller than the camera's
native resolution. The plus signs indicate that the output will be larger.

→ **Resolution:** This menu sets the output pixels per inch (or per centime-
ter). Enter the number of pixels required by the output device (a printer,
for instance).

Adobe Camera Raw 3 does indeed pack a lot of power
into a single dialog box. The next chapter gets you up and
working in the replacement for the Photoshop CS File
Browser—Adobe Bridge.

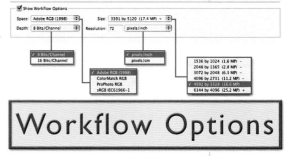

3.35

Chapter Four

Adobe Bridge and the Digital Archiving Workflow

The best and worst of digital capture for photographers is that the joy of instant feedback comes with the pain of becoming their own processing lab. Not a chemical lab as in the days of the darkroom—today, digital image processing is done in front of a computer monitor.

The procedure is not dissimilar to developing film, which involves going into a totally dark room, loading the film onto reels, putting the reels into a tank full of D-76 or ID-11 at 68 degrees, agitating it for the first 30 seconds, and then two more cycles every minute. At the end of the development cycle, the film is immersed in stop bath for one minute with agitation, rinse, fixer, wash, hypo clearing agent, wash, and Photo-Flo solution, then hung in a dust-free cabinet to dry.

After the film is dry, each frame gets an identification number written in the margin in India ink, is cut into strips, slipped into plastic pages, and contact prints are made. The film, safe in archival pages, is stored in numbered envelopes (acid free, of course) awaiting a decision on which one to print. You can count the steps if you like—there are somewhere around 20 of 'em. And that's just for black-and-white processing.

Color processing involves driving to the lab, dropping off the film for clip tests, driving back to the studio to wait the two hours it takes to process the clip tests, driving back to the lab to view the tests, deciding what roll to process and how, driving back to the studio to work on something else for two hours, driving back to the lab to pick up the finished transparencies, and finally driving back to the studio. The film has to be cut into strips if it was unmounted 35mm film in either medium or large format. The strips are slipped into plastic pages using lint-free gloves and then the photographer hunches over a light table with a loupe and a China Marker to select the hero images.

Processing film takes a lot of time. The feedback loop usually takes a minimum of two hours and in the case of color transparencies, processing often takes a whole lot of driving.

The steps described here are workflows—one for processing black-and-white film, the other for processing color transparency. They describe what had to be done to get the image that was captured by the camera on film developed so that it could be seen, edited, and ultimately delivered to the client.

Digitally recorded images have a lot in common with images shot on film. They have to be developed, too. The steps are different, that's all. The most difficult part about understanding a digital workflow is that it really is simpler, easier, faster, and more powerful than traditional film-processing methods. And it does not involve driving or pouring chemicals down the drain, which also makes it much more friendly to our environment.

Digital image processing may not seem easy to do because it is so very, very new. In fact, digital capture with high-resolution, digital single-lens reflex (DSLR) cameras has been possible for less than 10 years compared with more than a century and a half of making photographs on film or even longer with glass plates. The good news is that digital image processing is evolving at an extraordinary pace and is only going to get easier. The point to hold close to your photographic heart is that *digital workflow will never be harder than it is right now.*

The digital image-processing workflow outlined in this chapter follows the traditions of film-based photographic processing from developing all the way through creating contact sheets for client review. And the digital workflow offers the added advantages of electronic proofing as well as the ability to make perfect copies of digital negatives. It also produces bulletproof archive discs that you know are reliable because proofs of every RAW file shot have been made from the DVD copied from the original DVD. If the copy of the original DVD is good, then the original one is, too.

The balance of this chapter involves the software portions of the workflow and how to do them step by step. After you've worked through these projects, you'll have a workflow that works not only on photographs of women, but that also is great for landscapes, sports, weddings, portraits, architecture, nature, wildlife, fine art, or whatever form of photography fires your creative passion.

Digital Workflow Storage and Archiving

Two of the questions I ask during my Professional Workflow with Kevin Ames seminars are, "How many photographers shoot to CompactFlash media?" and "How many shoot tethered to a computer?" Usually 90% to 95% of the audience shoot to a CompactFlash card or MicroDrive and 5% to 10% shoot directly into a computer. Two concerns for photographers are choosing the media for the initial capture, and then managing the high volume of digital negative files comprising many gigabytes of data.

Managing refers to the workflow of copying the digital negatives from the CompactFlash cards or MicroDrives safely onto at least two copies of a permanent form of nonvolatile archiving media—one to keep in the studio and one in an off-site location. No matter what format you choose at the time of capture with your camera, the resulting files are your original work product. They are your *digital negatives*. They are what you use to create the files for editing in Photoshop CS2.

STORING DIGITAL NEGATIVES

The crux of the digital workflow is the storage medium. Hard drives contain moving parts and will eventually fail. This characteristic makes a hard drive a poor choice for a permanent archive. At the same time, the speed and high-density storage of many hundreds of gigabytes makes them ideal as working media. I recommend using three hard drives that are separate from the drive containing your computer's operating system when following a digital workflow. The first drive is the Archive RAW drive. The second is the backup drive. The third drive stores full-resolution JPEG files that are proofs made from the archive DVDs. After all, how do you really know the DVDs are good unless you make a JPEG from each of the RAW files they hold? Don't worry, it's an automatic process that puts Photoshop to work while you do other important things like eat, drink coffee, or sleep. Coffee and sleep are mutually exclusive to some, and I digress. . . .

The working hard drive in my studio is a 4-Disk RAID System Tower from LaCie (www.lacie.com). You can configure RAIDs (Redundant Array of Inexpensive Devices) to perform a style of self-backup. For example, if one drive in the RAID fails, it is replaced and rebuilt with the information from the other drives. A 1TB RAID formatted to RAID 5 like mine holds about 750GB. That gives me close to instant access to all of my digital negatives. (I keep my iTunes library on the RAID, too. Instant access to music is also very good.)

The Backup and JPEG drives I use are 250GB Mercury FireWire drives from Other World Computing (www.macsales.com). OWC Mercury drives are also available in USB 2.0, and you can reformat them for Windows.

ARCHIVING DIGITAL NEGATIVES

High-end, DSLR cameras allow photographers to shoot files that range from 8 to 17MB or 80 to 40 images per CD. However, burning and proofing to CD is a massive and, frankly, undesirable task.

Fortunately, good news is on the archiving front. DVDs hold 4.7GB of data and can store 560 8MB files and 240 17MB files. And they burn as fast as 16X. Even better news is that DVDs are now common storage media in all current computers.

Make a note of the fact that *permanent storage* does not mean *forever*. Having a plan for re-archiving existing CDs and DVDs to the next form of ubiquitous storage is important. This means that when new media becomes ubiquitous, you need to copy all the existing discs to hard drives and burn them to the new media. This step creates a rolling backup of digital negative archives ensuring that no matter how old the files are, a readable copy is always available (from a storage media standpoint, anyway).

Digital Workflow Overview

The flowchart shown here (4.1) illustrates a digital image-processing workflow. Storage media, CompactFlash cards, hard drives, and DVDs are in red, software processes are in green, and distribution choices of proofs for review are in blue.

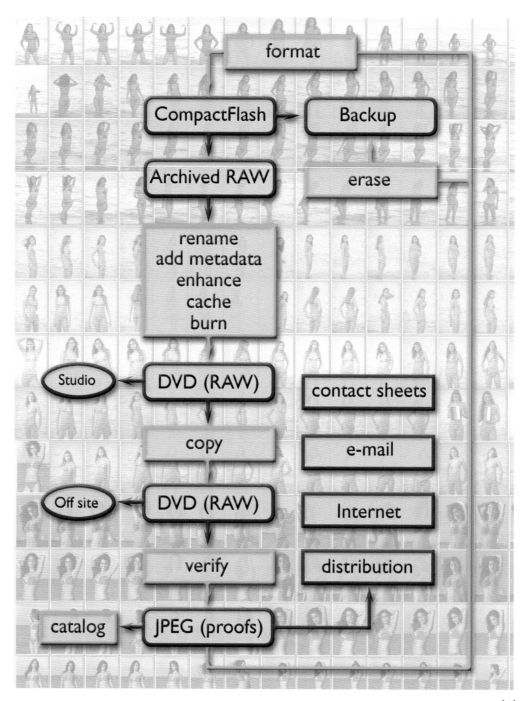

4.1

The digital workflow begins when the camera captures images on storage media. The task of this workflow is to safely store the files on that media to permanent media and then catalog them for retrieval, distribution for selection, and ultimately for publication. Let's go over each step in the process as outlined in Figure 4.1 before you do it step by step later in this chapter:

→ **Copy.** Indicated by the red arrows, this step transfers the files from the CompactFlash card to two separate hard drives—the Archive RAW drive and the backup drive. The backup drive holds an unmodified copy of the files from the CompactFlash cards. At this point in the workflow, the files are on three distinct and separate drives: the Archive RAW drive, the backup drive, and the CompactFlash card.

→ **Metadata.** The first software process deals with information about the data of the digital negatives. In this step you rename the files and add more specific metadata to aid in cataloging, retrieval, and image management. You then make enhancements including color correction and exposure adjustments and export the cache of the changes to speed access to the files when they are burned to DVD.

→ **Burn the first DVD.** Burn a DVD of the folder of RAW files, sidecar files (more on them in a minute), and cache.

→ **Copy the first DVD.** Use a second DVD burner and make a direct copy of the DVD made in the previous step.

→ **Verify.** This step proves that the digital negatives on the copy of the DVD are really there. This step is not to be confused with the verification step included in some DVD-burning software, such as Toast Titanium on the Mac. If a file becomes corrupted while copying from CompactFlash to the hard drives, all disc-burning software verification does is prove that the DVD holds a perfect copy of a corrupted file on the hard drive. This workflow verify step is initiated in Adobe Bridge and uses Photoshop CS2 to create full resolution, highest-quality JPEGs from every digital negative, sharpen each image, reduce color aliasing, and add a copyright notice in the document header and in the metadata about the file.

**JPEG
or RAW?**

The digital workflow described in this chapter is built around RAW files. Chapter 2 presents the case for high-bit-depth capture and explains the advantage of using RAW files over JPEGs. If you choose a JPEG workflow, please skip the section on enhancement in Adobe Camera Raw 3.0 (ACR3). You make JPEG enhancements as shown in Chapter 2. There is controversy about which format is best for capture: JPEG or RAW. In my years of shooting film as a commercial photographer, I mainly shot medium- and large-format cameras because my clients required the high resolution those tools provided. I began shooting digitally before JPEG was offered as a format choice. I believe that the RAW workflow offers more choices in post-production. If you currently shoot JPEGs, try doing the projects in this book using the supplied RAW files. It is my hope that you'll find information about RAW that is interesting and useful. It is not my intention to tout RAW capture over JPEG. RAW is merely my preference.

→ **JPEG Proofs.** The full resolution JPEG proofs are stored on the third separate hard drive. These files have the same name as their RAW counterparts on the DVDs with the exception of the file extensions (.jpg on the proof and .cr2 for a Canon RAW file, for example). They also carry the metadata added earlier in the workflow.

→ **Erase and Reformat.** After you've successfully created and stored the JPEG proofs on the third hard drive, you erase the files on the backup drive and reformat the CompactFlash card in the camera.

→ **Catalog.** You use the JPEG proof files to catalog both the RAW files on the Archive RAW drive and the DVD archives.

→ **Distribution.** You use the JPEGs for showing images to clients on the Internet, through e-mailable PDF presentations, and/or on printed contact sheets.

→ **Archive.** Next to each DVD step are red circles with *studio* or *offsite* written inside. These circles indicate that one of the DVDs is retained in the studio while a copy is kept in a secure off-site location for archiving purposes. The original RAW files are in three discrete places: on the two DVDs and the Archive RAW hard drive. They are also kept as full-resolution JPEGs on the JPEG proof drive. Three of these are kept in the studio. It is recommended that the JPEG files be burned to DVD and stored off-site to back up the JPEG proof hard drive. The JPEG files on this drive can be referenced by cataloging software to provide the highest-quality previews while searching without having to open the files in Photoshop. The JPEG proofs are faster when creating Web sites, PDF files, contact sheets, and even a higher resolution file for a quick use than building new image files from the original RAW files.

Naming Images

When you take a picture, the camera adds a really intuitive name for the pho-tograph—you know, something like: _img-00789.NEF. So what's in a name? The temptation in naming digital files is to put everything in the name that might be useful for finding the file later. For a swimwear shoot you might find a name like swimwearmiamifl2006-0001.RAF. Can you imagine that big long honker under every photograph on a contact sheet labeled Fashion Swim Wear, Miami September 2006? Talk about redundant.

I have seen a lot of naming conventions. Wedding photographers often use the bride's maiden name followed by the groom's last name and the year (for instance, black-chapman-20040001.CRW). Some photographers name by date—0609120001.ORF—where 06 is the year, 09 the month, 12 the day, and 0001 the image number.

These are well and good if not somewhat long. And they all have a flaw. The purpose of a name is to be able to keep track of a set of related digital nega-tives. The flaw is that there is no way to know whether a project is missing. What is the next logical couple after Black-Chapman? What is the next logical job after 060912? Does that photographer shoot every day? If not, what is logically the next job's name?

My naming convention uses serial numbers like the ones found on checks. Every job, event, project (personal or otherwise), vaca-tion, or hike gets assigned a number in consecutive order. The next logical number is always the next one in line. Keeping track of the projects is as simple as writing the serial number in a check register. The serial number provides a way of keeping the physical media (DVDs, model releases, expenses) from a shoot organized. If a number is missing, so is the project (4.2).

4.2

Note

Adobe has chosen to save all of the metadata added to RAW files in "sidecar" files that have the same name and the extension .xmp. This strategy preserves the integrity of the original RAW file by limiting the data written directly into it to changing its name.

A LITTLE DASH'LL DO YA. . .

When it comes to numbering images, it takes a dash not a village. The most critical component of the image name is the dash. Without the dash, a search for a low job number will show you every image with that number. Suppose you are shooting event number 17. Your image number without the dash would be 00170025.jpg. When you search for event number 0017, the computer will show you all the images for event 17. It will also show you every 17th shot for every event that has at least 17 shots in it. Prevent this inconvenience. Put a dash between the event number and the job number. Event 17, image 25 is now named 0017-0025.jpg. Much better. Sort by the job number and the dash. It's all good now.

I rename images using the project number followed by a dash, then I let Bridge assign the sequence. For example, 2062-001.dcr is the first image of project 2062. The folder holding the RAW files is named starting with the project number, as in 2062-01 Laura—lingerie. The 01 following the project number is the DVD number if there are more than one. If I shoot less than a DVD full, I leave the 01 off of the folder.

Computers are amazing at finding things. Ask them anything about the shoot that is in the metadata and they'll spit back the serial number. No problem. I have included an Excel spreadsheet you can use as a starter job journal among the download files for this chapter. To get started, download the files for Chapter 4 from www.amesphoto.com/learning. The code for the book is **PW48255**.

Now you are ready to begin the first project, which explains how to use Bridge to rename digital negatives.

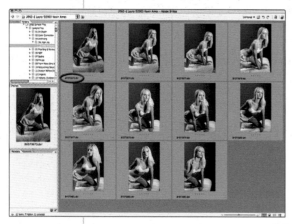

4.3

Using Bridge to Rename Digital Negatives

Step *1*: Using Adobe Bridge, navigate to the downloaded folder that contains images of Laura. Click the folder 2062 Laura.

The thumbnails appear in Bridge's content area. The filename created by the camera appears under each thumbnail (4.3). If none of the thumbnails in the content area are selected, Bridge works on all of them.

Step 2: **Go directly to the Batch Rename dialog box. Press ⌘/Ctrl+Shift+R or choose Tools ⇨ Batch Rename from Bridge's menu bar (4.4).**
The first time you use Batch Rename, click the + button to select the fields for the renaming process. The two you want are Text for the job number and Sequence Number for the image number. The file's extension is automatically added.

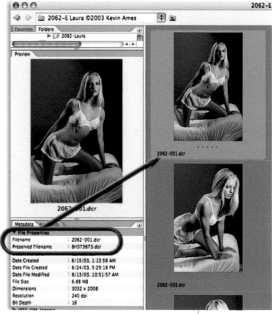

4.4

Step 3: **Enter 2062- in the text field. Click the Sequence number and enter 01.**

Step 4: **Choose Rename in same folder. Select Preserve current filename in XMP Metadata and then click Rename.**

Tip

Selecting Preserve current filename in XMP Metadata creates a field in the metadata with the original filename created by your camera. This feature is useful if a file became corrupted while transferring from a CompactFlash card to a hard drive (4.5). See for yourself. Select an image in Bridge by clicking it, and then click the Metadata tab. Look under File Properties. You'll see it in the Preserved Filename field.

4.5

Note

Canon's original full-frame camera, the 1Ds, saves its RAW file with the extension .tif. If you are shooting with this camera, click the + and choose New Extension. Fill the entry window with .crw. Using this extension will keep you from accidentally saving a Photoshop TIF file over your digital negative.

Metadata

Metadata in digital image files has been around for quite a while. The International Press Telecommunication Council (IPTC) set standards for adding information to digital files in a consistent format back in the days when news photographers carried LeafScan35s with them on assignments to digitize their photographs for transmission to their newspapers over telephone lines. Adobe has made Bridge and Photoshop CS2 compliant with the current IPTC standard for XMP (Adobe's Extensible Markup Platform) and the legacy Information Interchange Model (IIM) used back in the day. This section shows you how to add metadata, where it goes, and then how to create a metadata template of your own. Templates hold all of the basic data that you want in every file.

You can add additional metadata using Adobe Bridge, which ships with Photoshop CS2. The important point to remember is that metadata added immediately after capture in the camera and metadata you add will accompany all the subsequent photographs made from the file. Modern cataloging software (such as Portfolio 8 from Extensis and iView MediaPro from iView Multimedia) extracts the metadata from the files and stores the data along with viewable thumbnails in a database. The more metadata you add to a digital image, the richer the information to search and the easier it is to find exactly the photograph you want.

Two methods are available for adding metadata into files using Bridge. One is directly from the metadata and keyword panes. The other is via the File Info dialog box. We'll start there.

What Is Metadata?

The word *meta* means "after" in Greek. *Data* is information. Therefore, *metadata* is information added to the photograph *after* it is captured.

Digital cameras add the first metadata to a file including information about exposure, focal length, ISO, white balance, date and time of capture, camera make, serial number, and so on. This information is called EXIF metadata and it is written directly into the file whether the capture is JPEG or RAW.

If you shoot RAW files, any information added, including settings made in Adobe Camera Raw 3, is stored in .xmp "sidecar" files. Adobe opted to keep metadata in separate files with the extension .xmp to protect RAW files' forensic integrity and eliminate the possibility of corrupting the file by constantly writing into its header. Remember to keep the sidecar files with the RAW files when archiving them. To see the .xmp files, choose View ➪ Show Hidden Files from Bridge's menu bar.

Sidecar Files

Step 1: **Create a new document in Photoshop by pressing ⌘/Ctrl+N. Choose 1024 x 768 pixels, name the file** Metadata Example, **and click OK.**

Step 2: **Press ⌘/Ctrl+Option/Alt+Shift+I or choose File ➪ File Info.**
The metadata window for the document opens (4.6). You can find a copy of Metadata Example.psd complete with its metadata in the download files for this chapter.

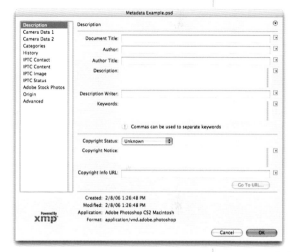

4.6

Step 3: **By default, the Description field in the left pane is highlighted. Fill in all the fields on the right with their names.**
For example, the Document Title window gets "Document Title" in it. Leave the Copyright Status as Unknown. Continue filling in field names for the IPTC Contact, IPTC Content, IPTC Image, IPTC Status, and Origin panes by clicking each one.

Step 4: **Save the template by clicking the disclosure triangle in the upper-right corner of the dialog box and choosing Save Metadata Template (4.7). Name it** Field Tracker Template **and click OK.**

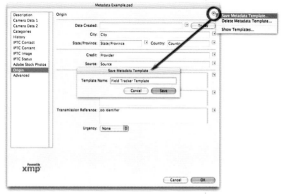

4.7

Step *5*: Close the dialog box by clicking OK. Save the file, Metadata Example.psd to a folder on your hard drive.

Step *6*: Press ⌘/Ctrl+Shift+O to browse in Bridge. Choose Window ⇨ Workspace ⇨ Metadata Focus. Navigate to the folder where you saved Metadata Example.psd. Click the file to select it.

Step *7*: Double-click the Favorites and Keywords tabs to collapse those panes. Close the File Properties and Camera Data (EXIF) panes by clicking their disclosure triangles.

Step *8*: Click the disclosure triangle in the upper-right corner of the Metadata tab and choose Preferences. Click the box next to IPTC (IIM, legacy), then click OK (4.8).

Step *9*: Double-click the folder holding Metadata Example.psd. Click the thumbnail for Metadata Example.psd to select it. Hold down ⌘/Ctrl+Option/Alt+Shift+I to open its File Info dialog box (4.9).

Here's the payoff: The information you entered in the panes of File Info appear in the Metadata tab in Bridge.

Step *10*: Click in each of the File Info panes and see how what you entered is displayed.

The Description pane carries legacy IPTC (IIM) data. Where appropriate it has been repopulated from the IPTC panes. They correspond almost exactly to the IPTC Core display in Bridge. Now you know where the data displays in Bridge and how it gets there.

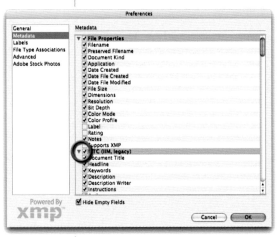

4.8

That's the metaphysics of metadata. The next section shows you how to create and apply your own template to an entire folder of RAW files and customize individual files quickly and simply.

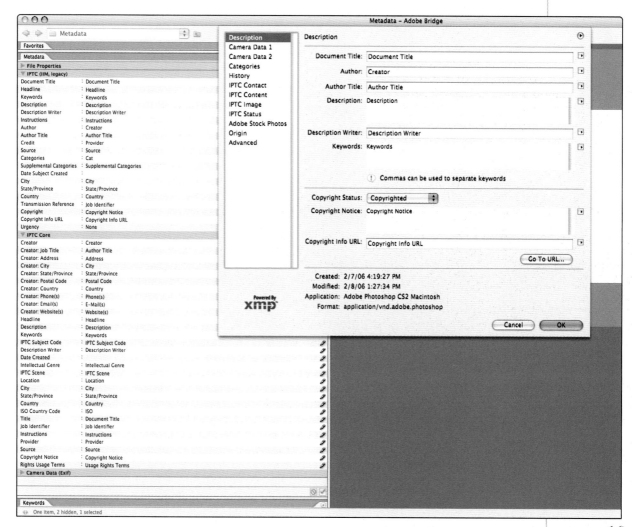

4.9

Creating a Basic Metadata Template

In this exercise you create a basic template that you will apply to every digital negative file going forward.

Step *1*: **Create a new document from the keyboard by pressing ⌘/Ctrl+N. The same size you chose last time is already in the dialog box. Press Return.**

4.10

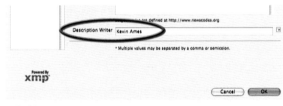

4.11

Step 2: **Press ⌘/Ctrl+Option/Alt+Shift+I to open the File Info dialog box.**
The Description pane is displayed. Fill in the Author, Author Title, and Description Writer. Leave the Keywords section blank. Enter your information into the Copyright Notice and Copyright info URL fields. Leave the Copyright Status at Unknown (4.10).

Step 3: **Go to the IPTC Contact pane using the keyboard shortcut ⌘/Ctrl+6 or click it in the column on the left of the dialog box. Fill in all of these fields with your information (4.11).**

Step 4: **Press ⌘/Ctrl+7 for the IPTC Content pane. Leave all of these fields blank.**
You'll add data that goes in these fields to groups of images later. Notice that the Description Writer field has been filled in with the data you entered in the Description pane (4.12).

Step 5: **Press ⌘/Ctrl+9 and move to the IPTC Status pane. Fill in Provider, Source, Copyright Notice, and Rights Usage Terms. The Copyright Notice will already be filled in with information from the Description pane (4.13).**

Step 6: **Save this template by clicking the fly-out triangle and naming it in the Save Template dialog box. Name it** [Your Name] Basic Template **and click OK to save.**
Saved templates are visible in the fly-out menu.

Note
All the fields in the IPTC (⌘/Ctrl+8) are left blank.

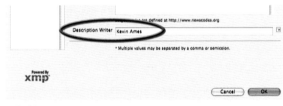

4.12

Pre-Archiving

Use the three sample RAW files of Heather you downloaded to complete this chapter's exercises to work through the following workflow with me. Where I apply my job number and metadata template, you apply yours. I'm starting with renaming even though it's been done once in this chapter so you'll have the entire workflow available step by step.

To get started, set up your working hard drive with the following empty folders: RAW files 2B Archived, Archived Digital Negatives, and Projects. (Hint: Insert a space before you type RAW. Doing so will place the folder at the top of the hierarchy.) Copy the downloaded folder 2202-Toni & Guy Fantasy Hair to the RAW Files 2B Archived folder. And yes, that is my iTunes music library (4.14).

When you work on your own project, begin by creating a folder with the project number and description in the RAW Files 2B Archived folder on the Archive RAW drive. For this exercise, we're using 2202-Toni and Guy Fantasy Hair as our project folder. Option+drag (right-click Copy then right-click Paste) your project folder onto the backup drive. Copy the files from your CompactFlash card to the project folder on the new folder on the Archive RAW drive backup drive. For this exercise, the images of Heather are already in the 2202-Tony and Guy Fantasy Hair folder.

4.13

4.14

Tip

Photo Mechanic 4 can copy files from CompactFlash cards to the Archive RAW drive and the backup drive at once while renaming and adding the base metadata. When finished, it even unmounts the CompactFlash card! It is a huge help in speeding up workflow. Download a trial version from `camerabits. com`. The current version costs $150.00 US and supports .xmp metadata.

RENAMING RAW FILES

Metadata
▼ File Properties
Filename   : 2202-001.CR2
Preserved Filename   : _V7Z3342.CR2
Document Kind   : Camera Raw

4.15

Step 1: Navigate to the folder 2202-Toni and Guy Fantasy Hair in Bridge and double-click it to populate the content pane with thumbnails. Press ⌘/Ctrl+Shift+R to open the Batch Rename dialog box (or choose Tools ⇨ Batch Rename).

The job number is 2202-, and I'll begin numbering the images at 1.

Step 2: The Rename in same folder and Preserve current filename in XMP Metadata options are selected. Click Rename.

If an image became corrupted during the copy process, having the original filename in the Metadata tab of Bridge facilitates finding the original file on the backup drive or the CompactFlash card (4.15).

ADDING METADATA

The power of adding metadata to the files before they are archived is that all subsequent uses, with the exception of images saved with Save for Web, carry this information. That means copyright and usage information and details about the shoot, including the edit history, accompany the images digitally everywhere they go. The information is especially useful for searching in digital cataloging software such as Portfolio 8 or iView MediaPro. Your digital photographic life will be a thing of beauty if you make adding metadata a must-do part of your workflow.

Step 3: Choose Edit ⇨ Select All or use the keyboard shortcut ⌘/Ctrl+A. Click the Metadata tab. Click the disclosure triangle to reveal the fly-out menu. Choose Append Metadata and select your basic template from the menu (4.16).

Bridge writes the new information to the .xmp sidecar file in the case of RAW images or directly into JPEG files. The added metadata appears in the IPTC (IMM, legacy) and IPTC Core panes. This is the base metadata. Next, add your job-specific information.

Step 4: **Spin down the IPTC Core metadata pane. Fill in the Description field with as much information as you can.**

4.16

The more information you fill in the easier time you'll have searching for the file later. This step adds metadata that is common to all the selected images. My example shows the model's name, Heather; that a model release has been signed; the model's agency, Click Models Atlanta; the client's name, Toni and Guy; and project information, Fantasy hair with tribal theme. Complete the Title field, using the name of the folder, which in this case is 2202-Toni and Guy Fantasy Hair (4.17).

Step 5: **Deselect all the images by pressing ⌘/Ctrl+Shift+A (or by choosing Edit ⇨ Deselect All).**

Now I'll highlight images that have something in common and are different from the rest of the shoot and add more information to the Description field. (Due to the large size of the RAW files, I have included only one of the close-ups.) You might choose to differentiate between close-ups and medium views, for example. A fashion shoot would list the clothes and accessories of each setup. The Description field is a good place to add the makeup artist, wardrobe stylist, and hair stylist. Think "Pertinent information goes here!" when filling it out.

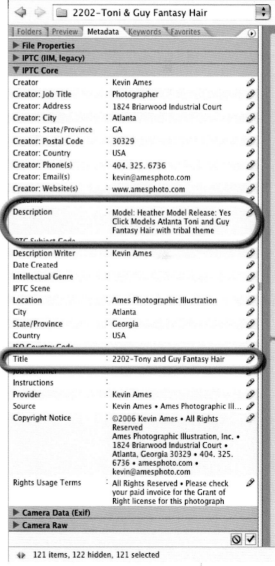

4.17

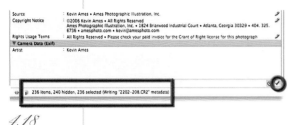

4.18

Step 6:
Click the apply check mark at the bottom of the pane or click OK in the "Do you want to apply these metadata changes to the selected files?" dialog box. If this box appears select the Don't show again check box.

Bridge shows you the status as it writes the metadata (4.18).

> Take description notes on your laptop during the shoot. Then copy and paste them into the Description field.

Notice that the Metadata tab contains no field for keywords. You add them in the Keywords tab.

Step 7: **Double-click the Keywords tab.**

I have created a set of fashion keywords by choosing New Keyword Set from the fly-out menu or by clicking the New Keyword Set icon at the bottom of the pane. Next to the New Keyword Set icon is the New Keyword icon. Use these icons to create your keyword sets. In this example, I will select all the thumbnails and then click the appropriate keyword in the Fashion set. Finally, I'll click the first image of Heather holding the Gray Balance Card and click the ColorChecker keyword. I like to have that as a sorting choice because the reference card is always the beginning of each section of a shoot (4.19).

Step 8: **Click back into the Metadata tab.**

Notice that it now has a Keywords field and the data you added in the last step is displayed.

> Select images in a range by clicking the first one and Shift+ clicking the last one. Hold down the ⌘/Ctrl key and click to select or deselect individual thumbnails.

ENHANCING RAW FILES

This section deals with making fast tweaks to color balance and exposure using Adobe Camera Raw 3. Make sure you have the current version of ACR3. Choose Photoshop ⇨ About Plug-In ⇨ Camera Raw. An About box appears with the version number (4.20). As of this writing, the current version is 3.3. Get the current version from www.adobe.com, click Support, click Downloads, and go to Photoshop CS2. Choose Macintosh or Windows. Follow the installation instructions on the download page for the Adobe Camera Raw update. ACR3 updates are free. Life is good.

4.19

Step 9: Click on the first thumbnail in Bridge (the one with the ColorChecker Gray Balance Card in my example). Shift+click on the last thumbnail in the sequence to select the entire range. Press ⌘/Ctrl+R (or choose File ➪ Open in Camera Raw) to open the entire set of selected thumbnails in Camera Raw.

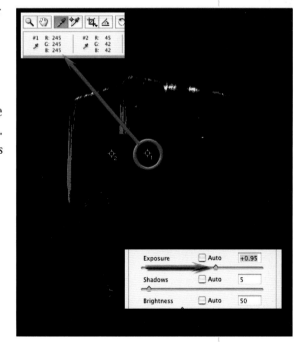

Adobe® Camera Raw Plug-in

© 2005 Adobe Systems Incorporated. All rights reserved.
by Thomas Knoll

4.20

Step 10: Click Select All at the top of the filmstrip or press ⌘/Ctrl+A.

The reference card shot has a blue border around it and is displayed in the preview pane.

Step 11: Click the Color Sampler tool (or press S). Click to place Sampler #1 on the white patch. Click the black patch to place Sampler #2.

Step 12: Click the White Balance tool (or press I), and then click in the white patch.

The color balance is neutralized. Sampler #1 reads R: 213, G: 213, B: 213. These readings are lower than the optimum of around 245.

Step 13: Hold down the Option/Alt key, click the Exposure slider, and move it to the right to increase exposure. The screen goes black, and as the numbers climb, areas of red appear in Heather's hair. These areas tell us that the red channel is at 255. The yellow means the red and green channels have reached 255 as well (4.21). The red and yellow are in the highlights and are specular highlights at that. (*Specular* means mirror. A specular highlight is a mirror of the source of light, in this case a Chimera softbox over the model's head. The specular highlight reveals the sheen of her hair as it curves forward.)

4.21

The values are right where they're supposed to be. The shadows are fine. The temptation is to boost them to increase contrast. Resist it with all your might. After you make a print, if it looks flat then boost the shadows in Levels or Curves. Don't do it in Camera Raw. Finally, I'll lower the Brightness to 40. Notice that Sampler #1 drops to 243.

Step 14: Hold down the Option/Alt key and click the Exposure slider.

The specular highlights are still showing red and yellow. Perfect. The Brightness slider affects the midtones, leaving the highlights and shadows alone.

Step 15: Leave Contrast alone and boost the Saturation to about 10.

Use the Saturation slider with care. The result might look wonderful on the monitor and be really bad in print.

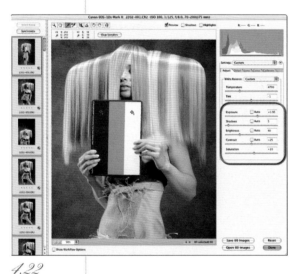

4.22

The payoff is that all the files in the filmstrip update with the changes as they are made because they are all selected. If you forget to select them before doing color balance and exposure tweaks, click Select All and then click Synchronize.

Step 16: Click Done in the Settings dialog box (4.22).

Step 17: Click Done in the Camera Raw dialog box.

Look at the content pane in Bridge. The thumbnails update to reflect the settings made in Camera Raw. Notice the settings symbol in the lower-right corner of the thumbnail. It tells you that changes have been applied in ACR3.

Step 18: Repeat the enhancements for the subsequent thumbnail in Bridge.

EXPORTING THE CACHE FILES

Cache means hidden. The cache files generated by Adobe Bridge store thumbnails and metadata so that the content pane will populate quickly, especially when reading from slow media like DVDs. You have two ways to get the cache files into the folder of RAW files on the working hard drive. Choose Tools ⇨ Cache ⇨ Export Cache or change Bridge's preferences. The latter is my favorite. Choose Bridge ⇨ Preferences ⇨ Advanced (or choose Edit ⇨ Preferences ⇨ Advanced) and select Use Distributed Cache Files When Possible (4.23).

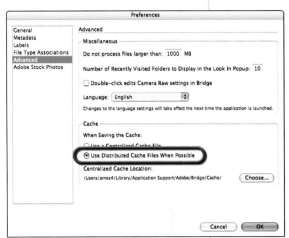

4.23

This setting automatically places cache files into folders on all local drives. It will not work over a network. If you are working on a network drive, choose Tools ⇨ Cache ⇨ Export Cache. Locate the cache files by choosing View ⇨ Show Hidden Files. All the .xmp sidecar files will appear, and after the last thumbnail you'll see the cache files. The rename, add metadata, enhance, and cache steps are complete.

Step 19: Launch your DVD-burning software and browse to or drag the folder on the Archive RAW drive that has the RAW files, .xmp sidecar files, and the two Bridge cache files into the burning window. Make one last check to make certain the cache files are there (4.24). Are you getting the idea that I think cache files are really, really important? If not, you'll believe me after you burn a DVD without them and then open it in Bridge. You'll get the point in the 15 minutes or so Bridge takes to build temporary cache files this time and every time you reinsert the DVD into the computer.

Step 20: Name the DVD exactly the same as the folder in the RAW Files 2B Archived folder. Burn the disc.

Note

The ColorChecker Gray Balance Card shows where the lighting has changed. When you get in the habit of shooting it at the beginning of each lighting set, click its thumbnail in Bridge, hold down the Shift key, and click the thumbnail in front of the next ColorChecker. Open the selection in Camera Raw 3 and repeat the steps for white balance and exposure tweaking.

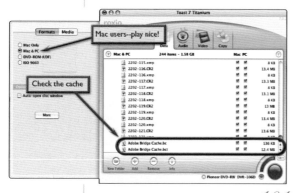

4.24

4.25

COPY THE DVD

Making a copy of the DVD is important. Do not make another copy of the folder on the Archive RAW hard drive. Make a copy of the DVD you just burned. In the next section you proof the *copy* of the DVD. If the copy of the first DVD is good, then the first DVD is, too.

The burning question is, "How do you know that every digital negative on the DVD is good?" The answer is, "You don't." Does this mean that you have to trust your luck? And if one of the files is bad, which one will it be (4.25)? (Don't kid me on this one. It will be the best photograph taken in the universe. Ever.) The only way to know that you have good files on the DVD is to make a proof of each one. No, don't groan. You can do this task automatically from Bridge using Photoshop CS2's Image Processor. You have to do some setup the first time, including naming the JPEG drive and building an action that adds some sharpening, reduces color aliasing, and flips the copyright status in File Info to Copyrighted. Consider this step to be halftime for the workflow process while you get this prep work out of the way. After you do this section, you won't ever have to do it again.

SAVING TO THE JPEG DRIVE

This external hard drive will hold all the JPEG proofs. Logic would have it named something intuitive like "JPEG drive." This name works fine on Windows. Windows sees it as F:\2202-Toni and Guy Fantasy Hair. The problem on the Mac is that cataloging software will read it as JPEG drive/2202-Toni & Guy Fantasy Hair in the case of the proofs about to be made. The solution on the Mac is to name it something that means nothing, such as the greater-than sign (>).

The cataloging software then shows the path on the Mac as >:2202-Toni and
Guy Fantasy Hair. This method works. So Mac users, name your JPEG drive
>. To copy the folder name to a new folder, Mac users highlight folder 2202-
Toni and Guy Fantasy Hair and press Return. Press Ctrl+C to copy the folder
name. Windows users right-click it, choose Rename from the pop-up menu,
and press Ctrl+C. Open the JPEG drive (>) and create a new folder. Paste
(press ⌘/Ctrl+V) the copied folder name onto the new one.

Note that the JPEG proofs are proxies for their RAW
files that have the same name. You want them to be in a
folder with exactly the same name as their RAW counterparts. This setup makes the cataloging software give
you the name of the DVD the cataloged proofs came
from (4.26).

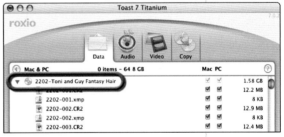

4.26

Creating a Proofing Action

Digitally captured or scanned images come into Photoshop slightly soft for many
reasons, none of which are important here. They are soft. That's what matters.

In the first part of this exercise you apply a small amount of unsharp mask to
the luminosity or the tone without the color of the image. In the second part
you apply a little blur to the color to reduce unwanted colors in the specular
highlights. In the third part you add the copyright symbol to the document's
header, which also appears in the File Info dialog box.

Step 1: Click the thumbnail named 2202-001.CR2 in Bridge. Press ⌘/Ctrl+R to open it in Camera Raw.

Step 2: Select the Workflow Options check box to reveal the choices. Set the options as follows, and then click Open.

Space: Adobe RGB (1998)

Size: 3328 x 4992 (16.6 MP)

Depth: 8 Bits/Channel

Resolution: 300 pixels per inch.

You made the other settings earlier in the enhance section of this chapter.

Step 3: Open the Actions palette, and then click the Create New Set icon at the bottom of the palette. Name the set Proofing.

Step 4: Click the Create New Action icon. Name it USM > Alias > ©.

On the Mac, assign F13 as the shortcut. On Windows, assign F12. You will use this action all the time when editing images in Photoshop. F13 on Macintosh and F12 on Windows are the last function keys of the typing keyboard. (Macs do not have preconfigured keys in the group above the arrow keys. They have three more function keys: F14, F15, and F16. As with the standard keyboard shortcuts, I will give the Mac function keys assigned in the book first followed by the ones for Windows.)

Note

The copyright symbol (©) is Option+G on the Mac. On Windows, hold down the Alt key and type **0169** on the keypad. It won't work using the numbers under the function keys. When you release the Alt key, the copyright symbol (©) appears.

Step *5*: Click Record.

Step *6*: Choose Filter ⇨ Sharpen ⇨ Unsharp Mask. Enter 100%, 1 pixel as the Radius, and leave the Threshold setting at 0. Click OK.

Step *7*: Choose Edit ⇨ Fade Unsharp Mask and change the mode to Luminosity. Click OK.

The result looks much sharper (4.27).

Step *8*: Choose Filter ⇨ Blur ⇨ Gaussian Blur. Enter 1.3 pixels and click OK.

That which was sharp is once again blurry. Hmmm. No sweat, there's more. . . .

Step *9*: Choose Edit ⇨ Fade Gaussian Blur. Change the mode to Color. Click OK.

The sharpness returns and the aliasing disappears. Woo-hoo! The change is subtle and you can see the effect at a magnification of 400% (4.28).

4.27

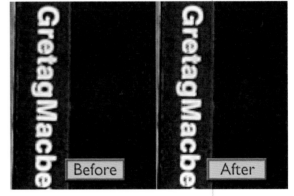

Step *10*: Choose File ⇨ File Info. Change the Copyright Status from Unknown to Copyrighted (4.29). Click OK.

4.28

Step *11*: Click the stop recording button at the bottom of the Actions palette (4.30). Highlight the Proofing set. Click the disclosure triangle in the upper-right corner of the Actions palette. Choose Save Actions. Click OK.

The action is saved in the Photoshop CS2 folder in the Presets folder in the Photoshop Actions folder.

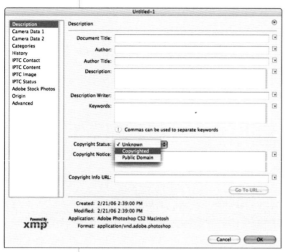

4.29

4.30

Actions are the easy way to have Photoshop do repetitive tasks for you. Do a procedure once while recording in the Actions palette and Photoshop can play it back on every file selected in Bridge. Photoshop does the work while you are free to do other things!

Verifying the DVD Copy

You know the reasons why you should verify your work. Here are the final steps of the archiving workflow:

Step *12*: **Put the copy of the first DVD in the computer.**
It appears in the Folders tab of Bridge. Click the Folders tab or go to View ⇨ Folders Panel if it's not visible. Click the first DVD; the content pane quickly fills with thumbnails thanks to the cache files burned with the RAW files back in Step 19 of "Exporting the cache files."

Note

Handing work off to Photoshop does not require any thumbnail to be selected in Bridge. If none are chosen, Photoshop processes all of them. This technique works with the Batch Rename command, too.

Step 13: **Choose Tools ⇨ Photoshop ⇨ Image Processor.**
Bridge hands you off to Photoshop and the Image Processor
dialog box.

The first section of the Image Processor offers a check box that will open the
first file so you can set ACR3's workflow options.

Step 14: **Instead of selecting the box, go
back to Bridge and highlight any
one of the thumbnails. Press
⌘/Ctrl+R to open it in Camera
Raw in Bridge. Click the Workflow
Options box to reveal them.**
The settings are shown in the figure (4.31).

4.31

Step 15: **Click Done. Press ⌘/Ctrl+Shift+A to deselect the
thumbnails in Bridge.**
If you forget to do this, the Image Processor will only proof
the selected file.

Step 16: **Click the Select Folder button in the second section
of the Image Processor. Navigate to the JPEG drive:
> on the Mac and a drive letter on Windows. Open
the drive and choose the folder 2202-Toni and Guy
Fantasy Hair created earlier. Click Choose.**
The third section of Image Processor is the File Type.

Step 17: **Click JPEG, set the quality to 12, and clear Convert
Profile to sRGB.**
The fourth section is Preferences.

Note

The Size setting in
ACR3 allows you to
reduce files as indicated
by a minus (-) sign after
the file size or enlarge
them as indicated by a
plus (+) sign after the
file size. No sign means
that the size is the
native resolution of the
camera. Choose this
size for the proofs.

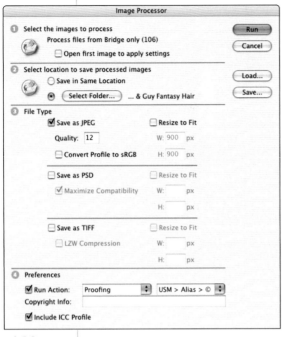

4.32

Step *18*: **Click Run Action. Choose Proofing from the first menu, and USM ⇨ Alias ⇨ © from the second. Select Include ICC Profile (4.32). Finally, click Run.**

That's it. The rest of the proofing runs in Photoshop, leaving Bridge free to do the work coming up in the next chapter.

Okay, there is one more thing. How do you know when Photoshop finds a corrupt file? A file that won't open crashes the Image Processor and presents the following dialog box (4.33).

4.33

Note

Although 16-bits per channel does offer the highest quality file for editing, the JPEG standard does not support it. Because the JPEGs produced here are for use for proofing on the Internet, e-mailable PDF presentations, cataloging, and proof sheets, the best quality is not required.

If this happens, go to Bridge and open a new window by pressing ⌘/Ctrl+N. Click the Folders pane, choose the JPEG drive, and click the folder. Scroll down to the last thumbnail. Highlight it, and then click the Metadata tab. Spin down the File Properties section and look at the Preserved Filename. Write it down. The next file is the corrupted one. Make another new window in Bridge. Click the backup drive in the Folders tab and click the folder with the copy of the RAW files. Find the corrupt file by its name. Click it and open it in ACR3. Click Open. If the file opens, replace the corrupt one on the Archive RAW drive with this one. If it doesn't, go to the CompactFlash card and check the corresponding file on it. Chances are one of these versions will still be good.

Yes, finding a corrupt file means you have to burn new DVDs. And if the file isn't the best photograph the universe will ever see, you can ignore it. Using the verify process means that you'll always know and never wonder what was shown in the one that got away.

Chapter Five

Distribution: Presenting Digital Photography

Back in the day, one challenge facing photographers was making catalogs of photographs. Computer databases did a good job of keeping records about each slide, transparency, or negative. The downside was that each one had to have information entered at the keyboard. This process took a lot of time. Plus, there was no way to include a digital thumbnail of the photograph in the database. Be that as it may, using a database for cataloging photographs was worth it to those of us who invested the time.

Most photographers relied on their memories of what they had shot. Those who made records of their work had an advantage in being able to quickly find a piece of film. A query gave a list of image numbers sorted by keyword or description. The photographer went to the physical files and pulled the film by its number. Then it was back to the light table with the loupe to choose exactly the right one. The rejects had to be refiled in order for the system to continue to work. Selected images had to be taken to the lab, duped (or printed), then delivered to the client, and the original refiled. Awkward as this method sounds, it was much better than relying on remembering what had been shot. "The shortest pencil is better than the longest memory," as the saying goes.

Another challenge was picking the best images from the shoot. This task meant hours bending over a light table looking at each frame with an 8X magnifying loupe. The picks were indicated with china markers on the sleeves or contact sheets. It was time-consuming, back straining, and frustrating when the shots you wanted to compare side by side were on different pages.

The last challenge was showing and delivering the chosen work to clients, potential clients, and others interested in it. Film has that romantic charm of being a one-of-a-kind original. Let me tell you right now that relying on film as the only copy of your photograph is not smart. Photographs captured on film—an emulsion on a flexible base—start degrading almost as soon as they come out of the chemical processor. The fading is a slow process that over time becomes way too real. The original is damaged, never to be the same. I have film in my library that has degraded to the point of complete uselessness.

Duplicating the very best photograph was always a compromise. Copying black-and-white negatives meant making a great print and shooting a copy negative with a loss of dynamic range. Color transparencies were duped by shooting them on low-contrast color transparency film. While quite good, they weren't perfect one-to-one copies. And they were expensive, costing from

$6 to $20 dollars depending on size for the best quality. Clients, of course, wanted the originals, so the photographer was stuck with the shoot's next best selections that weren't delivered, as well as somewhat inferior dupes of the heroes made at considerable expense in time and dollars at a photo lab.

This chapter addresses these three challenges—cataloging photographs, choosing photographs, and distributing photographs for review. The good news is that things are better now—much, much better. Today, the process of cataloging, proofing, and choosing the best images is easier, more reliable, and less work than ever before.

Cataloging Photographs

Once, cataloging photographs was at best a tedious, onerous, time-consuming task done in front of a black screen with green or amber characters. I know you want a huge and intricate discussion of cataloging your photographs of women. And here it is: Launch your cataloging software. It doesn't matter which one you use. Extensis Portfolio or iView Media Pro and others do much the same job. Once the cataloging window is open, drag the folders of proofs made in Chapter 4 from your JPEG drive on to it. Done (5.1).

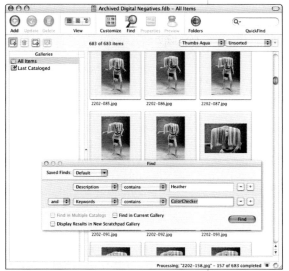

5.1

Yep. That's all there is to it. The JPEG proofs are placeholders for the RAW files they were made from. They are adjusted for color balance and exposure and carry all the metadata added to the RAW files before they are burned to DVD and proofed. The software pulls thumbnails and reads the metadata you added to the RAW files, as discussed in the last chapter. Now cataloging photography is so cool and easy. Did I mention you're done cataloging?

If you are familiar with Photoshop 7 or Photoshop CS, you know, use, and probably love File Browser. Rejoice! There is now more to love! File Browser has grown up into a stand-alone application called Bridge. It is automatically installed along with Photoshop CS2. You've already seen how some of Bridge works in the last two chapters. I'll use it here to show you how to solve two more challenges facing you as a soon-to-be master of your digital photograph processing universe.

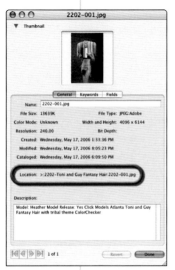

5.2

Finding a specific photograph is simple, too, thanks to the metadata you added to the files. For example, in your cataloging software, click Find and in the case of Portfolio 8, choose Description ⇨ Contains and type the model's name: **Heather**. To find the shot with the ColorChecker, click the + sign to add another search field. Then choose Keywords ⇨ Contains and enter **ColorChecker**. Click Find. You're done. The photograph named 2202-001.jpg appears in the catalog pane. Click its thumbnail to select it and click the Properties icon. The path shows the exact folder on the working drive or the name of the DVD that holds the original RAW file (5.2).

Choosing Heroes

The days of reviewing strips of film while bent over light tables are thankfully over. Adobe Bridge makes reviewing a shoot as easy as watching a slideshow. Imagine being able to rank slides as they were projected onto a screen without pulling them from the tray!

You've already seen how some of Bridge works in the last two chapters. I'll use it here to show you how to solve two more challenges facing you as a soon-to-be master of your digital photograph processing universe. Launch Adobe Bridge by pressing ⌘/Ctrl+Option/Alt+O or clicking its icon on Photoshop's Options bar (or by choosing File ⇨ Browse). Navigate to a folder of your own JPEG proofs or use the downloadable files for this chapter, which you can get from www.amesphoto.com/learning. The book code is **PW48255** and the folder to use for this section is called "Chapter 5 Bridge." Press ⌘/Ctrl+F1 to set Bridge to the default workspace (or choose Window ⇨ Workspace ⇨ Reset to Default Workspace).

Not all of my work is in the studio with models. I also shoot on location and quite often with women who aren't models at all. I find them amazingly beautiful and lots of fun to work with. LeAnn, a successful portrait photographer in her own right, and I decided (at the last minute) to make some photographs of her at an abandoned carwash I'd found in rural Tennessee. The sun was almost down when we arrived. Inside the carwash was way too dark, so I pulled my car into a position where its headlights washed the wall behind her. Tracy, LeAnn's assistant, held a Chimera 48" x 48" reflector while I made this series of photographs.

The files open in Bridge are copies of the JPEG proofs made when I verified the DVDs burned during the archiving workflow completed in Chapter 4. This project familiarizes you with selecting image thumbnails in Bridge, using the slideshow feature, and rating them there and in the content pane.

Step *1*: **Drag the Thumbnail Size slider until the content pane looks like this (5.3). Click the first thumbnail of LeAnn (2260-0012.jpg).**

Step *2*: **Shift+click the last thumbnail on the screen (2260-0030.jpg).**

Step *3*: **Scroll down to see the next row of thumbnails. Hold down the ⌘/Ctrl key and click the next two images in the sequence (2260-0031.jpg and 2260-0032.jpg) to add them to the selection.**

Tip

Bridge displays only the image name under the thumbnails by default. You can add up to three additional lines in the General Preferences pane by pressing ⌘/Ctrl+K (or by choosing Bridge ➪ Preferences and clicking General on Mac, Edit ➪ Preferences and clicking General on Windows). Click a check box and choose the data you want to see from the drop-down menus. Click OK.

5.3

Step 4: Enter the Slideshow mode by pressing ⌘/Ctrl+L (or by choosing View ➪ Slideshow).

The screen goes dark and the first selected thumbnail appears (5.4).

Step 5: **Press the right-arrow key to go to the next thumbnail.**

Continue pressing the right-arrow key after looking closely at each image. Look for expression, eyes, position in frame, posture, and hands—are they "pretty"? When you reach slide 2260-0019.jpg, press ⌘/Ctrl+1 on the keyboard. A single star appears in the caption (5.5). Press ⌘/Ctrl+1 for each of the following images: 2260-0020.jpg, 2260-0029.jpg, 2260-0030.jpg, 2260-0031.jpg, and 2260-0032.jpg. Finally, press Esc to exit from the slideshow.

Tip

Press the H key to reveal the slideshow shortcut keys.

5.4

5.5

5.6

Select a consecutive range of thumbnails by clicking the first one and Shift+clicking the last. Select additional thumbnails by ⌘/Ctrl+clicking on each one. Remove images from a selection by ⌘/Ctrl+clicking them. Select all the thumbnails in the content pane by pressing ⌘/Ctrl+A (or by choosing Edit ⇨ Select All). Deselect all the selected images using ⌘/Ctrl+Shift+A (or choosing Edit ⇨ Deselect All).

Step 6: Click the word *Unfiltered* in the upper-right section of the Bridge window. Choose Show 1 or More Stars (5.6).

The keyboard shortcut is ⌘/Ctrl+Option/Alt+1. The other unrated images are hidden, leaving only the five one-star thumbnails (5.7). Click the double triangles at the bottom-left corner to hide (and reveal) the panes on the side.

5.7

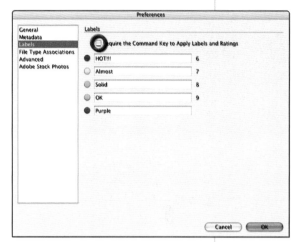

Bridge offers more rating options than stars. Would you believe it offers customizable colored labels, too? Click on the Labels section and name 'em whatever strikes your fancy (5.8)! (Super Tip: Uncheck the "Require ⌘/Ctrl Key to Apply Labels and Ratings" check box to assign ratings by typing only numbers. No modifiers required!)

5.8

Step 7: **Press ⌘/Ctrl+F5 (or choose Window ➪ Workspace ➪ Filmstrip Focus). Click the horizontal/vertical filmstrip button to orient the thumbnails along the right-hand side from top to bottom (5.9).**

Step 8: **Click a thumbnail for a large preview or use the up- and down-arrow keys. Choose your favorite and press ⌘/Ctrl+2 to give it a two-star rating. If you have more than one with two stars, choose Filtered ➪ Show Two or More Stars (or press ⌘/Ctrl+Option/Alt+2).**
Continue the process until you have only one hero, um, heroine chosen.

5.9

Did you hear a voice during Steps 7 and 8? Did it say something like, "Voice over on. Two two oh six LeAnn at the carwash Adobe Bridge scroll bar . . ."? Click the Apple on your menu and choose System Preferences. Click Keyboard and Mouse and then click the Keyboard Shortcuts tab. Under Universal Access, clear the "Turn VoiceOver on or off" check box (5.10). You will no longer hear the voice when you want the Filmstrip Focus workspace in Bridge. If you are hearing other voices, press Pause on your iPod.

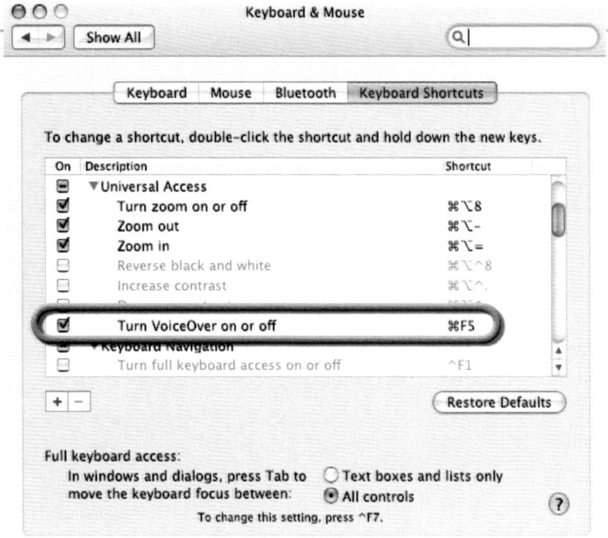

Macintosh:
Hearing
Voices

5.10

Putting Work Out There

Getting digital photographs to clients, family, friends, or the world in general has never been easier using Bridge and Photoshop CS2. Many ways also exist for getting your work out there. I think of distribution as a funnel. Some people love to see the whole shoot, so they get access to a Web site. Others want a presentation that they can e-mail, so they get their prints in a PDF document. Still others want prints on paper, so they receive a custom proof sheet. The absolute beauty of it all is that you can perform each process for the most part automatically using Bridge and Photoshop CS2.

I begin by showing you how to create an image gallery that you can post to your Web site or burn to disc for viewing on any computer. All of these projects start in Bridge.

INTERNET GALLERIES

Navigate to the Chapter 5 Gallery folder, which is in the folder for this chapter you downloaded earlier. The JPEG proofs I generate from my DVD are at the full resolution of the camera and saved at the highest quality using the lowest amount of compression. I have downsampled the files in the Chapter 5 Gallery folder and saved them at a higher compression to save you time downloading them from the Internet.

The model for this project is Virgina Morse with NEXT Management in Los Angeles. These proofs are from the cover shoot for this book. The gallery is for client review. In the following steps I use Bridge to sort and arrange the shoot so the gallery will be presented in the order I choose:

Step 1: **Choose Window ⇨ Workspaces ⇨ File Navigator. Select all the thumbnails by pressing ⌘/Ctrl+A, and then give all of them a one-star rating by pressing ⌘/Ctrl+1.**

Step 2: **Show thumbnails with a one-star (or more) rating from the Unfiltered menu or with the keyboard shortcut ⌘/Ctrl+Option/Alt+1, and then deselect all the thumbnails by pressing ⌘/Ctrl+Shift+A (or by choosing Edit ⇨ Deselect All).**

Step 3: **Click the first thumbnail of Virginia (2264-0001.jpg).** I'm fairly sure the client doesn't want to see the stylist working with her hair. Hide this image by pressing ⌘/Ctrl+0. It disappears and the next thumbnail is selected. Press the right-arrow key to move to 2264-0002.jpg. It's fine. Press the right-arrow key to highlight number 0003, which shows Virginia holding the ColorChecker reference card. I like it for my collection of chart shots, but the client doesn't want to see it. Press ⌘/Ctrl+0 to make it go away. By this time I'll bet you wish you didn't have to hold down the modifier key and could just press the 0 key instead.

Step 4: **Set it up in Preferences (press ⌘/Ctrl+K) by clicking the Labels pane and clear the box next to "Require the ⌘/Ctrl Key to Apply Labels and Ratings."**
I'll use the no-modifier-needed keystrokes from here on.

Step 5: **Continue pressing the right-arrow key to move through the thumbnails, pressing 0 for the ones that won't be shown in the gallery.**
You can resize the Preview panel (View ⇨ Preview Panel) by dragging the double lines on the top, bottom, and right sides to expand it (5.11).

5.11

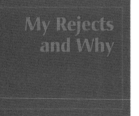

My Rejects and Why

Here are the photographs I chose not to share with my publisher—unless, of course, he's seeing them here (5.12).

Row 1 (left to right)—0001: makeup artist in shot; 0003: reference card; 0025: eyes droopy; 0027: makeup artist again; 0037: hands and mouth; and 0040: hand is flat to camera on shoulder.

Row 2—0041: she has a sort of ditzy look and I have always wanted to use the word "ditzy" in print; 0059 and 0060: makeup being applied; and 0061, 0062, and 0063: The flash on the background didn't fire, leaving it gray.

Row 3—0064–0066: no flash continues; 0078: out of focus big time; and 0080: hand and head are tilted toward the camera instead of away.

The cover of the book is on a white background, so I don't want to show 0061–0065. Yes, I could make the background white in Photoshop. Here's the question I ask when this sort of thing happens: "Why open myself up for a lot more work when there are lots of other great photographs in the take?" If these images were film, you would have hit 'em with the REJECT stamp, 'cause there was no Photoshop back in the day.

5.12

I spend considerable time reviewing my rejects and verbalizing why I chose to make them rejects. This step heightens my awareness of what happened and how to change it on future shoots. The more awareness the photographer has behind the camera, the more effortless the work in Photoshop becomes.

Step 6: Review the rejects to make certain they don't belong. **Choose Show Unrated Items Only from the Filtered drop-down menu in the upper-right corner of the Bridge window.**

If you rejected a photograph and then change your mind, highlight it and press 1. It's promoted to the chosen ones.

Usually I present the photographs in the gallery chronologically. Sometimes I have strong feelings about what work I want seen first. This is one of those times.

Step 7: Press ⌘/Ctrl+Option/Alt+1 to see the one-star thumbnails. Now select thumbnails 0067, 0071, 0074, 0077, and 0079 and press the 2 key to give them their second star.

Step 8: Press ⌘/Ctrl+Option/Alt+2 to see images with two or more stars, and then select all of them by pressing ⌘/Ctrl+A.

Step 9: Return to the one-star view by pressing ⌘/Ctrl+Option/Alt+1, click inside the thumbnail of 0067, drag the five selected photographs in front of 0002, and then release the mouse button when the vertical blue line appears (5.13).

Tip

Hide a photograph during a slideshow by typing 0, mode.

Note

Dragging a group of selected thumbnails will automatically scroll the screen down when they near the top of the window or up as they get close to the bottom.

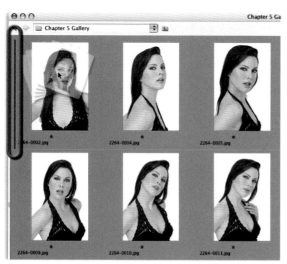

5.13

Step *10*: **Click 0079 to select it, and then click and drag it to the first position in front of 0067. Drag 0071 so it is just before 0002. Put 0074 next after 0079.**
This arrangement will lead with some close-ups of Virginia, show some medium views with many differing expressions, and wrap up with more close-ups. In the last photograph her eyes look toward the one preceding it.

Step *11*: **Move the thumbnail size slider to the left to reduce the thumbnails' size until they all fit in the view.**
This preview shows the flow of the gallery.

Step *12*: **Move any other images to suit (5.14), and then deselect all by pressing ⌘/Ctrl+Shift+A.**

Step *13*: **Choose Tools ➭ Photoshop ➭ Web Photo Gallery from Bridge's menu bar.**
The resulting dialog box is the same one that opens from Photoshop's File ➭ Automate menu with the exception that the Source Images are set to Use: Selected Images from Bridge.

Step *14*: **Choose the Simple template from the Styles menu. Type your e-mail address in the Email field. Click the Destination button and create a new folder on your computer's desktop named 2264-Virginia Simple (5.15).**

Note

Select all or deselect all? If all the thumbnails in Bridge are selected or if none of them are, Photoshop will process all of them when one of its scripts is called from the Tools menu.

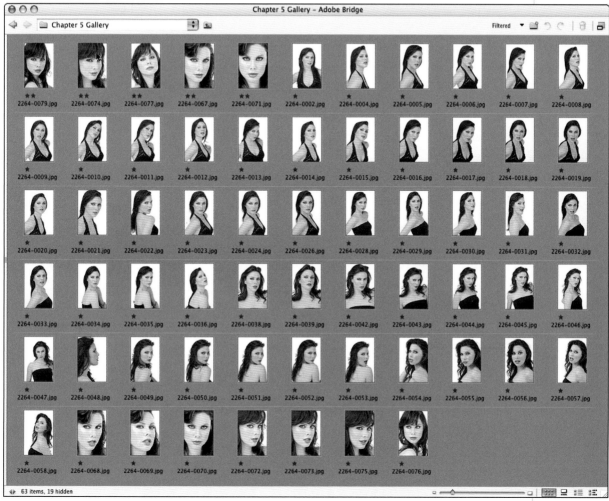

5.14

Twenty different templates are installed in Photoshop. A thumbnail preview of each appears under the OK and Reset buttons in the Web Photo Gallery dialog box. They are useful, though not as much as a completed gallery. Take the time to generate a gallery using each one and then save it to a different folder. Each one is different and some of the options available for the Simple template are grayed out.

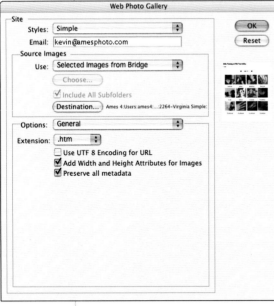

5.15

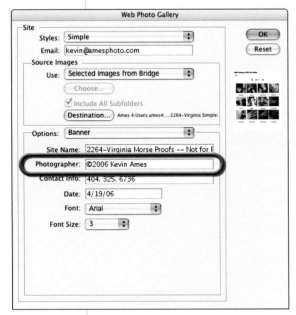

5.16

You can customize all the templates using Adobe GoLive! or Dreamweaver. I have two custom templates: one for sites for client review and one that makes my portfolio galleries. You can find the style templates inside the Applications/Program Files folder named Adobe Photoshop CS2 ⇨ Presets ⇨ Web Photo Gallery. Make a copy of the folder holding the template to be customized, name it, and modify it to your heart's content. (It's okay to have an HTML guru help. We are photographers, after all, not Web warriors.)

The next steps go through setting up the Options sections of the Web Photo Gallery dialog box for the Simple template.

Step *15*: **Choose Banner from the Options menu.** **Type** 2264–Virginia Morse Proofs–Not For Publication **as the site name.**

I took the photographs, so type **Kevin Ames** in the Photographer field (5.16). The current date is automatically added. Choose Arial as the font and leave the size at 3.

Step *16*: **Set the Options menu to Large Images.**

This step sets the image size for the enlarged view when a thumbnail is clicked in the browser. Only one photograph displays on a page, so there is room to make it big. Most monitors today display at least 768 pixels in height and 1024 pixels in width. The Resize Images box is selected by default.

Tip

Add the copyright symbol (©) and the year the photographs were made before your name in the Photographer text box. This is a valid notice of copyright for the photographs shown on the screen. To get the copyright symbol, press Option+G on the Mac. In Windows it's a bit more complicated: Make sure the Num Lock key is pressed. Hold down the Alt key and type **0169** on the number pad. Release the Alt key and the copyright symbol will appear. This method will not work using the numbers in the row under the function keys.

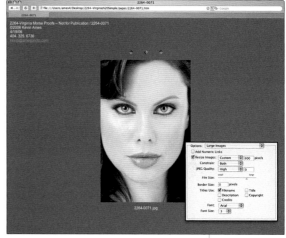

5.17

Step 17: Choose Custom and enter 600 **pixels. Choose Arial as the Font and set the Size to 3. (5.17).**

That leaves 168 pixels for the browser's header. My clients like to use these images for positioning on comp cards and in layouts, so I set the quality fairly high, in this case 9. (The highest is 12. The quality is excellent and the download is slow.)

Step 18: Leave the border at 0 for no border or 1 to 2 pixels if you want Photoshop to add one.

You can choose to add a lot of information under each photograph. Usually just the filename is sufficient. Too much information can clutter the page. On the other hand, if the metadata you learned how to add in Chapter 4 has important details in the Description field, selecting Description here is useful.

The Add Numeric Links check box is selected by default in the Simple template. It makes a bar of numbers across the screen above the previous, thumbnail view, and next arrows that represent each large thumbnail in the site. The shoot with Virginia resulted in more than a thousand images on the site. Using the Numeric Links feature would have filled two full screens with only numbers. I believe even on small sites it clutters up the window. Play with this feature and make your own decision.

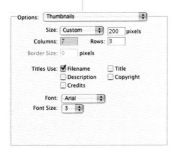

5.18

5.19

5.20

Step 19: **Choose Thumbnails from the Options drop-down menu, choose Custom from the Size drop-down menu, and enter 200 pixels.**

I have a wide monitor, so my choice is Columns: 7 and Rows: 3 with only the filename selected for Titles Use. Again the Font is Arial and the Size 3 (5.18).

Step 20: **Choose Custom Colors from the Options menu.**

Color is important to photographers. We love vibrant color in our photographs and really don't want them surrounded by anything on the Web site that might be distracting—shocking pink backgrounds festooned with lime green text, for example. My picks for Background, Banner, Text, Active Link, Link, and Visited Link are all neutrals.

Step 21: **Double-click on one of the colors to open the Color Picker (5.19). Select Only Web Colors in the lower-left corner of the dialog box.**

Six shades of neutral, including black and white, are right there for the clicking. My suggestions for each choice are shown here (5.20).

Step 22: **Explore the Security window from the Options menu (5.21).**

My choice is None because I don't particularly want to clutter up a photograph with a copyright symbol, its filename, description, credits, or title. And by the time the gallery link is sent to a client, I have already been paid or have received a significant deposit. If you want more security than the prominent copyright notice on each page, here's where you apply it. (You will add the copyright notice in front of your name when you make galleries of your work, won't you? Good. I knew you would!)

Step 23: **Click OK.**

Photoshop goes to work and builds a gallery of the proofs chosen in Bridge in the order you set. At this point you can go back to Bridge and do more sorting or rating or add metadata to a new block of RAW files.

5.21

Choosing Tools ⇨ Photoshop and selecting an automation in Bridge opens the dialog box in Photoshop, leaving Bridge free to work on other projects at the same time. That's right. Once you start Photoshop on a project, you can go back to Bridge and work in Camera Raw, review photographs, or prepare something else to send to Photoshop. Yes, I am a big fan of Bridge and its integration with the rest of the Adobe Creative Suite.

Teamwork:
Bridge and
Photoshop
CS2

When Photoshop finishes building the gallery, your computer's default Web browser launches and displays the thumbnail page (5.22). The entries from the Banner menu show in the upper-left corner. The filename appears under each image. Listed above the thumbnails is the number of total pages of thumbnails in the site. In this case, there are three. Click an image or the filename under it to see an enlarged view. Return to the thumbnail page by clicking the up arrow above the photograph. The visited links are shown in black so you know which ones you've seen enlarged.

5.22

My clients love the galleries for reviewing proofs. Usually they'll e-mail me a list of their choices. The names in the gallery are exactly the same as the original RAW digital negative. That makes finding them a snap!

PDF PRESENTATIONS

Once the client has chosen images, he or she often wants to send copies to colleagues and management. We have all received e-mail with 13 JPEGs attached and had to open them up in a browser or Photoshop after saving them. What a pain. Make it easy on your clients and their downstream e-mail recipients and send them a self-running presentation in PDF format that is small enough to e-mail.

Your e-mail application beeps. There's new mail for you! It's from your client. The first round of picks is 2264-0079, 0074, 0071, 0022, 0031, 0034, 0042, 0052, 0054, 0070, 0073, 0075, and 0076. Oh, and can you group all the medium shots first and then the close-ups?

Step 1: **Click into Bridge (hold down ⌘ and press Tab until Bridge's icon is highlighted on the Mac, or hold down the Alt key and press Tab to choose Bridge in Windows), navigate to the Chapter 5 Gallery folder, and choose it to display Virginia's thumbnails.**

Step 2: **⌘/Ctrl+click the 13 thumbnails chosen by the client (2264-0079, 0074, 0071, 0022, 0031, 0034, 0042, 0052, 0054, 0070, 0073, 0075, and 0076). Press the 3 key to give the selected photographs a third star. Press ⌘/Ctrl+Option/Alt+3 to display thumbnails with three or more stars.**

The chosen ones appear in Bridge's content pane.

Step 3: **Click 0022, then Shift+click 0054.**

The five medium-shot thumbnails are selected.

Step 4: **Click in the image of one of them, hold down the mouse button, and drag it in front of 0079.**

The photographs are in the client's requested order (5.23).

5.23

Step 5: Deselect all the thumbnails by pressing Shift+⌘/Ctrl+Option/Alt+A (or choose Edit ⇨ Deselect All).

Step 6: Choose Tools ⇨ Photoshop ⇨ PDF presentation.
The dialog box opens in Photoshop.

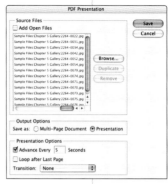

Step 7: Click the Presentation button and enter a time in the Advance Every window.
The default is 5. Leave Loop after Last Page cleared so the show won't run forever. There are lots of interesting transitions that don't work very well. Leave this one at None (5.24).

5.24

Step 8: Click Save. Enter 2264-Virginia First Round Picks and save it to the desktop by clicking Save again.

Step 9: Choose Smallest File Size from the Adobe PDF Preset menu (5.25).
Select Optimize for Fast Web Preview and View PDF After Saving.

5.25

Step 10: Click Security in the Preferences panel. Click Use a password to restrict printing, editing, and other tasks. Enter a password in the Permission Password window. Choose None for each of the Printing Allowed and Changes Allowed menus.

Step 11: Click Save PDF. A dialog box will open asking for a password confirmation. Enter your password and click OK.
Once again Photoshop gets to work and creates the presentation. When the job is done, Acrobat or Adobe Reader launches and plays the presentation against a black screen. Press the Esc key to drop the presentation back into Acrobat or Adobe Reader. Clients can click the pages to view them full screen (5.26).

5.26

Name 2264-Virginia First Round Picks.pdf
Kind Adobe PDF document
Size **1.4 MB on disk**
Created Today at 2:46 PM
Modified Today at 2:46 PM
Last opened Today at 2:46 PM

More info...

5.27

The PDF presentation is a great way to e-mail high-quality photographs for review on any computer. The file with all 13 shots of Virginia is only 1.4MB (5.27).

CUSTOM PROOF SHEETS

While we wait for the client to get back to us on which of the photographs of Virginia she wants to see printed, let's set up a template to customize the proof sheet. The template is a one-time-only project. Once you make it, you use it over and over.

The saying goes that "size doesn't matter." I hate to break it to you here. It does. Bigger *is* better. At least when it comes to making printed proofs. And bigger rocks not only because it is easier for the client to see detail in the prints, but also because it makes us as photographers stand out when our prints are compared to the prints other photographers make at local "big-box" stores. The following project is designed for use with the Super B 13" x 19" printers.

New

Name: 13 X 19 Proof Sheet Template

OK

Preset: Custom

Reset

Width: 13   inches

Save Preset...

Height: 19   inches

Delete Preset...

Resolution: 240   pixels/inch

Color Mode: RGB Color   8 bit

Background Contents: White

Image Size:
40.7M

Advanced

Color Profile: Adobe RGB (1998)

Pixel Aspect Ratio: Square

5.28

Step 1: Press ⌘/Ctrl N (or choose File ⇨ New) in Photoshop to open a new document window. Name the file 13 x 19 Proof Sheet Template.

Step 2: Set the Width to 13 inches, Height to 19 inches, and Resolution to 240 pixels/inch. Set the Color Mode to RGB Color, 8 bit, and the Background Contents to White. The Color Profile is Adobe RGB (1998) and the Pixel Aspect Ratio is Square. Click OK (5.28).

Step 3: Open another new document window and name it Stripes. **You will use it to define a pattern for the template. Make it 10 pixels wide and 8 pixels high with the resolution at 1 pixel. Duplicate the rest of the settings for this dialog box from Step 2. Click OK.**
A really small white rectangle appears in the new document. Drag the size slider in the Navigator palette all the way to the right to zoom the window to 1600%.

Step 4: **Click the Rectangular Marquee tool. Select Fixed Size from the Style menu. Enter** 0 **pixels in the Feather field,** 4 **pixels in the Width field, and** 8 **pixels in the Height field.**

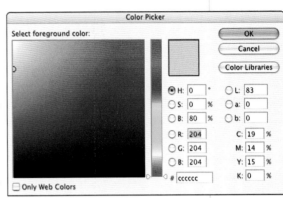

5.29

Step 5: **Click the upper-left corner of the file to make a 4 x 8-pixel selection. Double-click the foreground color in the toolbar to open up the Color Picker. Enter** 204 **into each of the R, G, and B entry fields (5.29). Click OK.**

Step 6: **Choose Edit ⇨ Fill and then select Foreground Color and set the Opacity to 100%. Click OK (5.30).**

Step 7: **Select the entire document by pressing ⌘/Ctrl+A. Choose Edit ⇨ Define Pattern.**

A dialog box opens with Stripes set as the name.

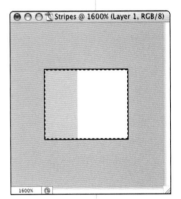

Step 8: **Click OK and close the file Stripes.psd without saving.**

Step 9: **Choose Window ⇨ 13 x 19 Proof Sheet Template. Make a new layer by pressing ⌘/Ctrl+Shift+N. Enter** Stripes **in the New Layers dialog box, and then click OK.**

5.30

Step 10: **Choose Edit ⇨ Fill. Select Pattern, click the Custom Pattern menu, choose the Stripes gray rectangle, and leave Opacity at 100%. Click OK (5.31).**

Step 11: **Press V to get the Move tool. Type 5 to set the Stripes layer opacity to 50%. Click the Lock Position icon (the four-headed arrow) in the Lock menu just above the layer stack.**

Photoshop delivers accurate screen views at 12.5%, 25%, 50%, and 100% (actual pixels). The zoom sizes in between are dithered and won't display patterns or details well.

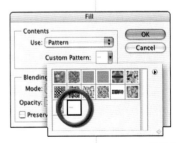

5.31

Step 12: Press ⌘/Ctrl+R (or choose View ➪ Rulers) to show the rulers. Find the center of the template by pressing ⌘/Ctrl+A (or by choosing Select ➪ Select All) to select the entire file. Press ⌘/Ctrl+T to enter Free Transform (Edit ➪ Free Transform). Finally, zoom in to 100% by pressing ⌘/Ctrl+Option/Alt+0 (or by choosing View ➪ Actual Pixels).

Step 13: Click inside the vertical ruler and drag a guide to the center indicated by Free Transform's reference point. Click the horizontal ruler at the top of the window and drag a guide down through the center of the reference point. If the guides aren't showing, press ⌘/Ctrl+; (semicolon).

The guides cross at the center of the template (5.32). Press Esc to exit Free Transform. Deselect by pressing ⌘/Ctrl+D (or by choosing Select ➪ Deselect). Zoom down to 25% (press ⌘/Ctrl+- [hyphen] four times). Click the Lock Position icon in the Lock menu just above the layer stack. Whew!

Step 14: Make a new layer and name it Alignment Border. Choose the Rectangular Marquee tool by pressing M. Change the Width to 10.5 in. and the Height to 15.5 in.

Step 15: Click in the template to make a selection. Choose Select ➪ Transform Selection. Drag the selection until the reference point is centered through the guides.

Step 16: Zoom in to Actual Pixels (press ⌘/Ctrl+Option/Alt+0) and fine-tune the alignment by pressing the arrow keys. Select the check box in the Options bar to set the selection transformation. Finally, drag another guide down from the top rule to 1.25 inches on the vertical rule.

Watch the Info palette while dragging the guide down. When the Y axis reads 1.250, stop dragging and release the mouse button. Done — to the thousandth of an inch! Woo-hoo (5.33)!

Step *17*: **Press D to set the default colors.**
Black is the foreground color and white is the background color showing in the toolbox.

Step *18*: **Choose Edit ⇨ Stroke. Enter 2 pixels for the Width and set the Opacity to 100% (5.34). Click the Outside button. Click OK.**
The layer Alignment Border has a 2-pixel border. Click the Lock Position icon.

Step *19*: **Deselect (press ⌘/Ctrl+D). Click the Move tool (V). Hold down the Shift key and drag the layer straight up until the top edge of the upper border aligns with the guide at 1.250. Press ⌘/Ctrl+R again to hide the rulers. Zoom back out to 25%.**

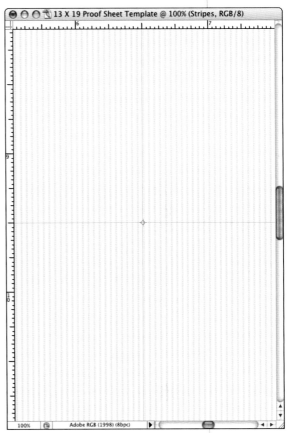

5.32

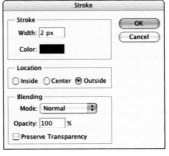

5.33

5.34

5.35

5.36

Step 20: Press T to select the Type tool. In the Options bar, choose Gill Sans as the font and Regular as the style. Set 36 points for the size. Click your cursor under the alignment border and type kevin ames photography. **Highlight the type. Click the Characters palette in the Options bar (5.35). Enter** 30 **in the Tracking window (5.36). Select the Commit check box.**

Step 21: Click with the Type tool under the first line on the center guide. Change the font size to 18 points, and then type 1824. Change the point size to 24 and enter briarwood industrial court. **Press Return, and then type** atlanta, ga.

Step 22: Change the point size back to 18. Type the ZIP code 30329. Hit the spacebar three times. Type the phone number 404. 325. 6736 and press Return.

Step 23: Type kevin@amesphoto.com, three spaces, and then amesphoto.com.

Step 24: Highlight the first line of type. Enter 105 for the tracking in the Characters palette. Highlight the second line and enter 150 for its tracking. Highlight the e-mail and Web site line and set its tracking to 110. Select the Commit check box.

The look is good, except the black type is too aggressive. I want to tone it down so it will still be there and won't detract from the photography.

Step 25: Hold down the ⌘/Ctrl key. Click the Text layer icon for the kevin ames photography line.

The text loads as a selection.

Step 26: Hide the layer by clicking the eye icon.

Only the marching ants remain.

Step 27: Click Stripes to highlight it. Press ⌘/Ctrl+J to make the selection into a new layer (or choose Layer ⇨ New ⇨ Layer via Copy).

Step 28: **Rename the layer** kevin ames photography. **Lock the position of this layer by clicking the four-headed arrow in the Lock menu.**

Step 29: **Click the Add a Layer Style icon and choose Bevel and Emboss (5.37).** The Layer Styles dialog box opens.

Step 30: **Set the Structure section like this:**
Style: Inner Bevel
Technique: Smooth
Depth: 181
Direction: Up
Size: 2
Soften: 0

Step 31: **Set the Shading section like this (5.38):**
Angle: 120°
Altitude: 30°
Use Global Light: selected
Gloss Contour: Linear (the icon in the upper left of the drop-down menu)
Anti-aliased: cleared
Highlight Mode: Screen at 75% Opacity and White for the color
Shadow Mode: Multiply at 75% Opacity and Black for the color

Okay. Take a breath. This is almost done.

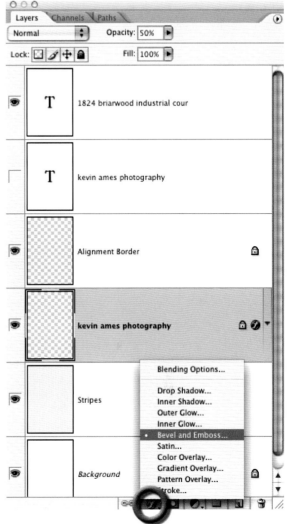

5.37

Step 32: **Click the word *Stroke* in the left pane of the Layer Styles dialog box.** The Stroke settings appear.

Step 33: **Set the Structure like this:**
Size: 1
Position: Center
Opacity: 100%
Fill Type: Color
Color: Black (R: 0, G: 0, B:0)

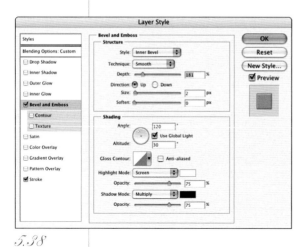

5.38

kevin ames photography
1824 briarwood industrial court
atlanta, ga 30329   404. 325. 6736
kevin@amesphoto.com   amesphoto.com

5.39

Step 34: Click OK.

That looks a lot better. Now for the address.

Step 35: ⌘/Ctrl+click the Text Layer icon for the layer 1824 briarwood industrial court.

The text loads as a selection.

Step 36: Hide this layer by clicking its eye icon. Highlight the Stripes layer. Press ⌘/Ctrl+J to jump the selection onto a new layer.

Hmm . . . jump the selection to a new layer, huh? Is that why the shortcut ends with J? Could be.

Step 37: Name the layer 1824 briarwood **and lock the position.**

Now I know what you are thinking. There has to be an easier way to apply the styles again. Well you're right on! Hold down the Option/Alt key, click on the style symbol in the kevin ames photography layer above, and drag it to the 1824 briarwood layer. Done. Almost. Click the disclosure triangle next to the Style icon you just dragged onto the 1824 briarwood layer. Double-click the word *Stroke*. When the Layer Style dialog box opens, lower the opacity of this effect for this layer to 50% (5.39). Highlight the layer Alignment Border. Done. Really. Click OK and save the template as a Photoshop document (PSD).

PROOF SHEETS FOR THE CLIENT

Checking e-mail from the client shows nine images from the PDF presentation that she would like to see in a printed contact sheet. And the order she wants them in is 0073, 0074, 0075, 0079, 0076, 0054, 0042, 0070, and 0071. Don't you love organized clients?

Step 1: Highlight the nine images listed previously from the Show 3 or More Stars view. Type 4 to add one more star. Hold down the ⌘/Ctrl+Option/Alt keys and press 4 to set the view to 4 stars or higher. Click the images and drag them into the requested order. Press Shift+⌘/Ctrl+A to deselect all images.

When you've finished, the gallery should look like this (5.40).

Step 2: Choose **Tools ⇨ Photoshop ⇨ Contact Sheet II.**

When the dialog box opens, we need to set it up to make the proof sheet that fits in the border of the template.

Step 3: Enter 10.5 in the **Width field,** 15.5 in the **Height field, and** 240 **for Resolution. This one is important: Clear Flatten All Layers (5.41).**

Look at the preview of the proof sheet. It shows the layout and underneath displays the dimensions of each photograph and the number of pages Contact Sheet II will produce.

Step 4: From the **Place menu, choose across first. Select Use Auto-Spacing. Enter** 3 **in both the Columns and Rows fields. Select Rotate for Best Fit and Use Filename As Caption.**

The default font is Helvetica, which is fine for now.

Step 5: Set the **Font Size to 9 pt. Click OK.**

Photoshop opens each of the chosen images from Bridge, resizes them, and then places each one in order in the proof sheet.

Step 6: Hold down the **⌘/Ctrl key, and then click each of the text layers to select them in the Layers palette.**

5.40

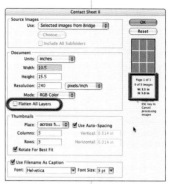

5.41

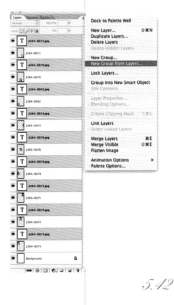

5.42

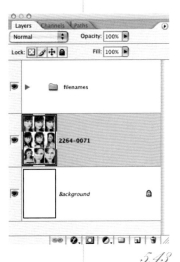

5.43

Step 7: **Press T to select the Type tool. Choose Gill Sans and Regular in the tool's Options bar.**

All the former Helvetica filenames change to Gill Sans and now match the template's typeface. Slick!

Step 8: **Click the Layers palette fly-out menu, and choose New Group from Layers. Name the group** filenames. **Click OK.**

The filenames group appears in the layer stack (5.42).

Step 9: **Hide the Background layer by clicking its eye icon. Click the top thumbnail (2264-0071) in the layer stack to highlight it. Hold down the Shift key and click the bottom image layer (2264-0073) to select all of your photo layers. Press ⌘/Ctrl+E (or choose Flyout ⇨ Merge Layers or Layer ⇨ Merge Layers).**

Now only three layers are in the stack (5.43).

Step 10: **Show the Background layer. Highlight the image layer 2264-0071. Click the Styles icon at the bottom of the palette. Choose Drop Shadow to open the Layers Style dialog box.**

Leave the Blend Mode on Multiply with black as the color. Lower the Opacity to 40%. Keep the Angle at 120° with Use Global Light selected. Distance should be 25px with a Spread of 0 and Size of 20.

Step 11: **Click the words Bevel and Emboss under the Styles pane. Set the Structure section by choosing Inner Bevel for the Style.**

The Technique is Smooth, Depth is 100%, Direction is Down, Size is 9 px, and Soften is 0. The Shading options are Angle 120° and Altitude 30° with Use Global Light checked. The Gloss Contour is unchanged; leave Highlight Mode at Screen with a 75% Opacity. Change the Shadow Mode Opacity to 40%.

Step 12: The borders of photographs shot against white merge with light-colored backgrounds. Click the word **Stroke** in the Styles pane. Set the Size to 1 px, the Position to Inside, and the Blend Mode to Normal. Set the Opacity at 50%. Fill Type is Color and the Color is black. Click New Style. Save the style as **Proof Sheet Style**. Click OK.

The style effects make all the difference in creating a professional look (5.44).

The new style appears in the Styles palette. The next time you make a contact sheet, skip Steps 8, 9, and 10 by clicking the Proof Sheet Style icon (5.45). Speedy!

Proofs and Template: Happy Together

This section brings the proof sheet together with the template. After you have done this a couple of times you'll think nothing of making lots of proof sheets with Bridge and Contact Sheet II and customizing them.

Step 1: Open the file 13 x 19 Proof Sheet Template.psd in Photoshop.

Step 2: Ctrl+tab to get to the file ContactSheet001.PSD on a Mac, or choose Window ⇨ ContactSheet001.PSD in Windows. Click on the filenames group, and then Shift+click the Background layer.

All the layers in the stack are selected.

Step 3: Press V to make the Move tool active. Click any of the highlighted layers, start dragging all three, and then hold down the Shift key and drop them onto the template.

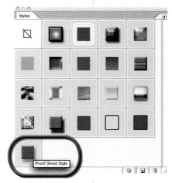

5.44

5.45

Tip

Adding the Shift key after beginning to drag the layers places them in the center of the destination file.

The proof sheet is in the center of the template. It covers up part of the name and address so you want to move it straight up.

Step 4: Hold down the Shift key and drag the layers up to the top of the black alignment border. Align the edge of the white border just inside the black outline of Alignment Border (5.46).

Step 5: Hide Alignment Border and Layer 1. The nine 3.5 x 5-inch proofs with beveled edge, stroke, and, of course, the drop shadow complete with their filenames are positioned perfectly in the template (5.47).

Step 6: Choose Image ➪ Duplicate. Name the file 2264–Virginia Proof 01. **Click OK.**

5.46

Note

The horizontal guide is on the inside edge of the stroke because the stroke was applied to the outside of the selection. You want to align the top edge of the proof sheet's white background with the guide.

5.47

Step 7: **Choose Layer ⇨ Flatten Image. Click OK to discard the hidden layers. Save the file in the TIF format.**
Save layered files as Photoshop Documents (PSD) and flattened ones for clients or for output as TIF. PSD files are always working files. TIFs are for clients. All that's left is to make the proof sheet on your printer. That can present issues as far as color management goes.

Here's how I make prints in my studio:

Step 1: **Choose Edit ⇨ Convert to Profile. In the Destination Space menu, choose the profile you have made for the paper and ink set you use in your printer.**
If you don't make your own profiles, choose the profile that was installed by your printer or download them from the paper manufacturer's Web site.

Step 2: **Choose Relative Colorimetric as the Intent and select Black Point Compensation. Click OK.**

Step 3: **Press ⌘/Ctrl+Option/Alt+P (or choose File ⇨ Print with Preview).**
The dialog box opens. Click Page Setup to select the Super B paper size. The dimensions appear in the Scaled Print Size section. If your printer can print borderless, set that up in its driver when you click Print. The Color Management section is important and a potential source of color issues. The Print section shows the Document with the profile applied in Step 1. The color management is complete.

Step 4: **Choose No Color Management from the Color Handling menu and then click Print.**

5.48

Step 5: **Set up your printer's driver Color Management to No Color Adjustment, None, or No Color Management depending on the manufacturer.**
The point is to make sure that your printer does not apply another profile (5.48).

Step 6: **Click Print One.**
The proof is on the printer.

Step 7: **If your printer maxes out at letter size, choose Image ➪ Image Size. Select Resample Image and then set it to Bicubic Sharper. Select Scale Styles and Constraint Proportions. Enter 11 inches into Height. Click OK.**
You are good to go for a borderless proof! And when you get a bigger printer, your proof sheets are ready to go supersized. (Trust me on this one—you will get a bigger printer. Bigger *is* better, remember?)

The JPEGs made by verifying the archive DVDs you learned to make in Chapter 4 aren't just proof that the disc is good. They are proofs for whoever you want to see your work in any way they want to see it: on the Internet, in a PDF document sent by e-mail, or on paper.

The archiving and distribution workflows seem complicated when you first do them. I remember how almost impossible developing film was when I was learning that workflow. Practice made it second nature. Now this digital work-flow is, too. The best part is that once you master it, you can teach it to an assistant. Then all you have to do is shoot!

The next chapter is on non-destructive editing in Photoshop. It sets the stage for the projects in the second section of the book. I even include a tutorial on how to use the Pen tool: an invaluable skill in the art of retouching photo-graphs of women. Wow! I can feel your excitement. . . .

Chapter Six

Unlimited Undos Forever: Non-destructive Photoshop

The "Way of the Fast Retreat" protects me from art directors who want things changed. They always want things changed.

Jim DiVitale

Adobe Photoshop CS2 offers its users many different editing styles for working on photographs. An image can be color-corrected, have its exposure tweaked, be retouched, and be sent to the client without your knowing a thing about layers. Photoshop's Auto/Magnetic/Magic style features can make most photographs close to good enough. Using the Image Í Adjustments method pragmatically, and often with heavy-handed finesse, works the image through color, exposure, and retouching. (The finesse part involves using the Edit Í Fade command. The heavy-handed part is the degradation of the original file that occurs that leaves no way to go back to the original image after the file has been saved and closed.)

The inevitable need to "go back" brings up the Photoshop style that causes the least damage to the image and creates the ability to easily rework the file long after it has been archived. What commercial digital photographer Jim DiVitale calls the "Way of the Fast Retreat," I refer to as unlimited undos forever—non-destructive Photoshop.

This style of editing is not new. As a matter of fact it goes all the way back to the first days of Photoshop. Before layers (Photoshop 3.0), non-destructive meant saving a copy of the file for every change. It also meant burning through hugely expensive (at the time) hard drive and CD space. Back then (a dozen or so years ago), blank CDs cost $15.00 each. They burned successfully three out of five times on $4,000 burners writing at 1x speed. A 1GB hard drive cost $1,500. The result was Photoshop users often gambled (unsuccessfully) against the possibility that no one would want to make changes later. It was balancing the cost of saving many versions against how much time doing the work over would take. Today that gamble is silly.

Still, we were thrilled to be able to work on our photographs, and these prices were cheap considering the control we gained. (The word *photographer* is a synonym for *control freak*.) Those were the "good old days." I, for one, am very glad to have them solidly in the past.

Today, computers are powerful. They have ultrafast processors, huge amounts of RAM and hard drive storage, and built-in high-speed optical recorders. They are cheap—less than the price of a

I know too many acronyms are in the world. For brevity's sake, allow me to create a new one: NDP for *non-destructive Photoshop.* Thank you very much.

1x CD burner of 10 years ago. Layers are available and Photoshop CS2 sports a limit of 300,000 pixels square for a single image. That's somewhere north of 250GB. Life is good. It is comforting to know that three years from now when a client wants the background color changed in an image, making it happen for them won't require reworking the entire image.

This chapter presents editing practices that always leave a way to get back to the present from the future. An added bonus is a simple tutorial on learning the most powerful tool in all of Photoshop—the Pen tool.

Non-destructive Photoshop involves using techniques that can be undone and/or modified after the file has been saved, closed, and reopened. The two areas for consideration in this style of working are Tools and Layers.

Avoiding Photoshop's "Forbidden" Tools

Sixty-three tools are available for you in Photoshop CS2's toolbar. Twenty-two are always visible on the palette. Of this formidable number of instruments, only four are destructive. One tool is useful and three have such destructive potential they must be banned outright. (These tools exist only to annihilate pixels.)

The Crop tool destroys pixels. Cropping an image throws pixels away. That process is destructive. It is also useful and safe when used on TIFs destined for

a client. The chances of using the Crop tool in the middle of editing a photograph are nonexistent. Cropping is the last thing done. The Crop tool gets the yellow caution square.

The tool that is banned for life from the world of NDP is the Eraser tool and its two buddies: the Background Eraser and the Magic Eraser tools. It's not that they are intrinsically evil; it's just that they kill pixels. Erasers don't kill pixels. People kill pixels. That's right. Their whole purpose in life is to destroy pixels. When the Eraser tool's work is finished there is no hope of recovering a single pixel after you close the file. ("The Eraser" sounds like an X-Men villain, doesn't it?) Take heart! A better way exists. You can do the Eraser's work using layer masks. This is not to say that there are absolutely no circumstances that the Eraser tool is not appropriate to use in Photoshop. I can think of a few. The problem lies in the huge potential of doing fatal damage with this tool. It's a good idea to never use it so you don't erase yourself into a corner. If you are willing to adopt the rule that the Eraser is a never-to-be-used weapon of mass destruction (WMD) and is banned from civilized Photoshop, you won't even select the tool. This means you won't ever use it inappropriately by accident, let alone on purpose. Therefore, the Eraser tool and its cronies receive the big red "Do Not Use" symbol with a drop shadow for foreboding emphasis (6.1).

The remaining 51 are fully cleared for use in NDP as long as you use them on layer masks and duplicate layers.

6.1

This section is not about rules other than no pixel killers allowed. It is a way of thinking when working in Photoshop to always leave a way back. After all the work is finished, the goal is to say, "No pixels were harmed during the creation of this photograph."

Getting to Know the Layers Palette

The Layers palette holds the canvas, paper, or graffiti wall upon which layers of pixels are brushed, sprayed, blended, or pasted. Each layer is a block building the final image. Layers can carry pixels, paint, type, adjustments, or vectors. The combinations are limitless. So are the creative possibilities. The potential for confusion seems to be limitless, too.

The Layers palette is powerful. It is the place in Photoshop where everything happens. It is safe to say that all the other palettes and menus support the Layers palette. This illustration has callouts naming each of the sections and functions that will be used in projects starting in the next chapter (6.2).

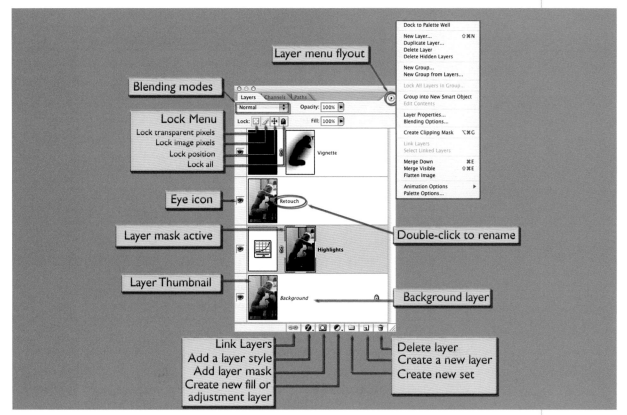

6.2

The temptation is to launch into a description of every feature and turn the book into a user's guide instead of one on photographing women. Instead, I explain the Layers palette as you complete each step-by-step project. This process is learning by doing. After finishing the projects in this book, you will have layers down cold.

THE BACKGROUND LAYER

The Background layer is a flattened version of the opened file. It is always locked and cannot be moved, blended (it is always Normal), or made transparent. Grayed-out areas indicate options not available. NDP practice is to duplicate this layer (⌘/Ctrl+J) when editing is required. This leaves the Background layer intact. Think of it as the Backup layer (6.3).

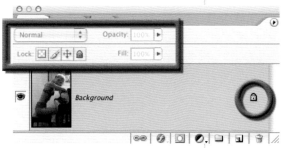

6.3

© 2062-M-0368 copy @ 25% (Retouch, RGB/16)

25%   © Adobe RGB (1998) (16bpc)

6.4

Creating a Vignette

This exercise introduces non-destructive Photoshop techniques. It involves brightening a photograph of model Carrie Thomas and creating a vignette. Download 2062-M-0368.tif from www.amesphoto.com/learning. The book code is **PW48255**. It is a 16-bit file. One of the best new features in Photoshop CS2 is the ability to work in 16-bit. This feature offers non-destructive Photoshop at its best.

Step 1: **Open 2062-M-0368.tif by double-clicking its thumbnail in Bridge.**
The Layers palette now has its first layer automatically named Background. The first best practice in NDP is to duplicate the background layer. Press ⌘/Ctrl+J or drag the Background layer to the New Layer icon (or choose Layers ⇨ New ⇨ Layer via Copy). Name the duplicate layer **Retouch**.

Step 2: **Hold down the ⌘/Ctrl+Option/Alt keys and press ~ (tilde, the key next to the number 1). Alternatively, click the Channel tab, and then ⌘/Ctrl+click the RGB composite channel. Click back into the Layers tab.**
This combination makes a selection out of the tones above middle gray (127) (6.4).

16-bit Info

The Info palette displays 16-bit RGB tonal values in 8-bit numbers by default. This option saves you from doing a lot of math conversions and having to recognize big numbers. To display the 16-bit values, click and hold one of the eyedroppers in the Info palette and select 16 bit.

Note for Mac users: If the keyboard shortcut in Step 2 doesn't work it's because the command is assigned to OSX keyboard shortcuts. Here's the fix: Launch System Preferences from the Apple menu. Choose Keyboard and Mouse. Deselect "Move Focus to the Window Drawer" under Keyboard Navigation. While you're at it, slip down to Dock, Expose, and Dashboard and deselect Hide and Show the Dock. That's the keyboard shortcut Photoshop uses to feather a selection. If you don't want to change your system keyboard, ⌘+click the RGB composite in the Channels palette. Feather is Select ⇨ Feather.

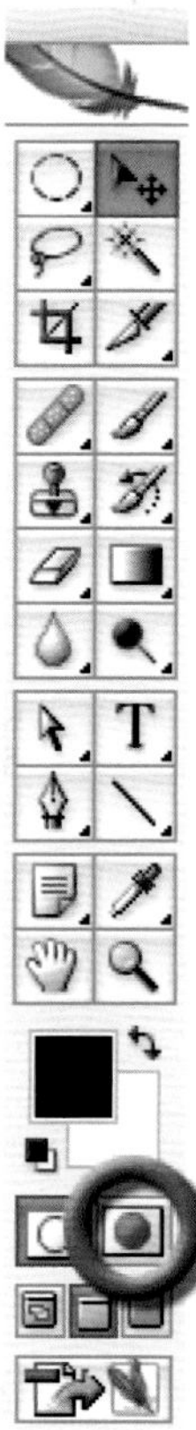

Step 3: **Double-click the Quick Mask icon in the toolbar (6.5).**
The Quick Mask Options dialog box opens. Click Selected Areas in the Color Indicates section. Set the Color Opacity to 100% (6.6). Click OK.

Step 4: **Choose Image ⇨ Adjustments ⇨ Levels (or press ⌘/Ctrl+L). Drag the highlight slider until the highlight input window reads 205 (6.7). Click OK.**
This adjustment is to the Quick Mask, not the image. The adjustment has increased the contrast of the Quick Mask, reducing the amount of highlights in the selection (6.8).

Step 5: **Press Q to exit Quick Mask.**
The marching ants of the modified selection appear.

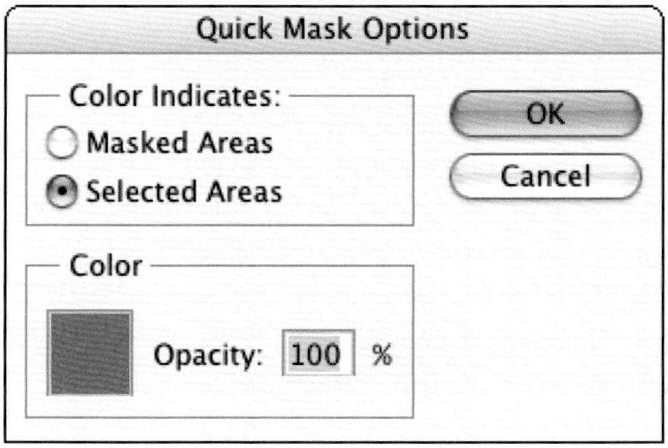

6.5

6.6

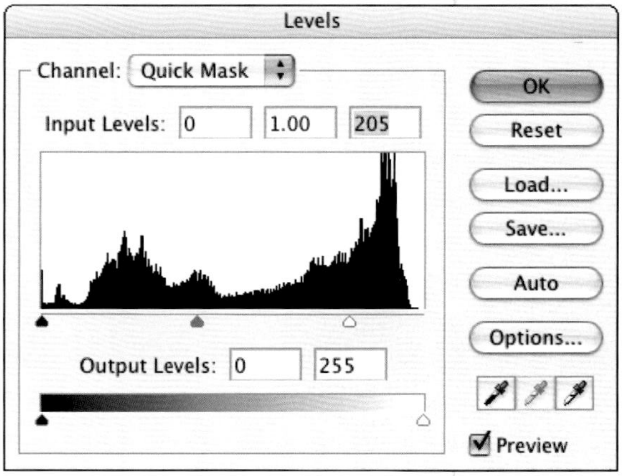

6.7

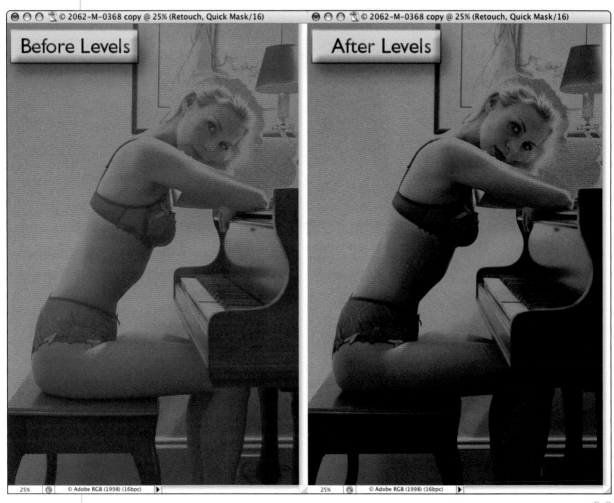

6.8

Step *6*: **Click the New Adjustment Layer icon at the bottom of the Layers palette. Choose Curves (6.9).**
The Curves dialog box appears. Option/Alt+click in the grid to set the fine grid.

Step *7*: **Count two boxes left and down from the upper-right corner. Click that intersection and drag the curve up one box. Count a box and a half up and right from the bottom-left corner. Click the curve at that point and drag it down half a box (6.10).**
The new curves layer appears in the layer stack above the Background layer (6.11). Click OK.

Before Photoshop, masks for placing color separations were cut by hand, using X-Acto knives, out of a red-colored material named *Rubylith*. Rubylith masks created clear areas on the film, which was blind to red. Color separations would later be stripped into clear places on the film. These negatives were used to burn the plates that ran on the printing press.

Setting up Quick Mask to show the selected areas mimics the convention of masking selected areas in the red of Rubylith. That's also the reason the default Quick Mask color is red.

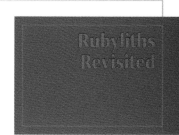

Step 8: Double-click the name *Curves* to edit the layer name. Type Highlights **in the highlighted field. Click outside the field or press Enter to accept the new name.**

The curves adjustment layer, Highlights, is active.

6.9

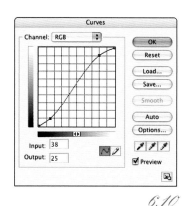

6.10

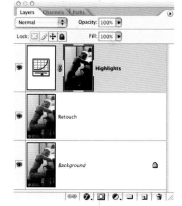

6.11

Note

When you create a new layer it always appears just above the active (highlighted) one in the stack.

Step 9: **Copy the newly brightened image to its own layer. Hold down ⌘/Ctrl+Option/Alt+Shift and press E.**
A layer with a copy of the layers merged to it appears in the layers stack.

Step 10: **Create a new empty layer by clicking the New Layer icon at the bottom of the Layers palette, hold down the Option/Alt key, and choose Merge Visible from the Layers fly-out menu. Rename the new layer** Retouch 2.

The Background layer, Retouch, and the effects of the curve adjustment layer, Highlights, are copied onto Retouch 2 (6.12). This is the layer that you will retouch. Upcoming chapters cover many techniques that you can use on this layer later. The best feature of NDP is the ability to come back and make changes later, even years later. I encourage you to return to Retouch 2 after you complete the work in Chapters 7, 8, and 9. You'll be ready to make your own strategy map and enhance this image beautifully. This section is about understanding NDP and the Layers palette.

6.12

Note

Duplicating the Background layer and naming it Retouch in this example is not really necessary because the Background layer and the curves adjustment layer, Highlights, are copied to a new layer. If you are new to non-destructive Photoshop editing, duplicating the Background layer is a very good practice. The most important principle of NDP is, "If you always make a copy of the Background layer first, you will never forget to." The second most important principle is if you start editing on the Background layer, choose File ➪ Revert and start over!

Now, about that pixel-killing Eraser . . .

Step 11: **Make a new layer by holding down ⌘/Ctrl+Shift and pressing N or by clicking the New Layer icon at the bottom of the Layers palette (alternatively, choose Layer ⇨ New ⇨ Layer). Name the layer** Eraser Vignette.

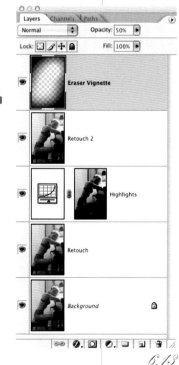

Note

Add the Option/Alt key to the command to suppress the New Layer dialog box.

Step 12: **Press D to set the default colors of black as the foreground and white as the background in the toolbox. (Click the black/white boxes below the colors in the toolbox.) Fill the Eraser Vignette with black by pressing Option/Alt+Delete/Backspace, or by choosing Edit ⇨ Fill ⇨ Foreground Color @ 100% or Black @ 100%. Press V to select the Move tool and then press 5 on the keyboard to set the layer's opacity to 50% (or click the Opacity arrow in the Layers palette and move the slider to the left until the entry window reads 50%).**

Step 13: **Choose the dreaded and deadly Eraser tool from the toolbox.**

No, I'm not telling what the keyboard shortcut is. You really don't ever want to use this tool! Okay. I give. It's E. Sheesh!

Step 14: **In the Options bar, set the brush to 400 pixels with a hardness of 0%. Paint over Carrie to create the vignette. Choose Filter ⇨ Blur ⇨ Gaussian Blur and enter** 250 **pixels. Click OK.**

Blurring smoothes the edges.

Step 15: **Choose a smaller brush and erase (shudder) over Carrie's face and torso to bring her all the way through the vignette. Now press ⌘/Ctrl+Option/Alt+Z three times to progressively undo the vignette. Redo it by pressing ⌘/Ctrl+Shift+Z three times. Finally, hold down the Option/Alt key and click Eraser Vignette's eye icon.**

All the other layers are hidden and you see the transparency coming through the pixels that have been erased (6.13). This looks pretty good.

6.13

Step *16*: **Duplicate the file by choosing Image ➪ Duplicate, save it to the desktop, and close the file by pressing ⌘/Ctrl+W (or by choosing File ➪ Close).**

Step *17*: **Choose File ➪ Open Recent and choose 2062-M-362 copy.psd. Press ⌘/Ctrl+Z or ⌘/Ctrl+Option/Alt+Z to Undo.**

Nothing happens. Undos are gone after you open and close the file. The Eraser has eliminated the pixels from Eraser Vignette. In this example, painting black ones back in is possible. Imagine if you were blending two images together by erasing one of them. After the file has been saved, closed, and reopened, what tool would you use to get those pixels back? (Not-so-subtle hint: There isn't a tool like that in Photoshop!) Close the copy file.

Now that you have experienced the limitations of the Eraser, I want to show you the super (non-erasing) Eraser—layer masks.

Step *18*: **Click Eraser Vignette's eye icon to hide it. Make a new layer and rename it** Vignette.

Step *19*: **Select the Elliptical Marquee tool and draw an oval around Carrie (6.14).**

Step *20*: **Choose Select ➪ Transform Selection from the main menu. Hover the cursor outside any corner of the bounding box. The rotate cursor appears. Drag the corner clockwise until her body fits inside the marching ants (6.15).**

Step *21*: **Pull the selection away from her head by dragging the top middle handle outwards. Repeat at the bottom and the sides.**

The selection surrounds her body without touching it.

Step *22*: **Click the Commit Transform check mark in the Options bar or press Enter.**

6.14

6.15

A layer mask shows everything on its layer when it is white. A white layer mask is called a "reveal all" layer mask. Clicking the Layer Mask icon creates a "reveal all" mask; adding the Option/Alt key makes the mask a "hide all" mask when you click the Add Layer Mask icon. A layer mask filled with black conceals everything on its layer. It is called a "hide all" layer mask. Remember which one is which this way: "White reveals, black conceals." Painting with 100% black on a "reveal all" mask makes it transparent. Lower the brush's opacity and the mask will blend the images on its layer with the one below it in the layer stack.

Hide All/Reveal All Layer Masks

6.16

: **Hold down the Option/Alt key and click the Add Layer Mask icon at the bottom of the Layers palette.**

The Layer Mask icon appears next to an empty thumbnail icon on the layer named Vignette.

Step 23 wants the selected area to hide the black that is put on the layer itself in Step 25. Fill the masked area with black ("hide all") by holding down the Option/Alt key then clicking to add the layer mask. The oval is filled with black and the edges are white.

Step 24: **Press D to set the default colors of black and white.**

Step 25: **Click the empty layer thumbnail icon of Vignette to make it active.**

A border appears around the layer thumbnail icon indicating it is active (6.16).

Step 26: **Choose Edit ➪ Fill. In the Fill dialog box, choose Foreground Color and 100%. Click OK.**

The result is a sharp-edged black oval with Carrie looking through it (6.17). This is a vignette, albeit harsh and obvious. Let's refine it.

Step 27: **Click the arrow next to Opacity: 100% in the Layers palette.**

A slider appears. Drag the slider that pops up to read 50%. The vignette reveals detail underneath it (6.18).

Tip

Select the Move tool by pressing V, then press 5 on the keyboard to set a layer to 50% opacity. Each number on the keyboard has its own opacity percentage. 1 is 10%, 2 is 20%, and so on. 0 is 100%. This method is easy to remember and much, much faster than using the Opacity slider.

6.17

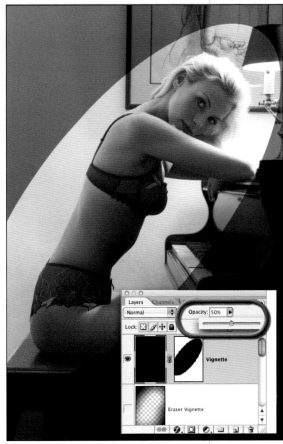

6.18

Step 28: **Click the Vignette layer mask thumbnail to make it active.**

The border moves from the layer thumbnail to the layer mask (6.19).

Step 29: **Choose Filter ⇨ Blur ⇨ Gaussian Blur from the main menu.**

In the Gaussian Blur dialog box, set the Radius at 250 pixels. Click OK.

Tip

Press two numbers quickly to get in-between values. For example, quickly press 2 then 5 for 25%.

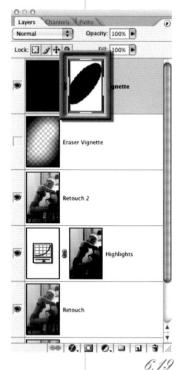

6.19

Changing the amount of blur on the layer mask makes the vignette go from a spotlight to a subtle darkening of the edges (6.20). There is even more variability. Move the layer's opacity back and forth to control the amount of the final effect.

Vignettes are great. They can have a beautiful soft edge that blends almost imperceptibly into the background. Large amounts of blur also blend into the subject. You can easily modify the mask to override areas of the effect. This is non-destructive Photoshop at its best!

Step *30*: **Choose Filter ⇨ Noise ⇨ Add Noise from the main menu. In the Add Noise dialog box, set 3% as the amount, Uniform. Monochromatic is grayed out because we're working with a layer mask that can only exist in black and white. Click OK.**

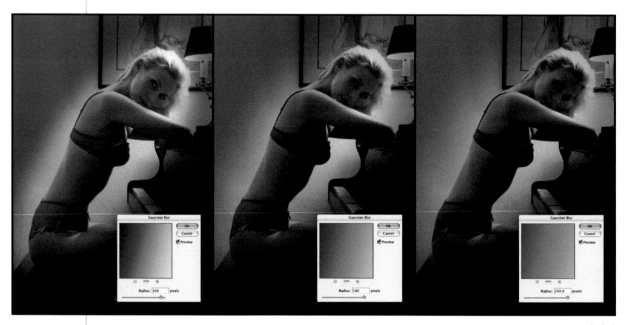

6.20

Step *31*: **The 250-pixel blur has left gray in the layer mask over Carrie. Select a soft-edged 200-pixel brush at 100% opacity with black as the foreground color. Paint over her face, letting the soft brush bring back the highlights in her hair.**
Use the brush to follow the line down her back and around her hips. A quiet highlight returns.

Photoshop is a tool to be wielded with subtlety. The lamp on the piano has fallen into the vignette's darkness.

Add noise? Yes, add noise. This layer has a massive blur applied to its layer mask. Without added noise, the vignette might band or posterize during output.

Step *32*: **Zoom into 200%. Reduce the brush to 20 pixels. Paint black over the inside of the lampshade. Paint down the stem (6.21).**

Painting a perfectly straight line is easy in Photoshop. Click the brush at the starting point. Hold down the Shift key and click the brush where the stroke should end. A straight line of paint appears (6.22).

6.21

Step *33*: **Use the click, Shift+click technique with an 8-pixel brush and bring back the highlight on the base of the stem. Change the brush opacity to 50%. Continue painting back just the highlights on the lamp (6.23).**
Dull highlights give away the vignette. Painting them back in on the layer mask makes the vignette appear natural.

Step *34*: **All the work on this file is finished. Create a new layer at the top of the layer stack. Name it Final. Merge the visible layers to Final.**
The final layer stack contains the layers Background, Retouch, Highlights, Retouch 2, Eraser Vignette (hidden), Vignette, and Final (6.24).

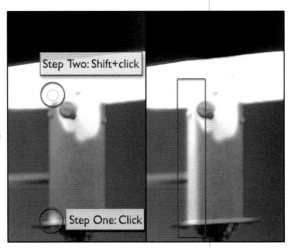

Step Two: Shift+click

Step One: Click

6.22

6.23

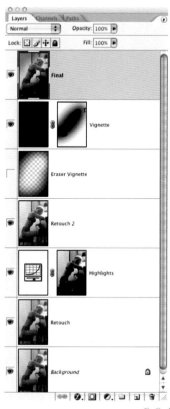

6.24

The Mask Revealed

Option/Alt+click on the layer mask thumbnail. The image is replaced with the mask itself (6.25). The areas in black are protected from the effects of the vignette. Reviewing the mask by itself is useful for seeing areas that you might need to clean up. This is an editable view.

Option/Alt+click to return to the normal view.

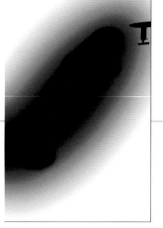

6.25

Study the layer stack. You can undo all the work that you've done in this project within the final image all the way back to the original that lives in the Background layer. You can modify every step at anytime in the future. The essence of non-destructive Photoshop is the question, "After this step is finished, can it be returned to the version before it?" When the answer is always "yes," you are a practitioner of the "Way of the Fast Retreat." Oh. Take a quick look at the Eraser Vignette layer. Can you think of a way to use the Eraser to create what you did with a layer mask? Now there's the power of NDP, and you get unlimited undos forever to boot! What a deal! (6.26).

Step *35*: **Save the file as a Photoshop document (.psd).**
Two files are now in the folder: 2062-M-0368.tif and 2062-M-0368.psd.

The next section is a tutorial for the most powerful and at the same time most avoided selection tool in the toolbar: the Pen. I'm sure you've heard the cliché that the pen is mightier than the sword. It is especially true in Photoshop! The projects that follow this chapter make serious use of the Pen tool. The sample files include the paths so you won't have to make your own to do the other work. And if you want to master Photoshop, pen tooling is a most useful skill.

6.26

When setting up a workflow, deciding which type of file goes to the client, which is a working file, and which file is for use on Web sites or e-mail is important. Here's how I assign file types to specific uses:

.PSD—These are working files and are the only files in my workflow that contain layers and 16-bit information. Output devices cannot use 16-bit (yet) so it is important to keep them in-house.

.TIF—These files serve two purposes. First, they are origination files. This means they have been built out of either Camera Raw or another manufacturer's RAW converter. They have not been edited. Second, after editing, the saved PSD is flattened and saved as a TIF overwriting the original 16-bit TIF. It is then converted to 8-bit for delivery to the client. After postproduction, all files with .TIF extensions mean that they are 8-bit flattened files. This is still non-destructive. The original RAW file has been archived. TIFs never contain layers. Layers are work products. They are proprietary to my studio. We do not deliver layers to clients. Inexperienced Photoshop users can cause much havoc and chaos playing with your layers.

.JPG—JPEG files are used for photographs on the Internet, e-mailable PDF presentations, and custom-printed proof sheets.

Using the Pen Tool

The Pen tool is considered by beginning and some advanced users of Photoshop to be intimidating and difficult. Back in the day of Photoshop 2.0 when I was dragged kicking and screaming into the digital world, my guru and part-time studio mate, Eddie Tapp, told me that the Pen tool was "the most powerful tool in Photoshop." Like you, I really didn't want to hear it. He was (and is) right. The power of the Pen tool is the ability to make very exacting selections with complete control. Now this capability appealed to the underlying control freak in me so I learned (go ahead, look up "photographer" in the dictionary—the first definition is "control freak." Okay, maybe it's the second one.) Slowly. I taught the Pen tool by giving students images of telephone handsets with coiled cords to outline—a method I now consider brutal and unkind, although very effective. Then another friend, Joe Glyda, head of photography for Kraft Foods and the man who took that venerable organization from film to digital, said, "Kevin, it's as easy as ABC." Here's how Joe teaches the Pen tool:

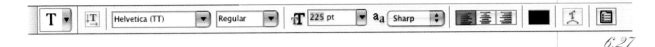

6.27

Step 1: **Press ⌘/Ctrl+N to open the New dialog box.**
Choose the 5x7 preset. Make it 7" wide and 5" high. Name it **Pen Tool**. Click OK to accept the rest of the default settings.

Step 2: **Click the Type tool.**
The Options bar setup is Helvetica, 225pt, Sharp, Left Align Text, and Black as the color (6.27).

Step 3: **Click inside the new file and type ABC in capital letters (6.28). Center the text with the Move tool if necessary. Select the Commit check box in the Options bar. Choose Flatten Image from the Layers palette fly-out menu.**

ABC

6.28

Step 4: **Click the Pen tool or press P on the keyboard to select it. Zoom in to 100%. Press F to invoke the Full Screen Mode. Click the Paths button in the Options bar and choose Rubber Band from the Pen Options drop-down arrow (6.29).**

My in-depth QuickTime movies on the techniques of NDP are available on CD-ROM from Software Cinema. They expand on this section of the book with additional step-by-step projects, a section-by-section explanation of the Layers palette, and exercises for working with layer masks. The title is Non-Destructive Photoshop. To order it, go to `www.software-cinema.com` and click on Workshops On Demand.

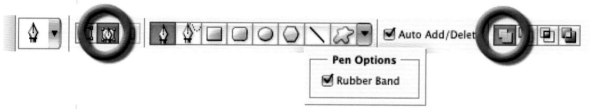

6.29

Step 5: **Start at the lower-left corner of the A and click to set the first anchor point. Move up the left side to the top of the A. Click to set another anchor point. Move to the next corner point and click.**

Continue around the A until the path is closed by clicking on the initial anchor point with the Close Path icon that appears automatically when a path is ready for completion (6.30).

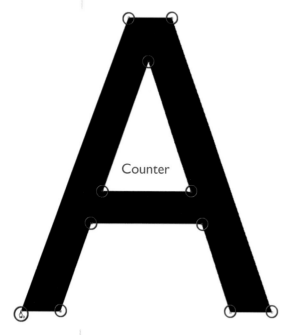

Counter

6.30

Tip

The Pen tool creates a vector path that can be resized without loss. Working at a view of 200% or more when creating outlines with the Pen tool is a good practice. Paths drawn at higher viewing percentages are that much more precise.

Tip

Hold down the spacebar to temporarily use the Hand tool. Click and drag to scroll around the image.

The three letters teach each of the outlining functions of the Pen tool: straight lines on the A, straight and curved lines on the B, and sweeping curves on the C.

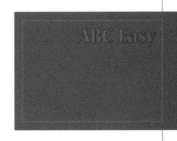

Step 6: **Outline the counter of the A. Click on the apex of the inside of the A to set an anchor point.**
Continue around the counter and close the path.

Step 7: **Click the Paths tab. Double-click the thumbnail.**
The Save Path dialog box opens and the default name Path 1 is offered. Click OK.

Step 8: **Click the lower-left corner of the B to set an anchor point. Go up the left side and set another point at the top-left corner. Follow the top of the B to the point where the curve starts and click and drag straight out.**
This action sets an anchor point and pulls out a direction handle. Actually you get two direction handles pointing in opposite directions. In this case, they follow the line between the last two anchor points exactly. The direction handles are the key to drawing paths around curves. They are powerful and require some practice to master. Be patient. This is a skill most worth learning.

Note

The enclosed or hollow part of a letter is called the *counter*.

Saving Paths

Every time you start a new path, Photoshop names it *Work Path*. Saving the path as a name preserves it. If a path is named *Work Path* and you begin a new path, Photoshop replaces the original work path with the new one. If this happens to you and you have not gone too far (20 undos is the default), you can recover by going back in the History palette and saving the work path. You lose the new work path when you do this. Saving paths saves a lot of time redrawing them, not to mention frustration and the occasional less-than-polite expletive.

Step *9*: **Release the mouse button. At the midpoint between the curves of the B, click and drag.**
The rubberband of the path is starting to bend around the bottom part of the upper curve of the B. When the bend matches the B, stop dragging. Release the mouse button (6.31).

Step *10*: **Hold down the Option/Alt key and move the cursor over the first direction handle.**
The cursor becomes the Convert Point tool. Keep holding down the Option/Alt key and click and drag the handle pulling the shape of the curve around the upper portion of the B. Continue working the direction handles until the path bends around the B, perfectly matching the curve (6.32).

Step *11*: **Once again, hold down the Option/Alt key and move the cursor over the direction handle that is in the lower counter of the B. Click and drag it out to the right until it is parallel to the baseline (6.33).**

Step *12*: **Release the Option/Alt key. Move the cursor down to the point where the lower curve of the B becomes a straight line. Click an anchor point and drag out the direction handles.**
The direction handle that you pull along the bottom line of the B rests on the baseline.

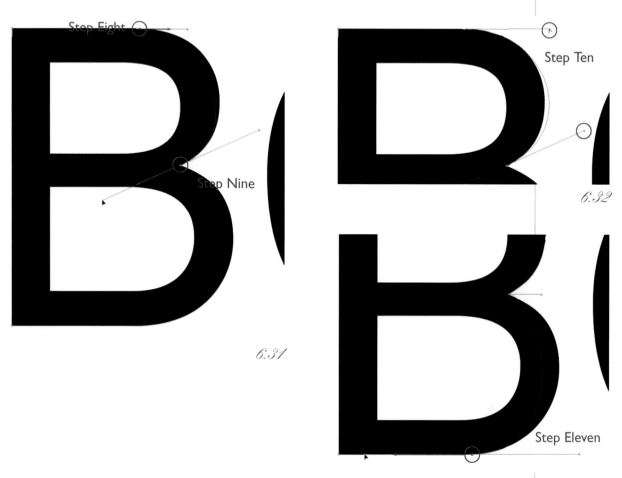

Step Eight

Step Nine

Step Ten

Step Eleven

6.31

6.32

6.33

Step 13: **Hold down the Option/Alt key. When the Convert Point cursor appears over a direction handle, drag it to bend the path around the B. Alternate until the path is close to the top and bottom parts of the lower curve.**

The path will bulge out at the front of the lower curve of the B.

Step *14*: **Hover the cursor over the bulge in the path. It changes to the Add Anchor Point tool. Click to set an anchor point.**

The direction handles automatically appear without being dragged. Press the left-arrow key to move the new anchor point into the curve. The path moves with it (6.34).

Step *15*: **Use the Option/Alt key to drag the new direction handles to smooth the path around the B (6.35).**

Hint: This technique works much better at 200% view. Close the path.

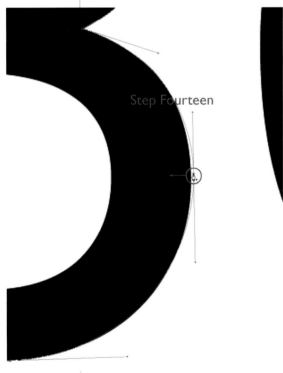

Step Fourteen

6.34

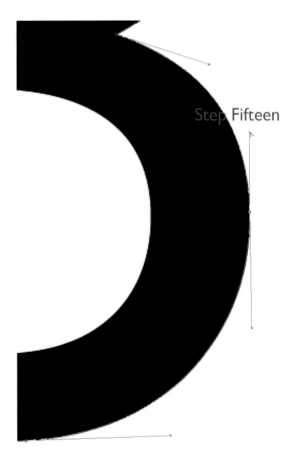

Step Fifteen

6.35

Step *16*: Outline the counters of the B using the procedures in the previous steps.

Step *17*: Now for the C; start by placing an anchor point and dragging down to create direction handles at the top outermost corner. After the handles are out, hold down the Option/Alt key without releasing the mouse button. Drag the lower direction handle until it bisects the straight edge of the C. Release the Option/Alt key (6.36).

Step *18*: Click to place an anchor point at the inside top corner and drag left to draw the direction handles out from it.

The direction line that appears along the straight edge of the C should be parallel to it; the handle bisects itself on that edge. Hold down the Option/Alt key and drag the direction handle under the mouse cursor along the curve of the C (6.37).

Note

The baseline is the imaginary line on which the capitals and most of the lowercase letters in a line rest.

Tip

An alternate way to move the anchor point is to hold down the ⌘/Ctrl key and drag the anchor point into position.

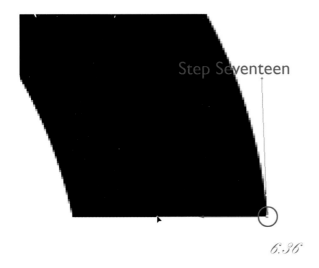

6.36

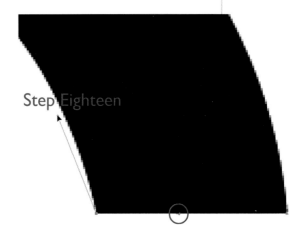

6.37

Tip

Drag the directional handle from the anchor, pointing it toward the route that you're drawing the path.

Step 19: Place an anchor on the inner curve of the C opposite the last anchor point.

Drag out direction handles and rough-in the upper curve. Hold down the Option/Alt key and drag the handle under the cursor in the direction of the next point. Release the mouse. Using the Option/Alt key, drag the inner handles to bend the path to the curve. Add an anchor point and smooth the path.

Step 20: Add anchors and drag out direction handles the rest of the way around the C.

When the path is closed, the handles will look similar to this figure (6.38). Note that the path for the entire letter was created using only ten anchor points.

Tip

You can also make a selection by dragging Path 1 to the Load Path as a Selection icon at the bottom of the Paths palette (6.39).

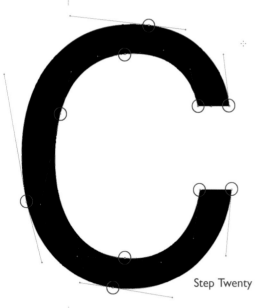

Step Twenty

6.38

6.39

Step 21: **Click on the Path tab.**

The thumbnail for Path 1 shows the ABC outline. ⌘/Ctrl+click Path 1 to make it into a selection.

Step 22: **Click the Layers tab. Cut the selection out of the background and into a new layer by pressing the shortcut ⌘/Ctrl+Shift+J. Click the Background layer eye icon.**

Step 23: **The ABC has been cut from the background by the selection made from the path. Click the eye icon on for the Background layer and off for Layer 1.**

The outline of ABC left behind looks like an emboss. Leaving a little of the edge behind is important because doing so ensures that the cutout will be sharp edged. An accurate path of the letters looks like this (6.40).

All right! This chapter wraps up Part I. You have learned the back stories of bit depth and RAW files, as well as how to use Adobe Camera Raw 3.0. You have also learned a lot about Bridge and how to use it to call Photoshop CS2 into action to make proofs of archive discs, e-mailable PDF presentations, photographic Web galleries, and even printed custom proof sheets. I show you more of the Pen tool's versatility as well as the new functionality of the Layers palette, Smart Objects, and the little things that make Photoshop CS2 the terrific tool it is in the projects in Part II. You may have already worked some of the upcoming projects in the original version of this book *Photoshop CS: The Art of Photographing Women.* Even though they may look similar, sometimes even using the same photographs, I have carefully gone through them for you and updated them to Photoshop CS2. Additionally, I have added lots of subtle new stuff that will make your workflow faster and easier. The projects also show specific retouching techniques that build on non-destructive Photoshop editing. Jump right in. The next chapter shows how to turn a normal woman into Barbie. Why anyone would want to is beyond me—unless it's to learn the basic techniques of body sculpting in a fun, campy way. Now if only Photoshop CS2 offered a "Good Taste" adjustment layer . . . Onward!

Note

When you close the path, the direction handles disappear. If the mouse button is still down, you can reshape the last handle. To retrieve the directional handles, ⌘/Ctrl+click on an anchor point.

Tip

The lure of placing lots of points along a curve is great. It is also the cause of rough, jagged paths. Use as few points as possible when making paths.

6.40

part 2

Projects: Behind the Camera and In Front of the Computer

Chapter Seven

Barbie: From the Ridiculous to the Sublime

I'm a Barbie girl in the Barbie world. Life in plastic, it's fantastic!
Lyric from "Barbie Girl" by Aqua

Barbie. You know her—the Barbie doll. She's the feminine ideal aspired to by generations of little girls who dream that their grown-up lives will be like that of Barbie's fantasy world. Fortunately, little girls outgrow Barbie and refine those dreams to become the real women we love. Fortunately, too, the techniques in this chapter are invaluable basics that when applied in subsequent chapters with finesse, sensitivity, and refinement turn the ridiculous into the sublime. It is important to start the project section of the book with an exploration of the global effects that make skin plastic and perfect. There is a sense that women in fashion aren't real.

Nothing could be further from the truth. At the same time, the camera records a moment, freezing it forever. It translates a four-dimensional breathing human being who lives in height, width, depth, and time into the two dimensions of monitor or print.

Men's magazines seem to consider Barbie to be the male ideal of physical feminine beauty. Flip through their pages. The photographs portray women whose faces feature full, bee-stung lips; wide, clear eyes of intense unworldly color; and skin that is smooth and flawless. Their bodies are perfect, too. Their curves flow in graceful lines with neither unseemly bumps nor unsightly creases. Midriffs are toned, sculpted with the precision of dreamworld perfection.

Barbie is perfect, you see. Her skin is perfect. So are her wardrobe, accessories, car, house, and life with Ken before the breakup and after as he works to win her back. Doesn't every girl want to be sought after? Yes, Barbie is perfect even though her figure is genetically unobtainable as you'll see during this chapter.

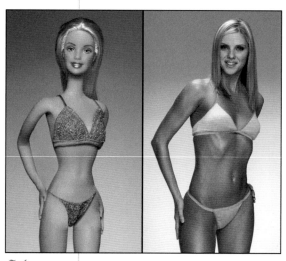

7.1

This chapter is about fantasy, not reality. It is about creating an "ideal," the digital Zen of "Barbie-ness." The stage is set. The players are pictured here (7.1). On the left is Barbie. On the right is Mindy, a woman desperately seeking to reveal to the world her inner Barbie. So it is that with a tongue-in-cheek, a quite ridiculous sense of drama, with not a single iota of seriousness at all, we shall wave that magic wand whose secret name is Adobe Photoshop CS2 and cast the spells that turn our heroine Mindy into Barbie . . . .

Strategies of Forms and Fancies

How will this transformation from normal girl to fantasy Barbie take place? In spite of the belief of most casual readers that this is done simply, the process is in fact quite complex. It encompasses four distinct postproduction phases: retouching, color correction, skin smoothing, and finally, body sculpting.

One of the things I do when planning a session is to create a retouching strategy map. Drawn on a separate layer in Photoshop, this map contains all the areas to be reworked. It serves as a guide during the retouching process and a warning in case something has been overlooked. To check your work against the strategy map, simply click the eye icon on the retouch layer on and off. If an area in the strategy map doesn't blink, you missed it.

The retouching strategy map for Mindy's ascension (or decline—you choose) to Barbie-ness shows that there is much work to be done (7.2). We'll start with the overall retouch.

Tip

The *strategy map* set has its eye icon turned off. To refer to the map, click the eye on. Inside the folder are two layers: one for the map and the other for the text boxes. You can toggle them on or off as desired.

Note

Files 2062-0-0032.psd and 2062-0-0130.tif have already been corrected for color and exposure. They have been unsharp masked and color anti-aliased.

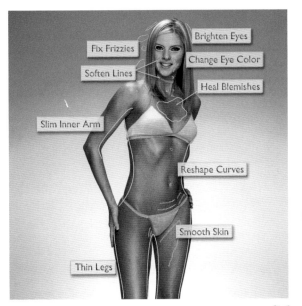

7.2

Tip

If you are using a Wacom graphics tablet, program the bottom rocker switch of the pen to Option, or Alt in Windows. That way you can sample the clone from a point without touching the keyboard. Your cloning and healing speed will improve dramatically, not to mention the quality of your work. This tip works with the Pencil, Brush, Clone Stamp, Healing Brush, and Eyedropper tools. Set the top switch to ⌘ or Ctrl in Windows. This key is used for selecting images in Bridge and layers in Photoshop.

Retouching

The first set of steps covers removing the frizzy hair; fixing blemishes; and softening the lines on Mindy's face, neck, and armpit, as identified in the strategy map. To get started, download the images for Chapter 7 from www.amesphoto.com/learning. The code is **PW48255**. Save them in your working folder.

Step 1: **Navigate to the folder in Bridge and click it. Select the files 2062-0-0032.psd and 2062-0-0130.tif by ⌘/Ctrl+clicking them. Double-click one of them to open them both in Photoshop CS2. Make the photograph of Mindy (2062-0-0032.psd) active by clicking it.**

Step 2: **Press F to invoke the full-screen mode and zoom in to actual pixels view (100%) by pressing ⌘/Ctrl+Option/Alt+0 (zero).**
Hold down the spacebar to temporarily activate the Hand tool. Drag the image until Mindy's face fills the screen.

Step 3: **Duplicate the Mindy layer by pressing ⌘/Ctrl+J or dragging the layer to the New Layer icon at the bottom of the Layers palette.**
Name the layer **Retouch**.

Step 4: **Press S or select the Clone Stamp tool and Option/Alt+click next to the frizzy hair to the left of Mindy's head.**
Clone out all the frizzies.

Step 5: **Make a new layer and name it** Healing.

Step 6: **Switch to the Healing Brush tool by pressing J on the keyboard.**
In the Options bar, select Sample All Layers.

Step 7: **Sample an area of clear skin on Mindy's forehead above the left eye (7.3).**
Heal the slight skin textures on her forehead. Now move to her cheeks and heal the blemishes and textures. Without resampling, heal under both of her eyes.

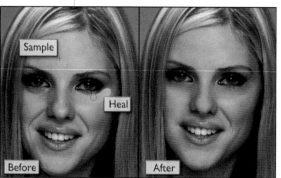

Sample

Heal

Before

After

7.3

Step *8*: **Sample just to the left of the laugh line on the left cheek. Heal down to the point where the line curves by her lip. Resample on her cheek and continue healing toward her chin. Heal the lines and textures on her chin.**

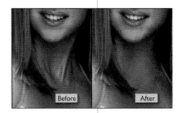

7.4

The goal is to have smooth skin for the make-it-plastic part of the show. Compare the healed left side to the unretouched right side of Mindy's face. The healing process takes time and a lot of small strokes to get a smooth result. Finish healing the right side of the face.

Step *9*: **Sample between the horizontal lines on Mindy's neck. Heal the lines.**

Overhealing is all right. In this case the goal is artificially smooth skin. In reality, you would lower the overhealed layer opacity, resulting in softer, not plastic, skin. Heal the tendons in Mindy's neck. Usually, you would soften only the shadows (7.4).

Step *10*: **Highlight the Retouch layer and then press Shift+J to switch to the Patch tool. Draw a selection around the wrinkles at the armpit (7.5). Drag the selection to her upper arm.**

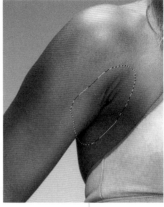

7.5

The original selection previews the area that the dragged selection is covering (7.6). When the selection looks clean, release the mouse button or lift the pen. The wrinkles are gone and, yes, it looks very weird (7.7). Remember, Barbie would never have wrinkles at her armpit.

Smaller, hard-edged brushes work best when you're using the Healing tool. This tool looks outside the actual sampled area. Notice that the color changes when you initially brush over an area. When Photoshop applies the stroke, the oversampled area is blended outside the healed area making the healing smooth and for the most part undetectable.

Brushes for Healing

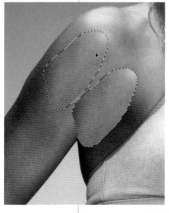

7.6

Step 11: Scroll over to Mindy's chest.

Now use the Patch tool to heal the blemishes here. Draw a selection and drag it to her stomach just to the left of the navel ring (7.8). Deselect.

Step 12: Scroll down to the lines just above the waistband of her bottoms. Patch these areas, too.

Step 13: Heal the blemish on the centerline of her breast-bone while you are at it.

You can use the Patch tool on it as well. Patch the line on the right knee.

One last bit of patching to do. Mindy's ribs have to be softened.

Step 14: Draw a selection around the ribs on the left (7.9). Drag it down to the smooth skin on her stomach.

Don't get too close to her bikini top or you'll get a pink sheen on the healed area. Patch or heal any artifacts. The major retouching is finished.

7.7

Note

{ The Blending Mode drop-down menu is not labeled *Blending Mode.* Unless you idle the cursor over it and wait for the tooltip to appear telling you it set the Blending Mode for the layer, you have no way of knowing it is, in fact, the Blending Mode drop-down menu. (Was that redundant?) It displays Normal and lives right under the Layers tab. }

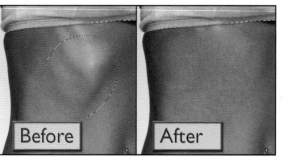

Before   After

7.8

Note

{ The Healing Brush can also take care of the fly-away hair on her forehead. Start the stroke at the end of the hair and brush toward the scalp. }

7.9

Brightening and Coloring Eyes

The two goals in this section are to first brighten Mindy's eyes, and then color them. Take a close look at Barbie's eyes (7.10). They are an intriguing shade of teal—Pantone 325C for the graphic designers in the audience. Mindy's aren't either bright or teal yet. They will be.

7.10

Step *1*: **Create a new layer above Retouch and name it** Retouch 2.

Step *2*: **Hold down the Option/Alt key and choose Merge Visible from the Layers palette fly-out menu.**
The visible layers are copied to Retouch 2.

Step *3*: **Make a new Curves adjustment layer. Click OK. Name it** Bright eyes.
Set the default colors (D). Press X to make the foreground color Black. Hold down the Option/Alt key, and then press the Delete/Backspace key to fill the layer mask of Bright Eyes with black. Change the Blending Mode to Screen. Your Layers palette should now look like this (7.11).

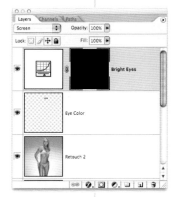

7.11

Step *4*: **Zoom in to 300%. Select a soft-edged brush with a 7-pixel diameter. The brush Opacity is 100%. Press X to set White as the foreground color. Brush over the catch lights in both eyes.**

Step *5*: **Press 5 on the keyboard to set the brush Opacity to 50%. Paint over the irises of her eyes. Avoid the pupils.**

Step *6*: **Press 25 to set the brush Opacity to 25%. Brush in the whites to lighten them some.**
This adjustment is rarely done in real life. The eyes are the windows of the soul—not the whites. Then again, we *are* bringing out her inner Barbie. . . . Compare the left eye (after brightening) to the one on the right without brightening (7.12).

7.12

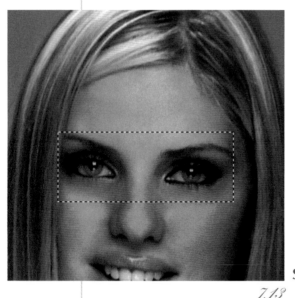

Step 7: Click the Retouch 2 layer to high-light it. Select the Rectangular Marquee tool. Draw a selection around both of Mindy's eyes (7.13).

Step 8: Press ⌘/Ctrl+J to jump the selection to its own layer. Rename it Eye Color.

Step 9: Choose 2060-0-0130.tif from the Window menu and then select the Eyedropper tool.

Set the Sample Size to 3 by 3 Average in the Options bar. Zoom Barbie up to 200% and click in the color of the iris of her eye.

Step 10: Return to 2062-0-0032.psd and select the Color Replacement brush from the Brush tools fly-out menu on the toolbar.

Select a 3-pixel soft-edged brush. In the Options bar, set Mode to Color, Sampling to Continuous, Limits to Contiguous, and Tolerance to 30%.

7.13

7.14 **Step 11:** Paint in the irises with the Color Replacement brush (7.14).

Yes, it looks artificial. So does Barbie.

Pen Tool Panic

If you are already friends with the Pen tool, skip this sidebar. Okay. Here it is—the time you have been dreading. It is time to use the feared, misunderstood, and much maligned Pen tool. A tutorial in Chapter 6 teaches you how to use it. If you still aren't quite ready to tackle the job, click the Paths tab and find the ones I have drawn for you. Here's hoping my fellow Pen tool fanatics will forgive me. . . . Don't put off learning this "most important tool in Photoshop." Remember, your photographs won't have the luxury of predrawn paths!

Click the eye icons on the Bright Eyes and Eye Color layers on and off to see the changes. Isn't it great to always be able to go back? Non-destructive Photoshop rocks!

Smoothing Skin, Plastic Style

One of the hallmarks of women in the magazines is their flawless skin. In the first section, you retouched Mindy's skin to remove blemishes and lines. The following steps show you how to turn a copy of it into the plastic perfection that we all believe is supermodel real (sure we do).

Step 1: **Use the Pen tool to outline Mindy's legs, midriff, arms, hands, chest, and face.**
Name each new path after its outlined part. Don't include the bikini or her hair. The areas to be pathed are shown in green (7.15). Next comes the setup for the skin smoothing.

Step 2: **Highlight the Bright Eyes layer. Create a new layer, name it** Retouch 3, **and merge the visible layers to it.**

Step 3: **Click the Paths palette. ⌘/Ctrl+Shift+click on the midriff, legs, right arm, face, and chest to select them. Choose Select ⇨ Modify ⇨ Contract and enter 1 pixel.**

Step 4: **Return to the Layers palette and copy the selection to its own layer by pressing ⌘/Ctrl+J. Name it** Skin.
Take a look at the sidebar "Seeing Feathers" before going on to Step 5.

Step 5: **Click the Lock Transparent Pixels icon in the Lock section of the Layers palette.**
This lock means that you can change only the existing pixels on the layer and not outside of their own edge. A padlock icon appears on the Skin layer.

7.15

Seeing Feathers

One of the not-so-intuitive functions in Photoshop is the Feather dialog box (available via Select ⇨ Feather). How much feathering is 3 pixels really? On top of being nonvisual, the effect of the command depends on the native resolution in the file. Whew. There is a better way. It requires some setup first, as follows:

Step 1: Double-click the Quick Mask icon on the toolbar. The Quick Mask Options dialog box opens. Change the Color Indicates to Selected Areas and set the Opacity to 100%. Click OK (7.16).

Step 2: The shortcut key for Quick Mask is Q. Press Q to turn off Quick Mask. ⌘/Ctrl+click on the Skin layer thumbnail to activate the selection. Press Q again to reenter Quick Mask, this time with the new settings. The selected areas appear as solid red (7.17).

Step 3: Here's the payoff. Zoom into 100%. Choose Filter ⇨ Blur ⇨ Gaussian Blur. Click on a red edge. The example shows her elbow. Move the Radius slider to 10 pixels. The glow around the solid edge is the feather and exactly matches a 10-pixel feather.

Step 4: Highlight 10 in the Radius window and enter **0.3**. This is just enough feather on the selection to keep the edge from being sharper than the image. A too-sharp edge is a dead giveaway that the image has been manipulated. Click OK.

Step 5: Press Q to return to Normal mode. The now slightly feathered marching ants reappear.

7.16

7.17

Step 6: **Choose Filter ⇨ Blur ⇨ Gaussian Blur. Set the Radius to 2.0 pixels.**

Notice in the preview that only the skin gets the blur. The transparent areas are unaffected because they have been locked (7.18). The blurred skin cannot bleed over its own edges. This step softens the edges. Click OK.

Step 7: Choose Select ⇨ Modify and contract this selection 10 pixels.

Step 8: Press Q to enter Quick Mask mode.

The red area shows the selected area. If it was blurred now, there would be a line on the edge of the selection. Not good.

Step 9: Bring up the Gaussian Blur filter by choosing Filter ⇨ Blur ⇨ Gaussian Blur. Enter 8 in the pixel Radius box.

Look at the preview. The Quick Mask softens. The edge is spread wide and into the previous 2-pixel blur (7.19). Click OK and press Q once more to exit Quick Mask mode.

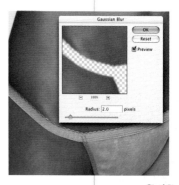

7.18

Step 10: Open the Gaussian Blur filter once again. Stay with the 8-pixel setting and click OK. Press ⌘/Ctrl+D to deselect.

Perfect. Mindy's skin is smooth and soft as, well, as soft as Barbie's. Of course, so are parts that need to be sharp: her eyes, lips, teeth, nostrils, belly button, fingernails, and ears, to mention a few.

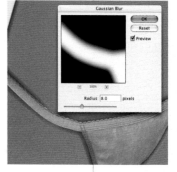

7.19

Step 11: Click the Add Layer Mask icon.

Step 12: Start in the center of Mindy's blurry eyes and paint black on the layer mask with a 30-pixel soft-edged brush at 100% Opacity.

Use the soft edge of the brush to bring out her eyelashes, lower lid, and corners of her eyes. Paint on her teeth and work the edge of the brush along her lips until they are once again sharp (7.20).

Step 13: Press 5 to set the Opacity of the brush to 50%. Start at the far-left edge of the left eyebrow and paint over it to the right and all the way down the left side of her nose, over her nostrils, and back up the right side of the nose.

Continue painting over her entire right eyebrow. Do this step without lifting the pen off of the tablet. If you are using a mouse, do the stroke without releasing the button. Press the left bracket ([) key twice to get a 10-pixel brush. Stroke over just the eyebrows (7.21).

7.20 *7.21*

Step *14*: **Use the 50% Opacity brush to bring her hairline back in where the transition is too sharp. Paint along the edge line of the jaw and chin, too.**

Step *15*: **Scroll down to the shadow line at the center of the lower bra strap.**

This correction requires a 100% Opacity and the 30-pixel brush. Paint out the line.

Step *16*: **Press X to exchange the colors. Set the Opacity of the brush back to 50% and brush the softness back in.**

The line was left in the path on purpose to make certain that this naturally occurring shadow continued to look natural. Don't worry about the noise in the unblurred shadow. You'll take care of that when you add noise to the Skin layer to prevent banding.

Soft focus filters were common when photographs were made on film. There was no cost-effective way to isolate wrinkles, lines, and other skin "imperfections" and smooth them individually. These tasks had to be done globally. Out-of-focus images are larger than sharp images. When these filters blurred the image focus, they caused a halo effect making highlights bloom and colors bleed into each other. One of the telltale signs of using Gaussian Blur over an entire photograph to smooth skin is this edge-bleed effect caused by blurring (defocusing and therefore enlarging) the whole image and painting sharpness back as desired.

Selecting only the areas to be blurred and constraining them to non-transparent pixels on a layer eliminates edge bleed and halos. Just the edge area is blurred, and then only slightly. The success of this technique is contracting the selection, blurring the Quick Mask until the selection barely overlaps the first blur, and *then* applying Gaussian Blur to the pixels after leaving Quick Mask. Look at the scallops on the waistband of Mindy's bikini. They are sharp while the skin is smooth. And there is no color bleed of the pink fabric into the skin. The technique fools the viewer by eliminating the visual cues of soft focus.

Step 17: **Go over all the skin and paint back areas that want a bit of sharpening.**

Be sure to paint her belly button back in. The navel ring needs to be brought all the way back to full sharpness. Brush the hand on the right back in a little. The important part is the contact shadow where the hand meets her leg. Paint in the contact shadows and fingernail on the hand on the left side.

Step 18: **Highlight the thumbnail of the Skin layer by clicking it.**

The border moves from the layer thumbnail to the layer mask indicating it is now active.

Step 19: **Choose Filter ⇨ Noise ⇨ Add Noise.**

In the Add Noise dialog box, set the Amount to 3%, the Distribution to Uniform, and select the Monochromatic check box (7.22).

7.22

Brushing with Opacity

When the brush is set to an Opacity less than 100%, it will build up paint only to the amount it is set to. This feature is useful especially when using a pressure-sensitive tablet and pen. Starting to brush with a light pressure allows the paint to build density gradually up to the opacity set point. In Step 14, the brush stopped adding paint at a density of 50%. Lifting the pen (or releasing the mouse button) allows another 50% buildup to begin.

Step *20*: **Merge the visible layers to a new layer. Name it** Smooth. **Save your work.**

We have come a long way. Mindy is looking softer and more doll-like. Barbie hasn't changed (duh). Compare this figure (7.23) to the one we started with. The next section shows you how to put some serious curves on the model to complete her transformation.

7.23

Tip

Photoshop CS2 can use more than 3GB of memory. Some filters such as Liquify are memory intensive. If your computer does not have oodles of RAM or if the files are huge, Photoshop will page the extra data to the hard disk. Make sure you have plenty of space on your scratch disc (by default the boot drive). Photoshop likes a combination of RAM and disk space that is at least four times the size of the file being worked on and really a whole lot more than that. You can assign additional drives as scratch disks in Preferences (choose ⌘/Ctrl+K then ⌘/Ctrl+7). You want these drives to be as big and fast as possible.

Body Sculpting

Mindy is slender and beautiful. In person she does remind one of Barbie. In a side-by-side comparison, injection molding beats nature every time—when it comes to unrealistic curves anyway. Remember, Barbie's proportions are fictitious and have absolutely nothing to do with the way living, breathing women look. This section introduces methods of body sculpting using the Pen tool and Liquify filter. This exercise is all done in good fun, and quite frankly, to point out that what appears in some magazines really has to be viewed with a skeptical eye.

Step 1: **Make a new layer and name it** Curves Guide.

Step 2: **Select the Pencil tool and set the size to 5 pixels. In the Swatches palette, click the third color from the upper-left corner, RGB Green, to set it as the foreground color.**

Step 3: **In the Paths palette, click Curves. From the fly-out menu, choose Stroke Path.**

The Stroke Path dialog box appears. Click OK. Click off of the paths to deselect Curves.

Step 4: **Click the Layers tab.**

The Curves Guide layer shows Mindy's new shape (7.24).

Step 5: **In the layer stack, click and drag Curves Guide under the layer named Smooth. Click the Smooth layer to highlight it.**

Step 6: **Choose Filters ⇨ Liquify. Select the Show Backdrop check box in the View Options section to the right of the preview window. Click the Use drop-down menu and highlight Curves Guide. Choose In Front for the Mode with the Opacity at 100%.**

It becomes visible in the preview. Curves Guide won't be affected by Liquify's tools so it will show us exactly how much Barbie to apply.

Step 7: **Zoom in to a 50% view. To do so, use the drop-down menu in the lower-left corner of the dialog box, or click the + next to it, or press ⌘/Ctrl++ (plus sign). Scroll until her arm guide is in the upper-left quadrant of the preview.**

7.24

Step 8: **Select the Forward Warp tool.**

In the Tool Options section, set Brush Size to 286, Brush Density to 22, Brush Pressure to 100, Brush Rate to 31, and Turbulent Jitter to 50. If you are using a mouse, reduce the Brush Pressure to 35 and leave the Stylus Pressure box cleared. This tool works more intuitively with a graphics tablet and stylus than with a mouse (7.25).

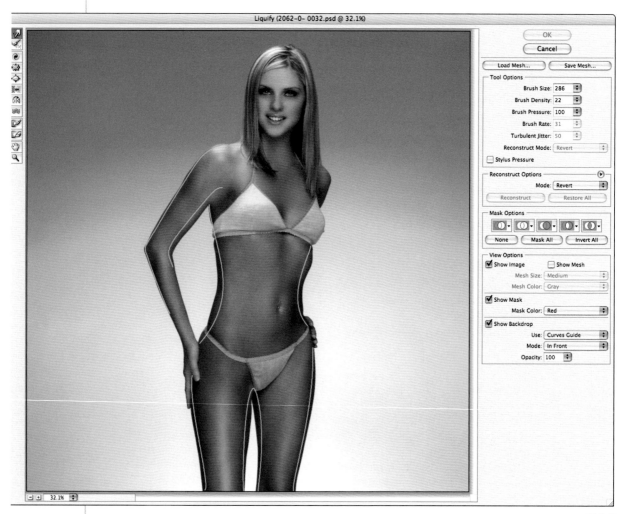

7.25

Step 9: Click the cross hatch in the center of the Warp tool cursor just below the top of the arm and drag the skin to the guide.

Work your way around the shoulder and down the arm to the wrist (7.26).

7.26

Step 10: Set the Brush Size to 150 pixels. Select the Freeze tool (press F) and paint red over Mindy's left side.

This step locks out the painted areas from being liquified (7.27).

Step 11: Reset the Brush Size to 286 pixels and select the Warp tool. Using very small and close-together strokes, pull the skin of her inner forearm and upper arm into the guide.

The work doesn't have to exactly match the guide (7.28).

Step 12: Use the Thaw tool (D) to unfreeze Mindy's side. Then freeze her upper arm (press F).

You might want to use a smaller brush.

Step 13: It's Warp tool time again. Start at the upper part of Mindy's side and pull the skin toward the guide. When you get below her top, work from the open area and push the skin to the guide. Push the hand and hip into the guide.

This step keeps the contour shadow from becoming too wide (7.29). Continue pushing until her outer leg matches the guide (7.30).

7.27

The Photoshop standard undo (⌘/Ctrl+Z) and redo (repeat ⌘/Ctrl+Z) shortcuts work in the Liquify tool. Step Back in history is the same, too: ⌘/Ctrl+Option/Alt+Z. Step Forward in history is ⌘/Ctrl+Shift+Z. Handy! The forward and backward in history shortcuts work in the filter and do not affect the History palette.

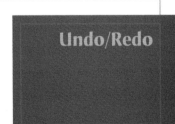

Undo/Redo

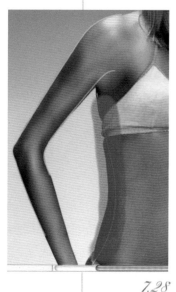

7.28

Step *14*: **Go to the right side and push the skin and the hand into the guide.**

Step *15*: **Clear the Show Backdrop check box and check the work.**

Reconstruct and rework as needed. Then click OK and save the file, keeping the same name.

Because all of the work is done in the non-destructive style, a single PSD handles all of the changes. Next up are Mindy's hips and then her inner thighs.

Mindy's shape is almost Barbie's. Barbie has teeny tiny hips. Mindy (only for the sake of this exercise) wants them, too.

Step *16*: **Duplicate Smooth by pressing ⌘/Ctrl+J, and name it** Barbie Shape 1.

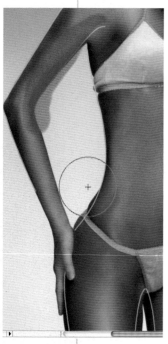

7.29

7.30

Note

Below the Freeze tool in the toolbar is the Thaw tool. Its icon looks like an eraser. It removes any of the frozen areas you paint over. The shortcut for the Thaw tool is D.

In the Liquify tool, reconstruction has nothing to do with the Carpetbaggers coming to the South after the *War of Northern Aggression* (a.k.a., the Civil War). It is a tool that allows the original image to be selectively painted back in to liquefied areas. The lower the brush size and pressure, the more strokes it takes to go back. This feature is very useful when you exceed the number of undos (20 by default).

Reconstruction

Step 17: **Open the Liquify dialog box by choosing Filters ⇨ Liquify. Select the Warp tool. Set the Brush Size to 600 and reduce the Brush Pressure to 51. If you are using a mouse, stay at 35.**

Gently push and pull her hips and hands toward each other, rounding down the leg. When you think it's right, click OK. Look at the result. If you don't like it, press ⌘/Ctrl+Z, go back into Liquify, and do it again.

Step 18: **There is a different technique to reduce her inner thighs. Click the Paths tab and ⌘/Ctrl+click Inner Legs to make it into a selection. Zoom into 300% view. Press Q to go into Quick Mask mode. Choose Filter ⇨ Blur ⇨ Gaussian Blur to open the Gaussian Blur dialog box.**

Compare the sharpness of the Quick Mask to the outer edge of her leg. Adjust the Radius until the mask matches the leg edge, about 0.3 pixel. Click OK. Press Q to exit Quick Mask.

Step 19: **Select the Clone Stamp tool (S) and set a 50-pixel soft-edged brush.**

Step 20: **Option/Alt+click on the background to the left of the left hand (7.31). Clone the background from the top of the selection down both of her legs. Clone in the center area so it will match the background.**

Do this cloning without lifting the pen or mouse button. Press ⌘/Ctrl+D to deselect the image when you're done.

Tip

Remember the Show Backdrop check box? Click it and choose the Smooth layer. Set the Opacity to 100%. Click it on and off and see how the new hip size looks compared to the original.

Keyboard Brush Sizing

Press the left bracket key ([ ) and watch the brush icon or pixel setting in the menu. The longer the key is held, the brush shrinks by 1 pixel. The right bracket ( ]) key makes the brush larger. Add the Shift key to decrease (Shift + [) or increase (Shift +]) the brush size 10 pixels per stroke.

Let's bring up Barbie and see how Mindy stacks up. Not bad. Not bad at all if you are into dolls. There is one difference that isn't explained in the text. Look at Mindy's lips. I used the Color Replacement brush to put some of the pink from her bikini onto her lips—digital lip gloss if you will (7.32).

Go back to the layer stack and click all the eye icons off except for Mindy and Barbie Shape 1. Click Barbie Shape 1's eye icon on and off to see just how much of Mindy's inner Barbie has shown through.

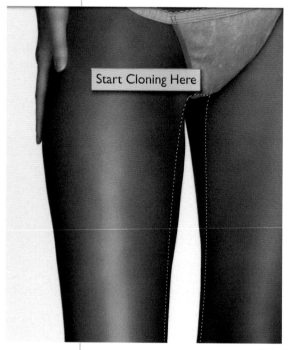

Start Cloning Here

7.31

7.32

Just Because We Can . . .

One little detail remains to be taken care of. Make sure that 2062-0-0130.tif is open. Put our Mindy makeover in a window next to it. View Actual Pixels. Click Barbie Shape 1 to make sure it's active.

There is one last little thing that really bugs me about Barbie. Have you noticed? She doesn't have a belly button. Let's fix that:

Step *1*: **Select the Lasso tool. Draw a selection around Mindy's navel (7.33).**

Step *2*: **Feather the selection 10 pixels (⌘/Ctrl+Option/Alt+D).**

Step *3*: **Choose Window ⇨ Arrange ⇨ Match Zoom and Location.**

Step *4*: **Hold down the ⌘/Ctrl key and drag the selection onto Barbie's tummy. Let go.**
Hmm, Mindy has a better tan than Barbie (7.34).

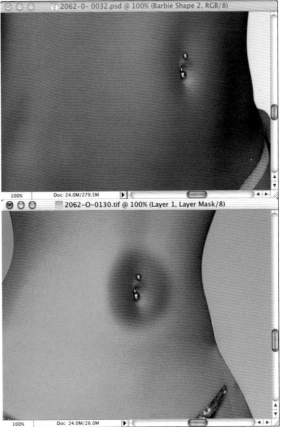

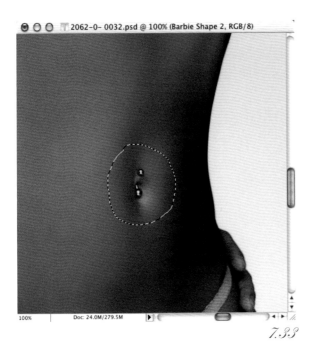

7.33

7.34

Step 5: Add a layer mask to Layer 1. Use a soft 60-pixel brush and paint out the tan skin leaving only the belly button and navel ring.

Step 6: Add a new Curves adjustment layer. Click OK. Press ⌘/Ctrl+G to group the Curves layer with Layer 1.

Step 7: Reopen the Curves dialog box by double-clicking the Curves icon in that layer. Count two boxes up and over from the lower-left corner of the Curves dialog box and click to set a point (7.35).

Step 8: ⌘/Ctrl+click on the navel skin just to the right of the navel ring.

Another point is set at exactly the value of the skin. Click the new point and drag it straight up slowly until the skin tones match (7.36). Click OK.

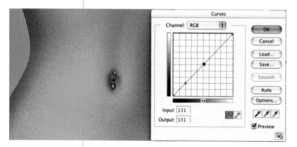

7.35

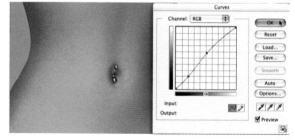

7.36

That's much better. Now Barbie looks just like Mindy (7.37)!

The next chapter refines the body-shaping techniques presented in this one as I help you explore a realm of photography that could never rival the work of painters—the pinup. That is, until Photoshop.

7.37

Chapter Eight

Pinups: Modern Girls in a Digital World

Pinups have a storied history in the art of the twentieth century. Today they hold a special place in the hearts of romantics around the world. The artists who painted them are many. Rolf Armstrong is considered the father of the American pinup. George Petty and Alberto Vargas created pinups for *Esquire* magazine. Vargas went on to paint for fan and admirer Hugh Hefner who published his pinups in *Playboy* during the 1960s and '70s.

Women also practiced the art. Zoë Mozert, protégé of Armstrong, was often her own model. Her images evoke charm, romance, and sex appeal. Joyce Ballantyne and Pearl Frush were also standout female artists of the genre. Pinups appeared on calendars, advertisements, movie posters, and magazine and romance novel covers.

So much for the history lesson. A burning question arises! What's wrong with this picture? Notice that it is only about painters. There is not a photographer in the bunch. "What's up with that?" you ask. Then you cry, "Not fair!" No, it isn't fair at all and it is easily explained. This art form has always been the exclusive purview of artists who turned their imaginations to painting fancifully sleek women featuring ever-so-slightly elongated legs, torsos, and accented curves. Their creations were simply beautiful and beyond the abilities of literal rendering cameras. Until now.

Pinups are back! And this time they are not paintings. Now they are photographs with all the qualities that made pinups so very popular. Girls with impossibly long legs and graceful flowing bodies in wonderful lingerie (or not) float on backgrounds in weightless-looking poses. They are modern romantic visions frozen forever by the shutter of a camera. What's so different now? Adobe Photoshop.

The previous chapter introduced several of the techniques that are applied to the pinup girls in this chapter. This time we apply those techniques with delicate and craftlike sensibility.

Pinups are art. Thanks to Photoshop we leave reality behind. We are now artists creating works of art.

Taking Pinup Photographs

Photographically, pinups are exaggerated, overposed, too expressive, and way too much fun to shoot. The set is simple—a roll of white background paper is enough. Having white or similar light tone behind your model's hair is important. The camera angle, too, is often not what it appears. Shoot your model upside down and flip the image later. Believe me, if she looks great upside down, she will look fabulous right side up. There's something about shooting a subject from above with the top of her head closest to the lens and her feet in the distance that is exceedingly nice.

The lighting is simple, too. Pinup artists used Rembrandt lighting on their moody efforts. Butterfly (Paramount) lighting has always been a favorite in high-profile pinups. The lighting is usually low contrast (not much brightness difference between shadow and highlight) and is somewhat harsh in quality (distinct shadow-edge transitions).

Rembrandt lighting is defined as the triangle of light on the cheek opposite the light source formed by the shadow cast by the forehead and nose. The light source is either 45 degrees up and behind the subject, which casts the shadow on the camera-forward cheek, or 45 degrees up and aimed at the cheek closest to the camera. The trademark triangle of light then appears on the cheek farthest from the lens (8.1).

Butterfly lighting is defined by the butterfly-shaped shadow cast by the nose on the upper lip. The light source is placed slightly to either side of the camera and up about 45 degrees. The shadow cast by the subject's nose should end somewhere halfway between the nose and upper lip. This butterfly example shows catchlights in the pupil produced by the model lifting her chin. The raised chin minimizes the telltale shadow (in the red circle).

Lighting Notes

Rembrandt

Butterfly

8.1

Sweater Girl

Cosmopolitan magazine cover girl Adair Howell from Elite Atlanta is wearing a Pringle of Scotland Georgina cashmere sweater dress and python shoes by Manolo Blahnik. Her pose and expression are pinup classics. This project includes dropping out the background to white; lengthening, smoothing, and slimming her legs; tucking her tummy; softening wrinkles; and appropriate healing work. Get the sample file 2062-K-0001.psd from www.amesphoto .com/learning. Use the book code **PW48255** and download the folder for Chapter 8. The 16-bit file has already been through the pre-postproduction process. The strategy map outlines the desired changes (8.2).

Step *1*: **Navigate to the Chapter 8 folder in Bridge, and double-click it to show the contents. Double-click 2062-K-001.psd to open it in Photoshop CS2. Use the Pen tool to draw a path around Adair and outline inside the wispy hair as shown (8.3). Save the work path as Path 1.**

A path is available in the Paths palette. As you can see, paths are very useful. I encourage you to embrace this most powerful tool.

Step *2*: **⌘/Ctrl+click Path 1 to make it into a selection.**

Step *3*: **Choose Select ⇨ Feather and feather the selection 0.3 pixels.**

Step *4*: **Return to the Layers palette. Make the selection into a new layer (⌘/Ctrl+J) and name it** Adair. **Click the eye icon on the Background layer off. Zoom in to Actual Pixels and scroll to her head.**

Her hair has been chopped into the shape of the path, which might be all right for a stylized pinup (8.4). Personally, I prefer a more natural flow to the hair that only the camera and a few photorealistic painters can execute. Click the Background layer's eye icon.

8.2

8.3

8.4

Step 5: **Activate the Background layer and then select the Elliptical Marquee tool.**
Draw a selection around the outside of Adair's head.

Step 6: **Click Path 1 to make it visible.**
Hint: Click the Paths tab.

Step 7: **Select the Lasso tool. Hold down the Subtract from Selection key (Option/Alt) and make a selection around her face and neck inside the line of the path.**

Step 8: **Press Q to enter Quick Mask mode, and choose Filter ⇨ Blur ⇨ Gaussian Blur to open the Gaussian Blur dialog box.**
Set the Radius to 15 pixels. Click OK. The soft edge of the Quick Mask does not cross the line shown by the path (8.5). Exit Quick Mask. Click in the Paths palette to deactivate Path 1.

Step 9: **Return to Layers. Press ⌘/Ctrl+J to make the selection into its own layer and name it** Adair's Hair.

Step 10: **Drag Adair's Hair above Adair. Activate the Background layer.**

Step 11: **Make a new layer named** White, **and choose Edit ⇨ Fill to fill it with white.**
Adair now has a full head of hair and a dirty-white halo, which would be fine if this was the Renaissance, she was a saint, and we were old masters. (It isn't, she isn't, and we aren't, thank goodness.)

Step 12: **Double-click the Adair's Hair thumbnail icon to open the Layer Style dialog box.**
A lot of power per square foot resides in this box. We are concerned with Blending Options and the Blend If section, in particular.

Step 13: **Click the highlight slider on the line labeled This Layer, drag it to the left, and watch Adair's halo.**
As the slider moves toward a value of 186, the halo fades to white. At 186 the halo is gone and her hair has breaks in it where it was light against the background (8.6).

Step 14: **Notice the line splitting the slider in half. Hold down the Option/Alt key and drag the right side to the right.**
Watch the hair. As the slider approaches 229, the hair is brought back. Move the slider farther to the right and the halo starts to return. Put it back to 229 and click OK (8.7).

8.5

Step 15: **Click the eye icons off for the Background and White layers. Make a new layer above Adair's Hair. Name it** Stretch. **Hold down Option/Alt and select Merge Visible from the fly-out menu to merge the visible layers to the Stretch layer (8.8). The keyboard shortcut is ⌘/Ctrl+Option/Alt+Shift+E.**

8.6

Step 16: **Choose Image ⇨ Canvas Size. Select the Relative check box. Enter 5 inches into the Height window and click OK.**
The expanded canvas is transparent. Activate the White layer, turn on its eye icon, and fill with white again. Turn off the eye icons for both the Adair and Adair's Hair layers.

8.7

Blending Magic

Any sufficiently advanced technology is indistinguishable from magic. This comment from Arthur C. Clarke, the author of *2001: A Space Odyssey*, pretty much sums up my reaction the first time I saw Katrin Eismann demonstrate this somewhat hidden feature of Photoshop. This layer-blending feature is powerful, cool, and fun to play with. It is important to remember that this is a blending feature, meaning that the layers blend with one another to create what you see on the photograph. If you move or modify one of the layers, the effect changes. To preserve the blending effect, you must copy it onto its own layer.

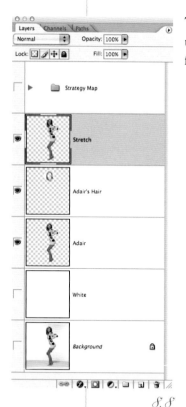

8.8

This is the first stretch of our artistic license. One of the characteristics of pin-ups is the models' extra long bodies and legs. Adair is tall already, almost six feet in her bare feet. She is about to become taller still.

Step 17: **Activate the Stretch layer. Press ⌘/Ctrl+T to enter Free Transform mode. Highlight H: 100% and type in** 106%. **Click the Commit check mark.**
Avoid the temptation to overstretch!

Step 18: **Click the Paths tab and duplicate Path 1 by dragging it to the New Path icon at the bottom of the palette. Rename it** Stretch 106%.

It sure is! Look under the Stretch layer. The layers White, Adair, and Adair's Hair are still available. The Way of the Fast Retreat: Merge them onto a new layer. In this project we've named it Stretch. To go back, you can make a new layer from the ones under it.

Kevin, Is This Non-Destructive Editing?

Step 19: Select the Path Selection tool and then click the path outline around Adair.

Filled anchor points comprising the path appear. Notice that the path no longer matches the pixel information. This is because you enlarged the data vertically 106%. Press ⌘/Ctrl+Shift+T to apply the last transform settings to the path. This command is called Transform Again (8.9). Click the path at the hole formed by her arm on her hip. Apply Transform Again to it as well. Click an area of the palette off the paths to deselect the path.

Step 20: Return to the Layers palette. Duplicate Stretch and name the duplicated layer Retouch. **Then heal the blemishes on Adair's legs.**

Before | After

8.9

When you apply a transform to a layer of pixels that was created with a path-based selection, the path is unchanged. Keeping copies of transformed paths is important in non-destructive Photoshop editing. Remember: *Every time* you transform pixels, apply the same transformation to a *copy* of the matching path. One never knows when the ability to make a precision selection will come in handy (like when an art director changes something. Nah. That *never* happens).

Keeping on the Path

8.10

Modifying Paths

One of my personal peeves is when an author assumes (and we all know about assumptions) that his readers already know how to do something. Especially when that something is as confusing and convoluted as paths can be. Granted, paths aren't easy to wrap your mind and hand-eye coordination around. If you are already hot on the path path, skip this section. On the other hand . . . maybe a refresher might be useful. This tutorial walks you step by step through modifying the path of Adair's back leg. The same techniques pertain to the path for the front path.

Step 1: Click the Paths tab. Duplicate Stretch 106%. Rename it Back Leg. **Duplicate Back Leg and rename it** Forward Leg.

Step 2: Activate the Back Leg layer and then select the Path Selection tool (press A). Its icon is a black arrow.

Step 3: Press Shift+A to change to the Direct Selection tool (white arrow) and draw a box starting above Adair's head and continue down to just above her legs.
All the anchor points in the box are solid, indicating they are selected (8.10).

Step 4: Press the Delete key.
The anchor points around Adair's legs are left. You will use them to isolate the back leg. Note that the remaining anchor points are now solid.

Step 5: Switch to the Pen tool (press P) and hold down the ⌘/Ctrl key.
The cursor changes to the white arrow. Click away from the path. The solid anchor points disappear. Still holding down the ⌘/Ctrl key, click the path with the white arrow again; they reappear, this time hollow. Click the anchor at the top of the dress and drag it down to the top of her knee (8.11).

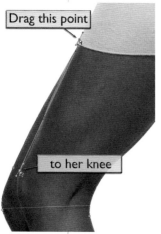

Drag this point

to her knee

8.11

Step 6: Release the ⌘/Ctrl key and hold down the Option/Alt key. Hover the cursor over the direction handles of the newly placed anchor point until it turns into the Convert Point cursor.

Step 7: Click and drag the handles until the path flows along the top of her front thigh.

Hint: The handles are reversed. The one pointing up her leg actually needs to be pulled toward her knee. The other handle will shape the existing path.

Step 8: Hover the cursor over the top of the path midway up her thigh.

The cursor changes to the Add Anchor Point tool. Click and add a point. Hold down the ⌘/Ctrl key and drag the anchor to the top of her quadricep, about two-thirds of the way up her thigh. Hold down the Option/Alt key and drag the new direction handles to shape the path to the muscle.

8.12

Step 9: This path has to be broken before it can be completed. Select the Direct Selection tool (white arrow) and click the first anchor point on the front of her shin just above her ankle, then Shift+click the anchor below that (8.12). Press Delete.

The path is now a segment.

Step 10: Select the Pen tool. Click the anchor point at the top of her shin.

This step picks up the anchor point at that end of the segment.

Step 11: Hold down the Option/Alt key and drag the downward-pointing direction handle up toward the knee. Close the path and adjust the direction handles until the top of the back leg is outlined.

Hint: ⌘/Ctrl+click an anchor point to reveal its direction handles (8.13).

8.13

Step *12*: **Hold down the ⌘/Ctrl key and click the anchor point at the back of Adair's front leg at the hem of her dress to select it.**
⌘/Ctrl+Shift+click the next three anchors, selecting them. Press Delete to remove them (8.14).

Step *13*: **Hover the cursor over the path at the top of the back high-heel shoe.**
When the cursor turns into the Add Anchor Point tool, click to set an anchor.

8.14

Step *14*: **Hold down the ⌘/Ctrl key and click the next anchor down the back of the shoe. Add the Shift key and draw a box around the anchors remaining on the shoes. Release the ⌘/Ctrl and Shift keys and press** Delete.

Step *15*: **Click the anchor at the top of the shoe to pick up the end of the path segment. Set a point at the overlap of the edge of the back shoe with the heel of the front one. Drag out a direction handle and point it up the calf. Adjust the direction handles until the path follows the lines of the shoes. Draw the path along the line of the calf of her front leg. Close the path.**

Step *16*: **Use these steps to modify the Forward Leg path (8.15).**

8.15

Smoothing Subtlety

This section covers the preparation of the skin on Adair's legs. Then you reapply the skin to achieve a painterly smoothness. Use the paths you created in the previous exercise or the ones provided to complete the next steps. Before moving on to Step 1, use the Healing brush to soften any blemishes on her legs and feet. (It is the same process you used in Chapter 7.)

Step 1: ⌘/Ctrl+click the Forward Leg path.

Step 2: Go to the Layers palette. Press ⌘/Ctrl+Option/Alt+D and feather the selection .3 pixels. Make the selection into its own layer by pressing ⌘/Ctrl+J. Name the new layer Front Leg Skin.

Step 3: Click the Preserve Transparency icon.
A lock icon appears in the layer.

Step 4: Choose Filter ⇨ Blur ⇨ Gaussian Blur and blur the layer 2 pixels.

8.16

Step 5: ⌘/Ctrl+click the Front Leg Skin layer thumbnail to make the pixel edge into a selection. Choose Select ⇨ Modify ⇨ Contract and enter 8 pixels. Click OK.

Step 6: Press Q to enter Quick Mask mode and apply a Gaussian Blur of 20 pixels. Click OK and exit Quick Mask mode (8.16).

Step 7: Gaussian Blur the selection 4 pixels.
See the difference in the skin texture between the front and back legs (8.17)?

Step 8: Go to the Paths palette and ⌘/Ctrl+click the Back Leg path to load it as a selection. Return to the Layers palette and feather the path 3 pixels.

Step 9: Click the Stretch Retouch layer in the Layers palette to activate it. Make the selection into its own layer by pressing ⌘/Ctrl+J. Name it Back Leg Skin. Click the Lock Transparent Pixels icon.

8.17

Step 10: ⌘/Ctrl+click the Back Leg Skin layer thumbnail to make the pixel edge into a selection. Choose Modify ⇨ Contract and enter 4 pixels. Click OK.

Step 11: Press Q to enter Quick Mask mode and use Gaussian Blur to blur the edge 40 pixels. Click OK.
The double-sized blur on the selection will help maintain the shadow cast from the front leg onto the back one. Exit Quick Mask mode (8.18).

Step 12: Use Gaussian Blur to blur the selection 4 pixels.
The skin on the back leg softens and the shadow is preserved. Deselect the selection by pressing ⌘/Ctrl+D.

Step 13: Click the Front Leg Skin layer to highlight it and then choose Filter ⇨ Noise ⇨ Add Noise.
In the Add Noise dialog box, set the Amount to 3%, the Distribution to Uniform, and click to put a check mark in the Monochromatic box (8.19). Press OK.

Step 14: Repeat Step 13 for the Back Leg Skin layer.

Note

Using greater Gaussian Blur pixel counts on the Quick Mask makes the skin-smoothing technique more realistic. The lower blur of the skin helps retain important shadow detail. It minimizes the "plastic" look that seems somewhat the rage in fashion photographs.

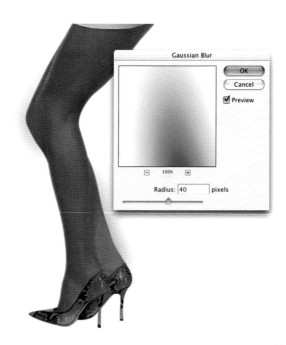

8.18

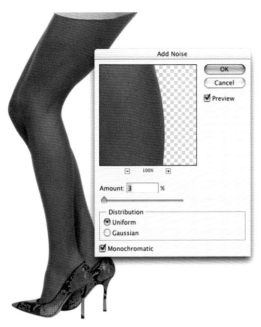

8.19

8.20

Retouching

This section goes over softening the lines on Adair's face,
fixing the flaws on the dress, smoothing her hand, and
brightening her eyes.

Step *1*: **Click the White layer's eye icon off. Create a new
layer above Front Leg Skin and merge the visible
layers to it. Name it** Retouch 2. **Make White visible.**

Step *2*: **Zoom in to 100% Actual Pixels view. In the Strategy
Map set, click the eye icon off of Strategy Blocks
and Strategy Map. Click the eye icon on for Strategy
Map 106% (8.20).**
After reviewing the work to be done, close the Strategy Map
set and click its eye icon off. Start by brightening the eyes.

Step *3*: **Create a new Curves adjustment layer. Click OK to
accept the defaults in the dialog box. Close the layer
and name it** Bright Eyes. **Move the layer below the
Strategy Map set and just above Retouch 2.**

Step 4: **Fill the layer mask with black. Change the blending mode to Screen.**

Step 5: **Select a 15-pixel brush with a soft edge at 100% opacity. Make the Foreground color white. Paint in the area of her eye from lid to lid.**
If you hit any of the skin outside of the lids, press X to exchange the colors and paint the skin back to its original tone.

Step 6: **Press V to select the Move tool and then enter 5 to set the Opacity of Bright Eyes to 50%.**

Step 7: **Make a new layer above Retouch 2 called** Healing.

Step 8: **Select the Healing Brush and click Sample All Layers in the Options bar.**
Use a 10-pixel hard-edged brush to sample high on the left cheek. Heal the laugh line from her nose to her lip in one stroke by painting up and down the line in order to make the finished stroke wide enough to cover the line (8.21).

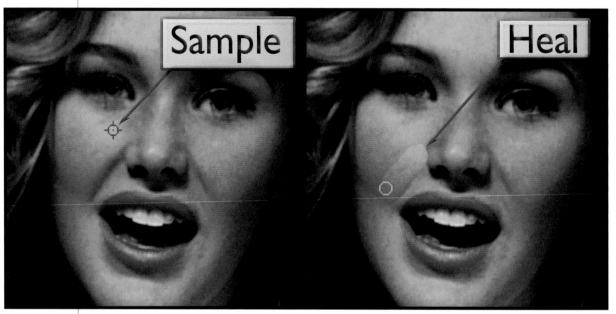

8.21

Step 9: Soften the result by choosing Edit ⇨ Fade Healing Brush or pressing ⌘/Ctrl+Shift+F. In the Fade dialog box, set the Opacity to 62% and click OK.

This setting causes a little bit of the laugh line to show through (8.22). Repeat Steps 8 and 9 on the remaining one.

Step 10: Heal the blemish above the right eyebrow, the lines on her neck, and anything else you might notice.

I like her freckles, so I left them alone.

Step 11: Click the eye icon for the White layer off. The layers Adair, Background, Adair's Hair, and Stretch are also hidden. Make a new layer and name it Body Sculpting. Drag it above Bright Eyes and merge the visible layers to it using the keyboard shortcut ⌘/Ctrl+Option/Alt+Shift+E. Make White visible. Click the Add Layer Mask icon at the bottom of the layers palette.

This step sets up the layer needed in the next section for transforming the photograph of Adair into pinup art.

8.22

Body Sculpting

The next part of creating Adair's pinup is to do a little bit of body shaping. This time you'll do the technique in Photoshop CS2 in 16-bit. Don't worry though if you have converted to 8-bit for the sake of speed. It is easy, clean, and painterly.

Step 1: Draw a path defining a slimmer shape for her tummy.

Close the path in front of her.

Step 2: Draw another path that slightly slims her bottom and makes a smooth line of her leg by removing her hamstring (8.23).

Remember, this is a pinup not an athletic poster.

8.23

8.24

8.25

Step 3: Draw one more path that will cut out her back elbow that shows through the hole created by her forward arm with its hand on her hip (or click the Paths tab to find Sculpting Path).

Remember to save your paths as you create them. They will disappear as soon as you start a new path, which can be frustrating!

Step 4: ⌘/Ctrl+click your path or Sculpting Path to make a selection. Return to the Layers palette and make sure Body Sculpting is activated. Invert your selection by choosing Select ⇨ Inverse or by pressing ⌘/Ctrl+Shift+I.

Step 5: Press Q to enter Quick Mask mode.

What you see is weird at first. The selection is the area inside the path (8.24). The challenge is to use Gaussian Blur to duplicate the edge softness of her back.

Step 6: Zoom in to 400% on a portion of her sweater that's visible next to a mask edge. Choose Filter ⇨ Blur ⇨ Gaussian Blur to open the Gaussian Blur dialog box.

Compare the edge of the Quick Mask with that of her sweater. To match up the edges, try using a .5-pixel Radius.

Step 7: In the Gaussian Blur dialog box, click Cancel. Zoom out to 50%. Exit Quick Mask mode.

Step 8: Invert the selection by pressing ⌘/Ctrl+Shift+I. Feather the selection .5 pixels.

Step 9: Repeat the preceding steps to slim her stomach. Deselect.

Step 10: Now select the Brush tool and set an 80-pixel brush. Paint with black on the layer mask to reveal the white background and cover her tummy where the selection outlines it.

The selection will keep the brush inside the lines and soften it, too. Do the same around her bottom and down her leg (8.25).

There you have it. Body sculpting is super-easy against plain, evenly lit backgrounds. The Pen tool allows the shape of the sculpture to be altered at the artist's whim. If you (the artist, that is) don't like it, undo the work, revise the path, and go at it until you do. How hot can this be (8.26)?

8.26

Note

The purpose of Step 6 is to determine the amount of blur to match the edges. When you invert a selection, it loses any applied feathering. That is why you cancel the Gaussian Blur in Step 7 and feather the inverted selection .5 pixels in Step 8.

Toning Down Wrinkles (Of the Fabric Persuasion, That Is)

One of my clients, Fred Mastroianni, designs apparel for men and women. He is also the art director on the shoots. Then he sits with me for hours creating the retouching strategy maps of every detail that he wants changed, softened, or slimmed. As the designer of the clothing, he knows the fabrics and how they must appear in print. The time I spend with him has given me a huge appreciation for how to make apparel look fresh.

To Undo, press ⌘/Ctrl+Z on the keyboard. Repeat the same keystroke to *redo*—literally *undo* undo. Add the Option/Alt key to the sequence to step back through history (perform multiple undos). ⌘/Ctrl+Shift+Z steps forward through history (perform multiple redos).

Undoing Undo

Wrinkles in fabric are really shadows. They are supposed to be there. The fabric would look painted on without them. The real problem is that these shadows are dark and the eye naturally is pulled to darker areas in a high-key photograph (a photo with more white than other tones). The trick, therefore, is to lower the contrast of the shadow. Reduce contrast by adding light to the shadows (discussed in Chapter 3). The following is one technique I developed to make such wrinkles less obvious:

Step 1: Duplicate Body Sculpting by pressing ⌘/Ctrl+J. Rename it Wrinkles. **Turn the White eye icon back on.**

Step 2: Make a new Curves adjustment layer. Click OK. Name it Lighten Wrinkles. **Fill its layer mask with black. Set the layer blending mode to Screen. Zoom in to 200%.**

Step 3: Select a 7-pixel brush with a soft edge.
This technique works better with a pressure-sensitive tablet and pen.

Step 4: Set the brush Opacity to 20% by pressing 2 on the keyboard. Make the foreground color White. Paint over a shadow in front of her arm to lighten it. Press ⌘/Ctrl+Z (undo) to see the original shadow. Press ⌘/Ctrl+Z again to redo.
If you want the shadow lighter still, paint over it again without lifting the brush. This method takes advantage of the feature that allows paint to build up to the limit of the brush opacity and not exceed it until you lift the brush (8.27).

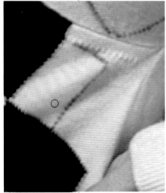

8.27

Step 5: Work throughout the sweater and reduce the shadows. Look at the work by zooming back to 100%. Click the Lighten Wrinkles eye icon on and off. Leave the eye icon off for the next step.

Step 6: Scroll down to the ribbing where the skirt of the dress begins. Click the Wrinkles layer to highlight it, and then select the Healing brush.

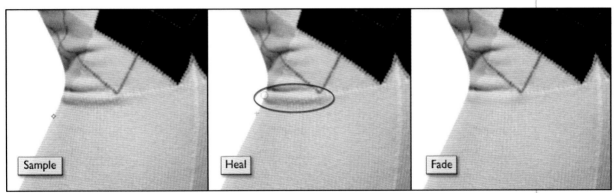

8.28

Step 7: Select a 10-pixel hard-edged brush.
Option/Alt+click the edge of the skirt just below the
shadow. Center the brush on the shadow and stroke
away from the edge without lifting the brush (8.28).
Choose Edit ➪ Fade Healing Brush and lower the
opacity to 25%. Click OK.

Step 8: Select the Healing Brush and set its size to 6 pixels.
Sample next to each of the pulls under her arm and heal them
(8.29).

8.29

Adding the Shadows

The pinup of Adair is almost finished. Without shadows she looks like she is
floating in (white) space. After we add the contact shadow and drop shadows,
our work here is done.

Step 1: Turn off the White layer's eye icon.
The only other layers with eye icons on should be Wrinkles
and Lighten Wrinkles.

Step 2: Merge the visible layers to a new layer by clicking
the Add New Layer icon, and then holding down
Option/Alt as you select Merge Visible Layers from
the Layers palette fly-out menu.
Name the new layer **Retouch Final**. Turn off the eye icons for
Wrinkles and Lighten Wrinkles.

Note

Aligning the sample
point with the healing
point is the trick to
healing textures.
Sample on the edge of
the texture and the
background in this
example. Align the
Healing brush so the
edge begins in the
same place relative to
the sample point. Brush
the entire area with one
continuous stroke.

8.30

Step *3*: **Duplicate Retouch Final and drag the duplicated layer under the original Retouch Final layer. Rename the duplicate** Shadow.

Step *4*: **Click the Lock Transparent Pixels icon.**

Step *5*: **Click the Retouch Final eye icon off. Fill Shadow with black.**

Adair's shape is filled with black (8.30). The transparency is unaffected. Make Retouch Final visible.

Step *6*: **Press ⌘/Ctrl+T to enter Free Transform mode.**

The Shadow layer is active.

Step *7*: **Press the Ctrl key (or right-click) inside the bounding box and choose Distort from the menu (8.31).**

Step *8*: **Drag the center point straight down to the middle reference point at the bottom of the bounding box. Click the top-middle reference point. Drag the shadow down and to the right. Release the mouse button. Click the bottom-right reference point. Drag it toward the center until the shadow of the right high heel slips under the rear shoe (8.32).**

Step *9*: **Select the Commit Transform check box. Make White visible.**
The layer mask icon appears. It is filled with black.

Step *10*: **Highlight Shadow. Set its Opacity to 50%. Click the Lock Transparent Pixels button off.**
The lock icon on the layer disappears.

Step *11*: **Press D to set the default colors.**
Black is the foreground color.

Step *12*: **Double-click the foreground color to open the Color Picker. Enter 20 in the B: text box of the HSB group. Click OK.**
This sets a dark gray as the foreground color.

Step *13*: **Exchange the foreground color for the background color. Double-click White to enter the Color Picker. Enter 80 in the B: text box. Click OK.**
The foreground color is now a light gray.

Step *14*: **Select the Gradient tool. Click the Linear Gradient button. Then click the Foreground to Background Gradient button.**
Both of these buttons are in the Options bar.

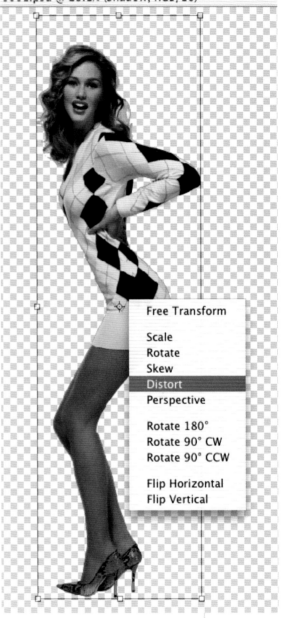

8.31

8.32

8.33

Step 15: **Add a layer mask to Shadow. Click at the point where the shadow starts under the toe of Adair's front shoe. Drag across the shadow to the top of her head (8.33).**

The shadow fades from being dark close to her feet to lighter the farther away it gets (8.34).

Step 16: Press the Ctrl key (or right-click) and click the Layer Mask icon on Shadow. Choose Apply Layer Mask.

Step 17: Duplicate the now layer mask-less Shadow. Hold down the option key and click the Add Layer Mask icon.

The new layer mask is filled with black. It is already named Shadow Copy.

Step 18: Highlight the Shadow layer and choose Filter ⇨ Blur ⇨ Gaussian Blur to open the Gaussian Blur dialog box. Set the Radius to 25 pixels. Click OK.

Step 19: Highlight the Shadow Copy layer. Set its Opacity to 20%. Highlight the layer mask.

With a soft 700-pixel white 100% opacity brush, bring in the sharpness of this layer under her feet. Let the big, soft edge fade the sharp edge into the blur of Shadow.

Step 20: Go to Actual Pixels view and scroll down to the feet.

The shadow is almost finished. Use a black, harder-edged brush on the layer mask to clean up the offset shadow (8.35).

There's a final touch to add on the shadow.

Step 21: Make a new layer above Shadow Copy. Name it Contact Shadow. Select the Contact Shadow layer. Set the Opacity to 50%.

Step 22: Get a 20-pixel soft brush. Highlight the layer mask. Paint with white under Adair's shoes at the balls of her feet.

Let the soft edge make a slightly darker shadow where the shoes meet the floor.

Step 23: Use a smaller brush and make a shadow under each heel.

These are very subtle. If you can barely notice them, they are right (8.36).

8.34

8.35

8.36

Contact Shadows

Contact shadows are the glue that keeps things from floating away, make drop shadows believable, and separate the photographers from art directors and graphic designers in Photoshop. It is that teeny-tiny shadow that is at the base of everything. It locks the object in the photograph to the background. It is a very deep dark shadow. It is the secret handshake that *only* photographers know. When it's missing, photographers look at the output then smirk, "It's fake! A graphic designer (or art director) must've made that shadow." Now I know that only photographers are going to read this so I'm not worried. Okay, maybe a little bit. Tell you what: If you are an art director or a designer, don't tell anybody. Everything will be just fine.

Behind the Scenes: Posing Pinups

Looking at photographic pinups might make you wonder for a moment, "How do those models hold those poses?" You might think they are at least Pilates masters with abs of solid steel. Ya think? Well it's all an illusion. Take a look at this pair of as-shot and after photographs. Photoshop CS2 makes this all happen.

Grip gear serves as Adair's armrest (8.37, 8.38). Amy props her feet on a light stand; note the sandbag keeping the stand in place and the color reference (8.39, 8.40).

8.37

8.38

8.39

8.40

Creating a High-Key Vignette

Subjects on a white background are called *high key*. The only lower tones are those of the subject herself. This project shows you how to drop out the background and remove both the clamps holding up the collar of the model's jacket and the white card that is bouncing light in on the left.

The model is Amy Lucas from Houghton Talent Agency. She is wearing a Gucci ski jacket with a fur collar (8.41). She has already been color and tone corrected, as well as retouched.

8.41

8.42

8.43

Step 1: In Bridge, open the sample folder you downloaded for Chapter 8. Open 2062-L-0031.tif by double-clicking it in Bridge. Make a copy of the Background layer by pressing ⌘/Ctrl+J. Rename the layer White.

Step 2: Select the Pen tool and set up the Options bar by clicking the Paths icon and the Subtract from Path Area icon (8.42). Draw a path around the background, skirting around Amy. Save your path. The path is outlined in green (8.43).

Step 3: Click the Paths tab to reveal the Paths palette. If you have drawn your own path, ⌘/Ctrl+click it to load it as a selection. You can use Path 1 if you haven't drawn one.

Step 4: Return to Layers. Choose Selection ➪ Feather Selection or press ⌘/Ctrl+Option/Alt+D to open the Feather Selection dialog box. Enter 1 pixel in the Feather Radius field. Click OK.

Step 5: Press ⌘/Ctrl+J to make the selection into a layer. Rename it Amy.

Step 6: Highlight the White layer. Set the default colors by pressing D, and then pressing X to make the foreground color white. Press Option/Alt+Delete/Backspace to fill the layer with white.

The background is now white (8.44). The tips of the clamps used to hold up Amy's collar were left behind. We are not going to rebuild the collar, just clean up the colors.

8.44

Step 7: Create a new layer above the Amy layer and name it Collar. Select the Clone Stamp tool. Set the brush to soft edge and 125 pixels in size. Click Sample All Layers. Sample the fur below the clamps. Clone fur over the clamp remnants all the way to Amy's hair.

Reduce the brush size as you get closer to her hair. Avoid overspraying the hair (8.45).

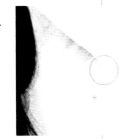

Step 8: Select the Healing Brush from the toolbox. Sample in the fur below the clamps and brush into the white.

Step 9: Select the Elliptical Marquee tool from the toolbox.

8.45

Step 10: Draw a selection around Amy that includes her hair and most of her lower hand (8.46).

Step 11: Click the Create a New Layer icon located at the bottom of the Layers palette. Rename the layer Vignette.

Step 12: Hold down the Option/Alt key. Click the Add Layer Mask icon at the bottom of the Layers palette to make a black layer mask on the Vignette layer.

The Layer Mask icon displays a black circle the same shape as the selection.

8.46

8.47

Step 13: **Click the Vignette layer thumbnail to activate it.**
A brush icon appears next to the eye icon. Set the foreground color to white. Hold down the Option/Alt key and press Delete/Backspace to fill the layer with white (8.47).

Step 14: **Click the layer mask to activate it.**
A Layer Mask icon replaces the brush next to the eye icon, indicating that the layer mask is ready for editing.

Step 15: **Choose Filter ⇨ Blur ⇨ Gaussian Blur. Enter** 114.3 **pixels in the Radius field and then click OK.**
If the blurred mask lightens some of her hair or face, select a black brush and paint it back in.

That's all there is to it (8.48). The major difference between a white and black vignette is that usually the white layer is left at 100% Opacity to bleed the image to paper white when it is printed.

There you have some of the secrets behind making glamorous pinups. The next chapter deals with creating the enhancements that make a beautiful face able to stand the scrutiny of long and up-close examination. I revisit the Healing Brush (this time in depth), enlarge a too-small eye, and work with realistic ways of making eyes more captivating. And I promise no pixels will be harmed in the effort!

8.48

Chapter Nine

From Many, One: A Digital Portrait

Artists have been piecing together images long before digital manipulation of imagery was even a dream. Stained glass windows, religious paintings, frescos, and mosaics are all examples of manipulated art. When stripped of semiotics, art is about manipulating materials to represent a concept. Sculptors shape stone and metal into their vision. Painters use pigments and dyes. Architects draft their dreams on paper for builders to build.

Photography is also an artist's medium, albeit rather new when compared to other forms. And photographers have experimented with and manipulated their work since it was possible to fix an image onto metal more than 160 years ago. They cut up photographs, pasted the parts together, and rephotographed the results. They made multiple exposures on a single piece of film. Film was boiled during development to form patterns of reticulation.

This constant push has helped evolve imagers who can see photographs as parts of a whole to be assembled after shooting. Ansel Adams taught himself to look at a scene and see the finished print in his mind before he released the shutter. He called this *pre-visualization.* Conversely, Jerry Uelsmann developed *post-visualization*—seeing an image after the exposure and then producing the finished image in the darkroom.

In-camera montages became predecessors to the more efficient digital techniques of today—teaching photographers how to see the components of a finished image. The photographers who learned to work within the compromises of in-camera composites on film and those created in the darkroom were uniquely ready to embrace the possibilities of digital postproduction. Digitally captured images moved the possibilities forward to a place dreamed of with film and accomplished only with extraordinary difficulty.

Often I shoot with the camera mounted on a tripod or studio stand. Yes, it limits my mobility and definitely keeps me from even vaguely resembling the fashion photographers on television and in the movies—and this is a good thing. An even better thing is that the lack of camera movement guarantees sharp images. Best of all is that nothing except the model moves. Everything is in register. Being able to choose the best elements from a series of the same image and putting them together in Adobe Photoshop becomes possible.

I often experience a visual flow while making photographs of a model. The feedback of seeing each exposure on a monitor as it

**Photographic
History Lives
in Photoshop**

Photography started with ephemeral images that faded in the light. The first permanent images were fixed on pieces of copper covered with silver. Then silver (or another light-sensitive metal) was made into emulsions and coated on paper, glass, and finally, on sheet or roll film. This media was exposed to light, and then developed. The chemicals tarnished the metal that had seen light. This became the negative. Silver-coated paper was used again, this time for prints made from glass plates and film.

Interesting, isn't it? A traditional silver gelatin photograph is really nothing more than tarnished metal on a paper base. The rate the density of the processed "tarnished" silver builds up in relation to the amount of light is called *densitometry*. Each film has a *characteristic curve* based on its own particular reactions to light and development. The adjustment curves in Photoshop work on digital images exactly the way the characteristic curve does on film.

is made shows me possibilities of combinations that can be evolved into one image in postproduction. I direct the model so that my postproduction options increase. This *real-time visualization* is what pushes my photography to be more than my original idea.

Constructing Christina

The project in this chapter is divided into three parts. The first part involves a critical review of the images of Christina, the model for this shoot. One frame that forms the base of the photograph is chosen. Then individual elements that will enhance the composite are selected. In the second part, the elements are assembled into an image for retouching. This section shares ideas about composition, positioning images using Photoshop's Free Transform and the Difference blending mode, and using layer masks to put it all together.

The third and final part covers the steps of retouching and finishing. It begins with creating a digital strategy map covering all the work to be done. Then we go step by step through smoothing skin, healing blemishes, expanding backgrounds, and even a bit of color changing.

To work along with the project in this chapter, download the folder for Chapter 9 from www.amesphoto.com/learning. The code for this book is **PW48255**. These files have already been color balanced and sharpened, anti-aliased, and of course, copyrighted. As with all the tutorial files, they are licensed to you only for purposes of learning these techniques. You may not use them in any manner for public display, including but not limited to posting on the Internet and inkjet prints.

Analyzing the Take

Take a close look at this figure (9.1). This is the entire take of this pose in the order it was shot. This section shows you how to analyze the photographs for overall composition and choose the best individual parts. Look carefully at the model's hands and feet. Pay close attention to the angle of her face. Which face works the best?

In selecting the components of the photograph, I often grid them out and then make a large print. I draw a green box around frames with possibilities. Then I circle the parts in those frames that I might want to use. I go through the grid quickly, relying on intuition more than reason. I can always change my mind later. The important thing is to connect with the creative side of the brain during this process, making logic secondary. That said, describing the intuitive process is impossible. So I must rely on the rational in this discussion. Please practice the gut-feeling style of selection on your own. The more you review your work, the more you'll notice new things about it.

A study of the pose in the first nine frames reveals a disconnected composition. Christina's right leg doesn't seem to be a part of the shot. There is nothing that connects it to the image. A more extreme example is in frame 10 (2062-B-0314). Her right arm is behind her back. This leaves her right leg completely disassociated from the rest of image. In the next three frames (2062-B-0315, 0316, and 0317) her right hand is resting on her right knee, under her knee, or behind it, respectively. This arm position connects her leg with the rest of the photograph. Frame 0315 has a relaxed feel to the arm.

Unfortunately, her hand is flat to the camera, making it less graceful. Frame 0316 is better with just the side of her hand showing. Frame 0317 is my choice because the shape of her hand follows the line around her knee (9.2). This one gets a green box. It might become the base image, too.

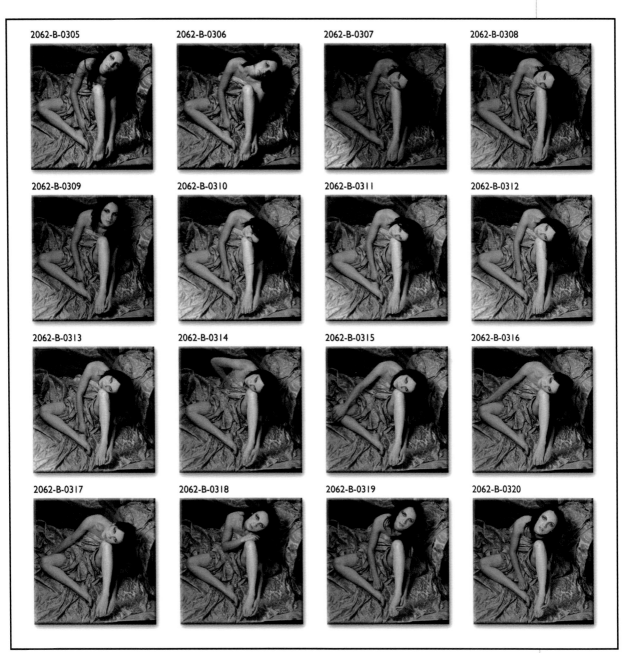

2062-B-0305 2062-B-0306 2062-B-0307 2062-B-0308
2062-B-0309 2062-B-0310 2062-B-0311 2062-B-0312
2062-B-0313 2062-B-0314 2062-B-0315 2062-B-0316
2062-B-0317 2062-B-0318 2062-B-0319 2062-B-0320

9.1

9.2

9.3

9.4

Look at her left foot and hand. In the first three frames there is little if any connection between them. In the remaining frames there is a connection of some kind. Become aware of them. Do any of these 13 images show a flow or particular sense of grace and femininity? Of these, which one is, well . . . pretty? Frames 0310, 0311, 0312, 0316, and 0317 are almost identical. Her hand is long and slightly under her foot. Her foot is wide and boxy-looking because it, too, is flat to the camera. That puts these five frames out of the running.

Frames 0308, 0309, 0313, 0318, 0319, and 0320 are very similar as well. Of all the frames, the first six show her hand curled, touching her little toe. In the last three frames her thumb is touching the top little toe joint. These last three are better, though not the preeminent choice. That leaves Frame 0314 as the best left hand and foot combo. Her hand gracefully caresses her foot and covers a portion of her toes. A green box for the frame and a circle around Christina's left leg and hand go on this one (9.3).

Let's choose a face and some hair. One of the problems with this type of pose is that the top of the model's head naturally goes toward the camera. Telling the model to look at the camera will only raise her eyes. Check out 0310. The solution is to have the model raise her chin to bring the plane of the face more closely parallel to the chip in the camera, as in frame 0312. If you were at one of my shoots, you would hear me constantly saying "chin up." Wherever the chin goes the face follows. I love the hair in 0313, so it gets a green box and a circle (9.4).

Now review all the frames for the shape of the face. I love the poses where Christina rests her cheek on her knee. That eliminates frames 0305, 0306, 0309, 0318, 0319, and 0320. The frames with her chin toward her chest are also out: 0307, 0308, 0310, 0311, and 0314. Frame 0312 shows too much forehead. In 0313 she is looking away. I think eye contact is important for the feeling in the final image. Her eyes are almost closed in 0316. Frame 0315's chin is lowered. The nod for the face is Frame 0317.

The base image has the most things in it that work. This is certainly the case for 0317. The right arm and knee, the body, and face all work well. In the steps that follow, you'll use Frame 0314 for the left hand, arm, foot, and leg, add hair from 0313, and then move on to retouching the composite.

This process has reduced the take from 16 frames to one hero and two supporting images (9.5). It seems like this is a lot of work. Editing is as important to the successful photograph as is shooting it and doing the postproduction. Each is one leg of the tripod that supports a great image. Next you'll assemble the parts.

2062-B-0313   2062-B-0314   2062-B-0315

2062-B-0317   2062-B-0318   2062-B-0319

9.5

Creating the Composite

Step 1: Open Adobe Bridge. Double-click the folder for Chapter 9. ⌘/Ctrl-click to select the files 2062-B-0317, 2062-B-0313, and 2062-B-0314. Double-click one of them to open all three in Photoshop.

Step 2: Select the Move tool from the toolbar or press V on the keyboard.
Make sure you can see 2062-B-0317. Click 2062-B-0313, hold down the Shift key, and drag the image over 2062-B-0317.

Step 3: Double-click Layer 1 in the Layers palette and rename the layer 0313 hair.
Close 0313 by clicking it and then pressing ⌘/Ctrl+W. Press D for "Don't Save" if prompted.

Step 4: Click 2062-B-0314 to make that file active, and then hold down the Shift key and drag 2062-B-0314 on top of 2062-B-0317.
Double-click Layer 1 in the Layers palette and rename it **0314 foot**. Close 2062-B-0314.

Step 5: Back in 2062-B-0317, double-click the Background layer.
The New Layer dialog box appears. Change the name of Layer 0 to **0317 Base**. Click OK. Only one file remains open: 2062-B-0317.tif.

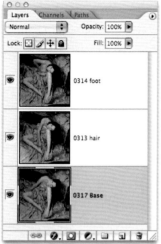

Step 6: **Press ⌘/Ctrl+Shift+S and save 2062-B-0317.tif as 2062-B-0317.psd.**

The layer stack should now look like this (9.6).

Step 7: **Click the 0314 foot layer to activate it, and then select the Lasso tool from the toolbar (or press L on the keyboard). Click and drag a selection around Christina's hand and foot (9.7).**

Step 8: **Press ⌘/Ctrl+J to copy the selection to its own layer. Double-click the words *Layer1* and rename the layer** hand & foot. **Click the eye icon in layers 0314 foot and hand & foot to hide them.**

Step 9: **Click the 0313 hair layer to activate it and draw a selection around Christina's head with the Lasso tool.**

It's okay to include her face, shoulder, and knee (9.8).

9.7

9.8

A .tif extension represents a photograph that is either ready for editing (in 16 bit) or for delivery to a client (8 bits). The .psd extension indicates that it is a working file containing layers of a work product. *PSD files are never supplied to clients.* Adoption of this protocol ensures that a quick glance at the extension of an image file tells the photographer what is in it. *Danger:* It is possible to save layers as TIFs. Don't do it—ever! Layered TIFs—as of this writing—open only in Photoshop and might cause problems for other software (non-Adobe page layout programs for instance). And besides, the layers are *your* working product.

What's in a Name? TIF or PSD?

Step *10*: **Press ⌘/Ctrl+J to copy the selection to its own layer and rename the layer** hair.

Step *11*: **Click the eye icon next to 0313 hair to hide the layer. Click the hair layer and drag it to the top of the layer stack.**
Only two layers are visible now: hair and 0317 Base. The next step aligns the hair layer with the base layer.

Step *12*: **Select Difference from the Blending Modes drop-down menu (9.9).**
Zoom in to 100% to view the actual pixels by pressing ⌘/Ctrl+Option/Alt+0. Select the Move tool (press V). Click and drag to align the layers until the catchlights in her right eye go black.

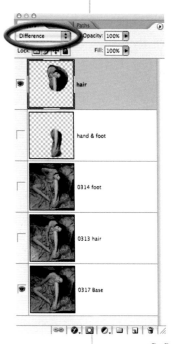

9.9

Tip

Naming layers is a useful habit to adopt when working in Photoshop. While it might not seem important during the heat of creating an image, naming layers is hugely valuable when you reopen the file for modifications at a later date. It saves time and experimentation when trying to remember how you accomplished an effect.

Registering Images: The Difference Blending Mode

The Difference blending mode finds areas of similarity between the active layer and the one visible below it. When areas are identical, they appear as black. The more black there is, the more perfectly registered an image is.

To see how this blend mode works, open 2062-B-0314.tif from the construction folder. Press ⌘/Ctrl+J to duplicate the layer. Make sure that the Layer 1 Lock icon is not active. The Lock icons are right under the Blending Mode drop-down menu. Change Layer 1's blending mode to Difference. The photograph is completely black. Press V to activate the Move tool and press the down arrow on the keyboard five times. The two layers are now out of register with each other (9.10). Now press the up arrow five times and watch the whole image become black again as the two layers reregister. This technique is useful for registering images when compositing them. It is most often used when registering scans from two or more pieces of film shot at the same time.

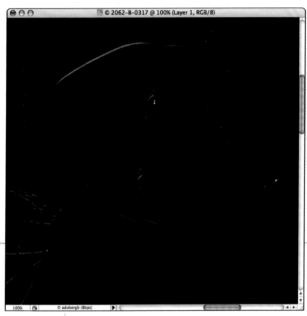

9.10

Step *13*: **Zoom out by pressing ⌘/Ctrl+– (minus sign) until you see the whole selection and press ⌘/Ctrl+T to go into Free Transform (or choose Edit ⇨ Free Transform).**

A bounding box appears. Locate the Reference Point and drag it over the aligned right eyes (9.11).

9.11

Long-time Photoshop users will notice that things are missing in the Layers palette. The brush/layer mask indicator has been replaced. A layer ready for editing is highlighted in blue and its layer thumbnail has bold corner outlines. The layer mask has the bold border when it is active or editing.

Step 14: Zoom back in to 100% by choosing ⌘/Ctrl+Option/Alt+0.

At this magnification the bounding box is not visible.

Step 15: Highlight the Rotate field in the Options bar. Hold down the Shift key and press the down arrow 10 times. Fine-tune the adjustment by releasing the Shift key and pressing the down arrow three more times.

The number in the Rotate field reads –10.3 degrees (9.12). The left eye catchlights should be almost completely black indicating that they are also in register. Press Enter to complete the Free Transform or double-click inside the Transform bounding box.

Step 16: Change the blending mode of hair back to Normal.

9.12

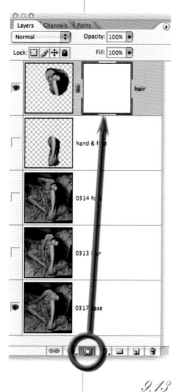

9.13

Step *17*: **Zoom out to fit the image onscreen by pressing ⌘/Ctrl+0.**

Now let's get rid of the broken leg, shoulder, and face, leaving only Christina's hair. The bottom of the Layers palette has several tools.

Step *18*: **Click the third tool from the left to add a layer mask to hair (9.13).**

Step *19*: **Press B on the keyboard to select the Brush tool. Press X to make black the foreground color.**

Step *20*: **Using a soft-edged 150-pixel brush, paint over the leg and shoulder areas and around her head.**

Do not paint out any of her hair. Zoom in to 100% by pressing ⌘/Ctrl+Option/Alt+0.

Step *21*: **Click the eye icon of 0317 Base to turn it off. Refine the mask with a smaller brush.**

Only the areas of the hair layer not brushed are visible. It is helpful to leave some of the background and blend it in with the brush. This avoids the helmet hair look of so many composites (9.14). Clean up any skin or background that doesn't belong. Click the eye icon of 0317 Base on and off to check your work, and then leave it on.

Tip

Just as the arrow key will nudge an active layer 1 pixel for each stroke, pressing an arrow key while in Free Transform affects an image in units of 1 depending on the function selected. Holding down the Shift key and pressing an arrow key moves the image in units of 10.

9.14

Tip

The left and right bracket keys make the brush smaller and larger, respectively. Hold down the Shift key. Now the bracket keys make the brush softer and harder, respectively.

Step 22: **Select the Move tool (V) and nudge the hair layer with the down arrow until the hair meets the model's right cheek. Refine the work on the layer mask of the hair layer until you achieve a natural cheek line.**

If the skin line that blends into the shoulder doesn't quite match, don't worry; that gets touched up later (9.15).

Okay, now on to the hand and foot. The procedure to replace them is mostly the same as for the hair.

Step 23: **Click in the foot & hand layer to activate it. Change the blending mode to Difference to see how well it lines up with the base layer.**

It is important that the top of the leg is registered with the base layer. Use the Move tool (V) to nudge the layer until the leg becomes black (9.16). Change the blending mode back to Normal.

Tip

Pressing the X key eXchanges the foreground and background colors. When working on a layer mask, painting with black conceals the underlying image. Press X to switch to white. Painting with white reveals the underlying image.

9.15

9.16

9.17

Step 24: **Click the Add Layer Mask icon at the bottom of the Layers palette to add a layer mask to the hand & foot layer.**

Press B to select the Brush tool. Select a 60-pixel soft-edged brush. Set Black as the foreground color.

Step 25: **Brush with black around the hand and foot on the layer mask and blend the leg layer with the one beneath it. Blend in the arm and the surrounding fabric.**

Click the eye icon of the 0317 Base layer on and off to see whether there are any places where it doesn't blend perfectly. Look for hard sharp lines. Paint on the layer mask as needed. If something is accidentally painted out, press X on the keyboard to exchange the colors and paint it back in. Press X once again and refine the layer mask. The hand & foot layer will look similar to this figure (9.17).

Step 26: **Zoom out to the Fit on Screen view by pressing ⌘/Ctrl+0.**

Click the Look icons of the hair and hand & foot layers on and off several times. Look for areas at the edges of these layers that seem to jump or look out of place. Examine any you might find and refine their layer masks before continuing with the next step.

Tip
What went wrong? If all the visible layers disappeared when you chose Merge Visible from the Layers palette fly-out menu, you didn't hold down the Option/Alt key.

Tip
Another way to align images is to lower the Opacity of the top layer to around 50%. The shortcut from the keyboard is to press 5 when the Move tool is selected. You can set other opacities as follows: 1 = 10% opacity, 2 = 20%, and 5 = 50%. Pressing two number keys in rapid succession sets an in-between number; for example, 7,5 =75%.

Tip
Pressing D on the keyboard sets the Default colors, which are black and white. Black is the default foreground color. Pressing X exchanges the foreground color with the background color.

Note

Some Photoshop users feather the selection before floating it so that it will blend in without using the layer mask. I am an admitted control freak and believe my eye is better than the "how much does feather feather?" question raised by its no preview dialog box. To each her or his own.

Note

The number of frames shot for this project offer many other construction possibilities. A challenge for you is to download the sheet of images (2062-B Pull Sheet.psd), print it out, and build your own version. The file 2062-B-03XX.psd has individually named layers of the 16 images on the grid. In Photoshop hide all of the layers except the ones you want to composite. Choose File ⇨ Scripts ⇨ Export Layers to Files. Make sure you select Visible Layers Only.

The compositing of the three frames is now complete. Indicate that by merging the visible layers onto a new layer.

Step 27: **Click the hair layer to activate it and then click the Create a New Layer icon (next to the trashcan icon) at the bottom of the Layers palette.**

A new layer called Layer 1 appears at the top of the stack (9.18). Hold down the Option/Alt key and choose Merge Visible from the Layers palette fly-out menu. The visible layers, 0317 Base, hand & foot, and hair, are merged and copied onto Layer 1. (Shortcut: Do all of this from the keyboard by pressing ⌘/Ctrl+Option/Alt+Shift+E. Done!)

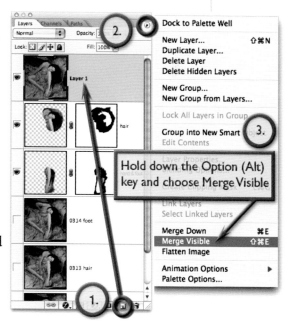

9.18

Step *28*: **Double-click the words Layer 1 and rename the layer** Retouch.

This layer is the one from which you will build all the retouching in the next section of this chapter. Save the file as **2062-B-0317.psd**.

Wow. Photography certainly has come a long way since 1888 when Kodak's motto was "Push the button—We do the rest." There are those who think that those were the good old days when someone else did the heavy lifting. Digital photography has pretty much killed the chemical darkroom and plopped the photographer down—kicking and screaming in many cases—in front of a computer monitor instead.

Nobody said that working with digital photographs was easy. If it was, everybody would be doing it at this level. Because doing really great finishing work is possible, it is important that we do it. Capture on film forced us to degrade the image before developing it. We used soft-focus filters, vignetters, and cross processing to achieve an imagined result. This meant that in the name of making a photograph "pretty," we had to forego control in postproduction. For the most part, we could only dream.

Now we have the tools. The control is ours. The following section shows you how to exercise of some of this power.

Strategic Retouching

The previous two chapters have shown the concept of the strategy map. Now it's time for you to create one. Here's how to go about it.

Step *1*: **Create a new empty layer (press ⌘/Ctrl+Shift+N) and name it** Strategy Map.

This is the layer that maps out the work to be done in the retouching of the photograph.

Step *2*: **Zoom in to 100% (press ⌘/Ctrl+Option/Alt+0). Hold down the spacebar and drag the image until Christina's face is centered in the window.**

Step *3*: Double-click the foreground color to open the Color Picker. Select a green that you like and click OK (9.19).

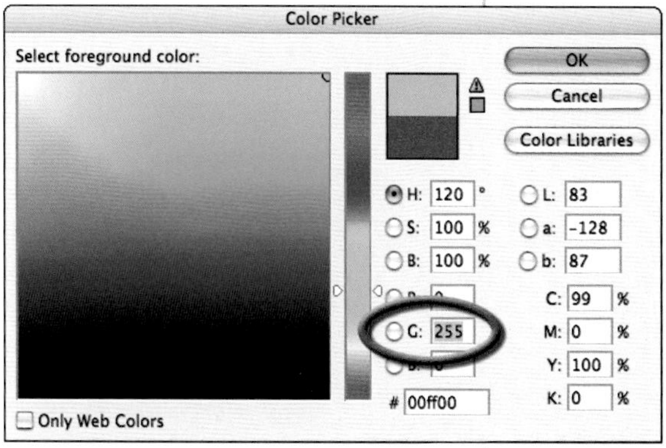

Step *4*: Select the Pencil tool (press B, then Shift+B). Choose a 5- to 7-pixel brush.

The pencil is hard edged.

Step *5*: Draw a circle around the lines under her left eye. Draw under her right eye, around her forehead, and along the bridge of her nose. Circle the blemish on her chin and the one just above her beauty mark.

We could remove it, but because it is a beauty mark—not a mole—(Christina loves it) we'll leave it alone.

9.19

Tip

Pressing F on the keyboard will fill the background with neutral gray and display the image without the window. Press F again. The background turns black and the Menu bar is hidden. Press Tab to hide the toolbar and palettes. (If you still see rulers, press ⌘/Ctrl+R to hide them.) This is called *Presentation mode*. Only the image against a black background is on the screen. Press Tab again to bring the toolbar and palettes back. Press F once more to display the Menu, Options bar, and Document (image) window.

Note

Text boxes are helpful if the retouching is being handed off to another artist or for creating postproduction estimates for clients. They are really amazed to see all the work that goes into a final photograph.

9.20

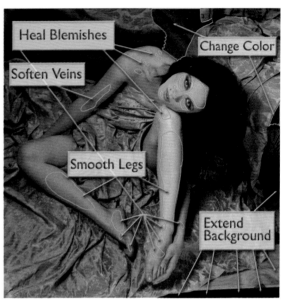

9.21

The strategy map is a reminder of the work to be completed. Click Retouch on and off after finishing an area to see whether everything is finished. If an area does not blink when you turn off the eye icon, it has not been retouched.

Step 6: **Scroll around the image and circle the areas that need retouching with the green pencil (9.20).**

I added text boxes and arrows to the strategy map to explain the work to be done on this image (9.21).

Step 7: **Zoom in to 100%, and then scroll to center Christina's face in the window. Highlight Composite by clicking it in the Layers palette. Press ⌘/Ctrl+J to duplicate the layer and rename it** Retouch.

All the work will be done on this layer instead of on Composite, which now serves as a backup for your work. If something gets ruined on Retouch, you can get it back. Click the eye icon next to Strategy Map off.

Step 8: **Press J on the keyboard to select the Spot Healing brush, a new tool in Photoshop CS2. (Press Shift+J to toggle the tool to the Healing brush, again for the Patch tool, and once more for the Color Replacement brush.)**

Choose a hard-edged 10-pixel brush from the Options bar. Make sure that Source is set to Sampled and that Aligned is not selected. Option/Alt+click to set the sample point in an area of smooth skin (9.22). Heal the blemishes by brushing over them using short strokes.

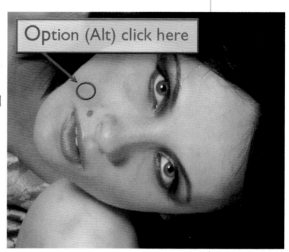

9.22

Step 9: **Sample the area under the blush on Christina's left cheek and brush under her left eye without lifting the stylus or mouse button until the bag is completely covered.**

When you lift the stylus or release the mouse button, Photoshop heals the area. Using the same technique, heal under Christina's right eye (9.23).

Step 10: **Click the Look (eye) icon on for the Strategy Map layer and scroll over to her shoulder.**

Click Strategy Map off. Heal the blemishes using the same technique as in Step 8.

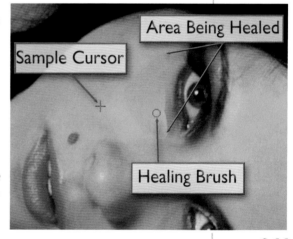

9.23

Step 11: **Scroll down her left arm to the vein that runs from the upper arm to the joint.**

The note on the strategy map is to soften the veins.

Step 12: **Press Shift+J to switch to the Patch tool.**

Be sure the Source button is selected in the Options menu.

Tip

The keyboard shortcut for the Fade command is ⌘/Ctrl+Shift+F. This command works with most tools and filters to control the effect immediately after the fact.

Step 13: **Draw a selection with the Patch tool around the vein (9.24) and click inside the selection and drag it up her arm to an area of clear skin and release.**
The selection jumps back and the patch is applied. The vein is completely gone—not exactly what is called for.

Step 14: **Choose Edit ⇨ Fade Patch Selection and drag the slider in the Fade dialog box to 34%.**
The vein is subtly revealed. Click OK. Repeat the process with the other veins on her arm.

Step 15: **Continue healing using the brush and Patch tool on the large blemishes and bruises on her right leg. Move on to the left foot and patch the shoe impressions on top of it.**
Be careful not to select right up to the edge of her hand. Heal the blemishes on her foot, hand, arm, leg, and knee. Click the eye icon of the Retouch layer on and off to see the progress so far. The next step shows you how to heal that shaving stubble.

Step 16: **Duplicate the Retouch layer by pressing ⌘/Ctrl+J. Rename it** Soften Legs.

Note

The Healing brush and the Patch tool sample areas outside of the edge of the brush or selection. When you use the healing tools too close to an area that is a different color or tone, the sample that extends beyond where the tool indicates it is working will blend and cause a discolored result.

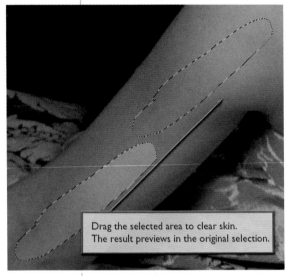

Drag the selected area to clear skin.
The result previews in the original selection.

9.24

Step 17: **Choose Filter ⇨ Blur ⇨ Gaussian Blur and set the Radius to 8 pixels. Click OK (9.25).**
The whole image becomes blurred.

Step 18: **Choose Filter ⇨ Noise ⇨ Add Noise and set 3% as the amount.**
Set Distribution to Uniform. Select the Monochromatic check box (9.26). Click OK.

Step 19: **Add a black layer mask by holding down the Option/Alt key and clicking the Add Layer Mask icon at the bottom of the Layers palette.**
Everything's sharp again.

Step 20: **Select the Brush tool (press B, Shift+B, and Shift+B again to get from the Pencil back to the Brush) and choose a soft 70-pixel brush at 100% Opacity.**

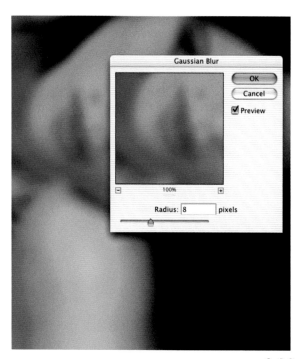

9.25

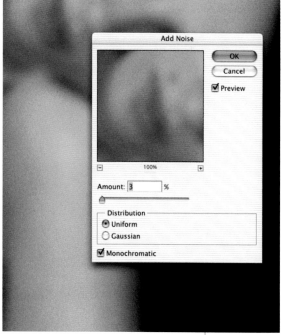

9.26

Be Shiftless

If you find yourself getting really tired of using the Shift key and a tool's shortcut, press ⌘/Ctrl+K to get into Photoshop's preferences. Clear Use Shift Key for Tool Switch. Now pressing just a tool's letter selects it. Pressing the same letter cycles through nested tools.

Note

If any layers below the Retouch layer are visible, they won't appear on the merged Retouch 2 layer. The Merge Visible command merges only what can be seen on the monitor to the new layer.

Step 21: Make white the foreground color and brush over the legs, being careful to stay inside them.
If the edges should become blurry, press X to switch to black and paint them back. Switch back to white and complete the smoothing. Yes, they do look like plastic. There is just one more thing. . . .

Step 22: Change the blending mode of Soften Legs to Darken.
The darkest stubble is softened and there is enough of it left to make the photograph believable. If there's still too much stubble for you, heal it in the final version.

Free Transform

Modifying selections or layers in the Free Transform mode often means working outside the document window. Before entering Free Transform, press F on the keyboard to go into the Full Screen mode with the Menu bar. You can also activate this mode from the toolbar. Access Free Transform from the Edit menu or by pressing ⌘/Ctrl+T. Zooming using ⌘/Ctrl++ (plus sign) or − (minus sign) is available while using Free Transform.

Extending the Background

Continuing along, the last two to-do's on the strategy map are extending the background and changing the color of the fainting couch behind Christina.

Step 23: Press ⌘/Ctrl+Option/Alt+Shift+E to copy the visible layers to a new one. Name it Retouch 2.

Step 24: Select the Lasso tool (press L) and draw a selection like the one here (9.27).

Make the selection into its own layer by pressing ⌘/Ctrl+J. Rename the layer **Extra Background**.

Step 25: Enter the Full Screen mode by pressing F.

See the nearby sidebar, "Free Transform," for more information about Full Screen mode.

Step 26: Choose Edit ➪ Free Transform or press ⌘/Ctrl+T.

A bounding box appears. Pull the lower-right handle diagonally toward the lower right of the screen until the fabric covers the cellphone and the plywood. Drag the upper-left handle toward the upper-left corner of the screen until the gap formed by the first drag is covered (9.28). Select the check mark in the Options bar to apply the transformation.

9.27

9.28

Step _27_: **Click the Add Layer Mask icon or choose Layer ⇨ Add Layer Mask ⇨ Reveal All from the menu bar to add a white layer mask to the Extra Background layer.**

Step _28_: **Select the Brush tool (B) and make a soft-edged 70-pixel brush.**

Set black as the foreground color. Zoom in to 100% by pressing ⌘/Ctrl+Option/Alt+0. Blend the image on Extra Background with Retouch 2 below it. Extending the background does double duty in this case by covering the red fabric at the right edge of the fainting couch. You can take care of minor gaps on the final retouching layer (9.29).

Scroll to the maroon fabric above Christina's shoulder. The last step is to change the color to one more in keeping with the golden fabric.

Step _29_: **Using the Pen tool, create a path around the fabric. Double-click the work path and save the path as Path 1.**

Step _30_: **⌘/Ctrl+click Path 1 in the Paths palette to make it into a selection.** Feather it (choose Select ⇨ Feather or press ⌘/Ctrl+Option/Alt+D) and set a feather radius of .3 pixels. Click OK.

Step _31_: **Return to Layers and click Retouch 2 to activate it. Make the selection into a layer by pressing ⌘/Ctrl+J.** Rename this layer **grayscale**.

_9.29_

During the time around the War of Northern Aggression (hey, I live in the South!) or Civil War, chaise longues were placed at the top of the stairs in plantation houses. The corsets in vogue at the time were often laced so tightly that a woman wearing one would nearly faint from lack of breath by the time she reached the top, so she had to "sit a spell." Hence the name *fainting couch*. A fainting couch is a wonderful prop when posing fashion and figure models.

Corsets, Couches, and Catching Her Breath

Step 32: **Convert this layer to grayscale by choosing Image ⇨ Adjustments ⇨ Desaturate.**
Duplicate the grayscale layer (⌘/Ctrl+J).

Step 33: **Use the Eyedropper tool (press I) to pick a golden color from the fabric. Click the grayscale copy layer to activate it. Rename it** multiply. **Click the Lock Transparent Pixels icon for the layer.**

Step 34: **Choose Edit ⇨ Fill from the menu bar.**
In the Fill dialog box, set Use to Foreground Color, Mode to Normal, and Opacity to 100%. Duplicate the multiply layer. Rename the multiply copy **layer overlay**. Duplicate the overlay layer and rename it **color**. Change color's blending mode to Color.

Note

If you are not familiar with the Pen tool yet, click the Paths tab in the Layers palette. ⌘/Ctrl+click the fainting couch to make the selection. Click back on the Layers tab to return to the Layers palette.

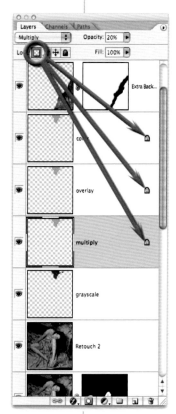

9.30

Step 35: **Change the blending mode of the overlay layer to Overlay.**

Done! Almost.

Step 36: **Select the Move tool (press V), click the multiply layer, and then press 2 on the keyboard to change the Opacity to 20%. Change the blending mode to (you guessed it) Multiply.**

Look! Some of the fabric texture is showing and it's the right color (9.30)! Fabulous! Play with the opacities of the multiply, overlay, and color layers to change the tone of the color. Hint: Higher opacity on multiply will darken the tone.

Step 37: **Click the Extra Background layer to activate it. Use the keyboard shortcut ⌘/Ctrl+Option/Alt+Shift+E to merge the visible layers to a new layer. Name it** Final **and save your work.**

Step 38: **Zoom in to 100% (⌘/Ctrl+Option/Alt+0) and scroll over the entire image.**

Look for any artifacts from the work that has been done. Usually all that's needed is a bit of attention from the Healing brush or the Clone stamp. When your review and finishing touches are complete, save the .psd file again.

Step 39: **Option/Alt+click the eye icon of the Final layer.**

This turns off all the looks except the one for Final. Scroll down to the bottom of the layer stack and turn the eye icon on for the 0317 Base layer. Scroll back up to Final and click the eye icon on and off to see where this all started and just how far it has come (9.31).

Step 40: **Flatten 2062-B-0317.psd and save it as 2062-B-0317.tif.**

This file is the one that goes to the printer or a client. Archive the .psd. It is your work product.

Learn More

Some of the compositing and retouching techniques are easier to learn when you can watch someone do them. A companion CD-ROM with QuickTime movies and the image files is available through Software Cinema. You can watch and work along with me, pausing or rewinding the movie at any time, as I show you how to use Layer Masks, Free Transform, the Healing brush, and Patch tools. For ordering information go to `www.amesphoto.com` and click Training.

A lot of work goes into finishing a file after it has been captured. This has always been the case. The big difference is that now the work is sourced to labs, printers, and retouch artists. It is important to remember that keeping the original vision intact is difficult when other vendors are in the loop.

The next chapter examines the techniques for retouching beauty photographs. You'll study methods of smoothing skin without losing texture, healing without tonal bleeds, and even making eyes the same size.

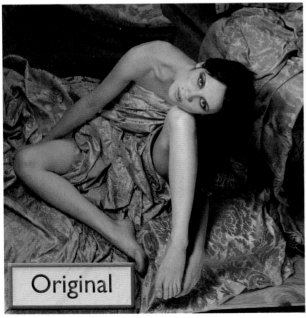

Original

Composite

9.31

Chapter Ten

Retouching Beauty

There is certainly no absolute standard of beauty.
That precisely is what makes its pursuit so interesting.

John Kenneth Galbraith

I visited the Metropolitan Museum of Art in New York with an eye toward looking for examples of retouching done in the past, before Adobe Photoshop, and even before photography. The purpose of the visit was to look at paintings from European portraitists and see how they painted women. I saw wondrous works that have the most incredible detail in the gowns, fabrics, and tapestries. Every thread is visible. The textures look amazingly real. I felt a subconscious urge to reach into the canvas and feel the cloth.

The women in these paintings are beautiful. Their hair is portrayed right down to single strands. And the most amazing thing I saw was how these artists treated their skin, eyes, and lips. They're perfect. Intellectually I know that they were flawed. Oil of Olay did not exist in the Renaissance after all. I asked myself, "What's going on here?" (Okay, what I really asked myself was, "What were those painters doing way back then?")

The answer rocked my world. And it is going to rock yours. What were they really doing with their art back in the Renaissance? Here is the answer in one word—*Photoshop*.

That's right, painters and portraitists wielding brushes and oils on canvas have been doing Photoshop since, well since the very beginning of making likenesses of people, especially women. (In some of the paintings the men looked downright gnarly, yet never the women!)

Now, the tools were different then, and they certainly didn't have computers, scanners, or cameras—digital or otherwise. These painters and portraitists had an eye for beauty, the skill to paint it, and the wisdom to use both. Use them they did, often and to very good purpose. Theirs was skill more than enough to make skin show texture, pores, wrinkles, scars, acne, goiters, warts, and crooked noses. Their wisdom told them that accuracy has its place, as does artistic license. And when it came to the women whom they loved to paint, why, the results are all beautiful, flawless, and intriguing. Their "Photoshop" was just as much about idealizing beauty then as it is now. There isn't a soul who really wants anyone to study a non-moving, silent image of herself, or himself for that matter, without it first being retouched. True in the Renaissance, even truer today.

This chapter is about retouching beauty with that artistic license. It encourages us to make photographs that draw the viewer in, while withholding that which would never be noticed if the person was present, breathing, laughing, crying, and being. The techniques are focused on women.

They are applicable to men as well. It is certainly all right to soften the lines on a man's face, brighten his irises, whiten his teeth, and remove some blemishes. Most men don't pursue beauty with the same fervor and passion that women do. Men are not idealized in the same ways, either. The techniques will work as well on men as on women; you just apply them with a lighter touch.

Remember that men are distinguished. Women are flawless. This is a rule of the universe and is not debatable in spite of contrary evidence such as the "Does this make me look fat?" question of death. Enough said.

Look at the structure of the face as it is photographed. The human face is not symmetrical. Close scrutiny (of the photograph) often reveals that one eye is larger or maybe a nostril is. Note: Be careful looking at the people you are photographing. They can get really weird if you just look at them like the photograph they are going to be. It is useful to let them know why you are studying their features. Say something innocuous like "I'm watching the way the light is working on you." They calm down then. There are photographic techniques that solve a lot of the size issues. As you go through this chapter, you will become aware of these facial differences and compensate for them in the camera. Sometimes, though, the circumstance demands making the photograph and fixing the sizes later.

Retouching a Face: Part 1

Christina is our model (Elite Model Management /Atlanta). The photography is for an Atlanta makeup artist, Janeen Loria (www.moodymakeup.com), who also has a line of skin care products and makeup. The set was ready and Christina was in place. I noticed that her left eye was smaller than her right. My first reaction was to flop the set so that her small eye would be closer to the camera, making it appear larger. Then two things came to mind: First, "This is a simple fix in Photoshop . . ." and second, "It is important not to draw attention to the model's flaws." Yep, that last one is very important.

In photography of a non-model, changing the set would not be a problem. She would have no idea why I would do this, and the universal reason ("the light is better") comes into play. Models, on the other hand, are totally aware of their features. Christina knows her left eye is smaller. And I know she knows because she favors her left side toward the camera. It's one of the subtle communications that develop between photographer and model.

Resizing Christina's eye is only a part of this chapter's project; I'll go through many beauty retouching techniques that are useful in developing your own style of artistic enhancement in photographing beauty. To get started, download this chapter's folder from www.amesphoto.com/learning. The book code is **PW48255**.

Step *1*: **Open this chapter's folder by double-clicking it in Bridge, and then double-click 2062-B Christina CU.tif to open it in Photoshop CS2.**
The file has already been through the pre-postproduction process. (Notice the © in the document header.)

16-Bit Editing

One of the professional features of Photoshop CS2 is the increased ability to work in 16-bit using layers. This editing style is about producing the highest output quality. The screen captures follow the 16-bit workflow. They are of the full resolution file. The file on www.amesphoto.com/learning is provided in 16-bit format at full resolution. The high resolution files take longer to download and provide a much better experience learning retouching.

Step 2: Zoom to 50% so that both eyes are visible.

Step 3: Select the Measure tool under the Eyedropper icon in the toolbar, and then click and drag a line from the left side of her right eye across the eyeball to the tear duct.

The Info palette shows the size across her right eye. In this case it is an inch and an eighth across. Now click and drag across the left eye using the same constraints. The result is less than an inch, showing the left eye is, in fact, significantly smaller (10.1).

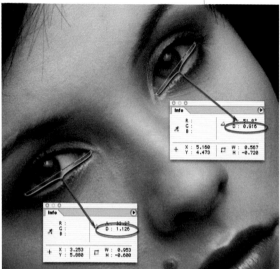

10.1

Step 4: Make a copy of the background layer by pressing ⌘/Ctrl+J and rename the layer Retouch.

Step 5: Press L (or select the Lasso tool from the toolbar) and draw a big selection around the left eye.

In the selection include at least half the nose and the area outside of the face to the right (10.2).

10.2

Step 6: Press ⌘/Ctrl+J and rename this layer Left Eye.

You have two ways to do this next step. One is to enlarge the Left Eye layer, by eye, using Free Transform until it looks right. The other is to use the right eye as a guide. The latter method is the one shown here so that you can get a feel for the process. After you do this to several photographs, the "by eye" method will be easy.

Step 7: Press V to select the Move tool and then press 5 to set the Left Eye layer to 50% Opacity. Drag the layer until the tear duct of Left Eye is over the leftmost (as you look at the screen) edge of her right eye (10.3).

10.3

Tip

Photoshop CS2 allows you to change the layer's opacity from within Free Transform. Use the layer's opacity slider. Keyboard short-cuts don't work.

10.4

10.5

Step 8: **Choose Edit ⇨ Free Transform or press ⌘/Ctrl+T. Drag the reference point over the place where the tear duct and the left edge of the right eye are aligned. Click the link icon (Maintain Aspect Ratio) in the Options bar and highlight the W field. Press the up arrow on the keyboard four times.**
The Left Eye layer enlarges from the tear duct.

Step 9: **Now position the cursor just outside the upper-right corner handle of the bounding box. The rotate cursor appears. Click and drag clockwise until the eyeballs align (10.4).**
Check the size. They are very close. (It's okay as long as Left Eye is not larger than the right eye.)

Step 10: **Select the check mark in the Options bar to finalize the transform or press Return/Enter.**

Step 11: **Press ⌘/Ctrl+Option/Alt+Z three times to undo the transform, the move, and the opacity change.**
Left Eye has returned to its original size, location, and transparency (none).

Step 12: **Now press ⌘/Ctrl+T to open Free Transform again. Click the Maintain Aspect Ratio link icon. Enter 104% in the W field. Select the commit check box to apply the transform to the Left Eye layer (10.5).**

Step 13: **Click and drag the Left Eye layer to the right until the edge on the bridge of the nose disappears (10.6).**

Step 14: **Create a layer mask on the Left Eye layer by choosing Layer ⇨ Add Layer Mask ⇨ Reveal All or by clicking the Add Layer Mask icon at the bottom of the Layers palette (10.7).**

Step 15: View actual pixels (100%) by pressing ⌘/Ctrl+Option/Alt+0 (zero). Press B to select the Brush tool. Make it soft edged by clicking Shift+[(the left bracket key on the keyboard) with 100% Opacity and a size of around 100 pixels.

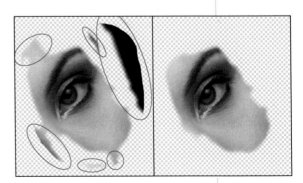

10.6

Step 16: **Press D to set the default colors. Press X to make the foreground color black. Paint over the cheek, edge of the face into the hair, eyebrow, and nostril to blend Left Eye with the image under it (the Retouch layer) (10.8).**

Step 17: **Check the blending by clicking the Background and Retouch layers off.**
Look for hard edges. Continue painting on the layer mask with black until they are gone (10.9).

Step 18: **Click the eye icon on the Retouch layer to turn it on and then click the eye icon on the Left Eye layer on and off to see what a difference 4% makes.**
This step is also a check to make sure the blending is perfect. Remember that the skin texture on the Left Eye layer is 4% larger, too. You take care of that later.

10.7

Step 19: **Save the file as 2062-B Christina CU.psd.**

10.8

10.9

Note

The Pen tool makes the very best and most controlled selections of all the tools in Photoshop. The importance of a photographer/retoucher being strong in the use of this tool cannot be stressed enough. Yet it seems that this tool is the one that everyone works to avoid at all costs. There is a lesson on the CD from Software Cinema for this chapter that explains how to use the Pen tool to draw paths. For more information on this CD, go to www.amesphoto.com and click Training. If you are not comfortable drawing your own paths yet, click the Path tab; it is included in the file. Its name is Path 1.

Retouching a Face: Part 2

The next set of steps involves fixing the stray hair that falls under Christina's chin and across her shoulder. Later, you'll brighten her eyes, soften the skin texture and lines under her eyes, and remove the blemishes on her shoulder.

Step 1: **Copy the visible layers to a new one by holding down ⌘/Ctrl+Option/Alt+Shift and then pressing E.**

Step 2: **Name the new layer** Retouch 2.

Step 3: **Select the Pen tool from the toolbar or press P to select it.**

Step 4: **Zoom in to 200% and draw a path along the very edge of Christina's cheekbone starting just below her left eye.**

Be sure the path is outside of the very fine hairs that show up against the dark background. Continue it along her jaw line and around her chin. Complete the path across her shoulder and up the edge of the frame and back across to the first anchor (10.10).

Step 5: In the Paths palette, double-click Work Path.

The Save Path dialog box opens and suggests the name Path 2. Click OK to accept.

Step 6: ⌘/Ctrl+click Path 1 (the supplied path, or Path 2 if you drew one and saved it) to make it into a selection.

Step 7: Return to Layers. Make a new layer at the top of the layer stack and name it Heal.

Step 8: Select the Healing Brush from the toolbar and set up the Options bar as shown here (10.11).

It is important that Sample All Layers is checked.

Step 9: Carefully Option/Alt+click the edge of Christina's shoulder for your sample and start healing at the edge where the loop of hair is on her shoulder (10.12).

The point is to get rid of the loop of hair for the next step. Sample the edge of her shoulder again and continue healing, progressing down the jaw line. Use strokes parallel to the shoulder line as you go down the jaw and chin line. When you do this, one of the strands of hair might be duplicated. Don't worry. Keep going. A smaller brush using overlapping strokes works better when the healing happens. The trick is to cover the area as shown without lifting the brush (10.13).

10.10

10.11

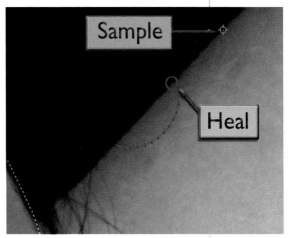

10.12

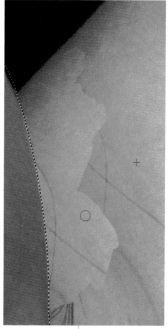

10.13

Resist the temptation to clean up the hair strands on her shoulder. You'll get those in a minute. Start from the same place on Christina's shoulder that you did in the last step and heal up into the dark area along her cheekbone. Heal enough to get the hair away from the line the shoulder makes against the background.

Step 10: **Resample (Option/Alt+click) in the background and continue healing up the cheek.**

Clean up the stray hairs in the background and within the selection. You can fix hair outside the selection later.

Step 11: **Resample the Healing brush on the skin of her shoulder and clean up the remaining hairs from Step 10. Finish healing the hair along her chin.**

Step 12: **Press ⌘/Ctrl+H to hide the marching ants of the selection.**

Look closely along the chin line. Make sure the healing has blended and that the tones all match. If you can see a line that is out of place, resample in a similar tone and heal the area again.

As long as we're here, let's clean up the areas on her neck and shoulders, especially the lines and blemishes. There is also a scar just below the right side of her chin. I have circled the areas in red (10.14).

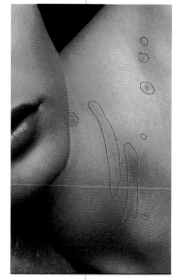

10.14

Note

If Photoshop won't do what you want it to do, stop doing what you're doing! Often a hidden selection is keeping things from working. Go to the Select menu. If Deselect is not grayed out, a selection is active. Choose Deselect or press ⌘/Ctrl+D and go on with life.

Step *13*: **Press ⌘/Ctrl+D to deselect.**

Step *14*: **Go around Christina's head and heal any hair frizzies that annoy you.**

Retouching a Face: Part 3

This section is concerned with bringing out the quiet simplicity and beauty of Christina's makeup by healing the small blemishes on the right side of her face. I created a map of the work to be done (10.15). The dots along her eyelid indicate that the area is to be softened, not healed completely.

10.15

Step *1*: **Make sure the Heal layer is active and that you are working in actual pixels view (100%).**
Start above her eyebrow and heal the blemishes that are outlined in the map. When it's time to heal the lines under her eyes, sample (Option/Alt+click) directly below the line and heal toward the nose (10.16). The brush size is still 10 pixels. There is a separate step for softening the eyelid, so leave it for now.

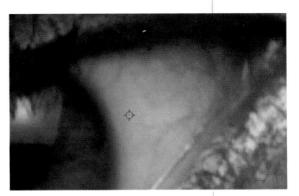

10.16

Step *2*: **Zoom in to 200% and look at the whites of the eyes.**
Bloodshot? Well, not really. Let's clean them up anyway.

Step *3*: **Sample in a clear part of the eye white (10.17).**
Use a fairly small hard brush and heal the blood vessels. Be subtle. Don't overdo it.

10.17

Step 4: **Sample in the eyelid below the lowest line and heal toward the tear duct using short strokes. Resample often to avoid brushing in a pattern.**

The before and after eyelid healing are shown here (10.18). Yes, it is a subtle change. Subtle is good.

Step 5: **Now to soften the eyelid line, make a new layer and rename it** Eyelids.

You'll use this layer again for the other eyelid.

Step 6: **Sample from the left and above the line in Christina's lid.**

Stroke across the eyelashes, down, and then back up to get the thickness that is shown here (10.19).

Step 7: **Now choose Edit ⇨ Fade Healing Brush or press ⌘/Ctrl+Shift+F to open the Fade dialog box. Set 35% in the Opacity field.**

Sample just above where the last strokes ended and finish healing the lid. Remember to fade the selection to around 35% as well. Click the eye icon on the Eyelids layer on and off to see the effect.

10.18

Okay, I admit it. The next two steps are totally anal retentive. . . .

Step *8*: **Click the Add Layer Mask icon at the bottom of the Layers palette, press B for the Brush tool, and pick a really teeny-tiny brush (yes, it is supposed to be hyphenated; see the sidebar), say 1 pixel. Make black the foreground color.**

Step *9*: **Zoom in to 300% and brush the individual eyelashes back in where they had been slightly faded by the healing step.**
Sheesh. Okay. No one will ever notice that there are 35% fewer lashes there. I'll know. And I want it right. And I know how to make it right. So I did. And now you know how to make it right, too. It feels good doesn't it?

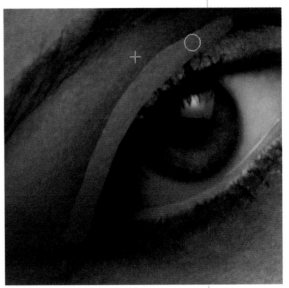

10.19

Now it's time to brighten the iris of her eye.

Step *10*: **Create a new Curves layer by clicking the Create New Adjustment Layer icon at the bottom of the Layers palette and selecting Curves from the pop-up menu.**

Step *11*: **Click OK in the Curves dialog box.** No changes have been made. Rename the layer **Irises**.

Step *12*: **Press Option/Alt+Delete/Backspace to fill the layer mask with the foreground color (black).**

Step *13*: **Click the Blending Mode drop-down menu and choose Screen (10.20).**

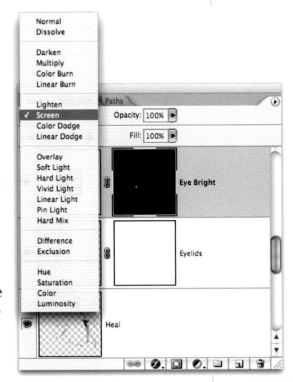

10.20

Well, it depends. When anal-retentive appears immediately before a noun it is an adjective and is hyphenated. If it occurs after a linking verb it becomes a complement (or predicate complement) and would not be hyphenated. Use it to qualify a verb and it's an adverb and is not hyphenated. Here's an example: *The anal-retentive photographer not only seems anal retentive but also works anal retentively.* Being very picky, especially during the shoot, makes the work in Photoshop easier. And you have to admit it's more than the other Photoshop books offer—grammar and photo tips all in the same sidebar!

Step 14: Zoom into 200% and select a 10-pixel, soft-edged brush at 100% Opacity.

Press X to exchange the colors, making the foreground color white. Carefully brush over the catchlight in the eye.

Step 15: Change the brush Opacity to 50% by pressing 5 on the keyboard or using the "scrubby-slider" by dragging over the word Opacity in the Options bar.

You can also use the regular slider or enter 50 in the field.

Step 16: Paint in the iris of Christina's eye without lifting the brush.

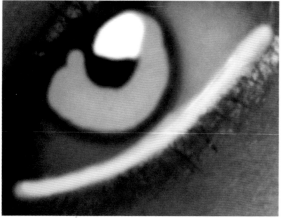

This guarantees that the paint is 50%. Leave the pupil and the dark band at the edge of the iris alone. Brush a line along the lower lid. If you overpaint, press X to make black the foreground color and paint the mistake away. Do not brighten the whites of the eyes. This figure shows the layer mask superimposed over the eye to show the painted areas (10.21).

10.21

Noted retouching artist Rob Carr told me once that when art historians look back on the dawn of digital retouching, they would call it the era of the "too–white-eyes." As our conversation evolved, he explained that eye whites are really gray, so they bring out the true windows into the soul of the subject.

Eye Whites Are Really Gray

Step *17*: **Zoom out to 50%.**
That eye is scary-bright. Let's tone it down some.

Step *18*: **Press V to select the Move tool. Press 5 to set Eye Bright to 50%.**
That looks so much better.

By now you have probably noticed that only half of the work is finished. Take the time to brighten her other eye, and smooth the rest of her skin.

This chapter has just barely gotten your feet wet in the possibilities of retouching beauty. Don't fret, though. More on the subject throughout the projects is to come. And you'll have lots of opportunities to practice techniques like brightening eyes and removing lines.

More than sixteen million gray tones are available in an 8-bit RGB color photograph. The next chapter goes through the many methods of making color files into black and white and discusses how they work, and which ones do the job with the most control. The chapter also includes lots of step-by-step demonstrations to help you make the best black-and-white images ever.

Tip

Screen is a blending mode that adds brightness uniformly to the layers below it. A good way to think of Screen is to imagine two projectors showing identical photographs aimed in perfect register with each other on the same screen *screen* (cool way to remember this, huh?). One of them is on. Turn the second one on and the projected image doubles in brightness.

Chapter Eleven

Sixteen Million Shades of Gray

I know they'd never match my sweet imagination.
And everything looks worse in black and white.
"Kodachrome" by Paul Simon

Now I'm not suggesting that things look worse in black and white at all. As a matter of fact, listen to Simon and Garfunkel's performance of "Kodachrome" during their Concert in Central Park. They change *worse* to *better—Everything looks better in black and white.*

I believe that a good black-and-white photograph is one of the most visually sensuous art forms going. There are so many tones and relationships in a good black-and-white image that I feel compelled to become lost in it. A great print can be so rich I want to pull it over me as if it were a great down comforter on a brisk winter's night.

Black and white seems to be a mystery. Where are all of those cover-me-up tones hiding? How come when the film comes back from the drugstore they look flat? One of the all-time masters of black-and-white photography, Ansel Adams, wrote extensively about producing optimal negatives and prints. This chapter does not pretend to explore black and white anywhere near the depth that Ansel did. My goal in this chapter is to demonstrate several methods of making high-quality black-and-white images from color photographs that exist in the digital space. It doesn't matter if they were scanned from color film or if they were captured digitally. The important consideration is all the information contained in the three black-and-white channels known as RGB.

Chapter 1 explored how digital color consists of three channels of black and white, each shot through a red, green, or blue filter. To illustrate this concept even further, imagine taking three Wratten color separation filters from Kodak—a number 29 Red, a number 58 Green, and a number 47 Blue—and laying them down on a light table so that they overlap. Where red overlaps green, yellow appears. Where green overlaps blue, cyan appears. Where blue overlaps red, magenta appears. Where all three colors overlap the light is white (11.1). Russell Brown, Adobe's Senior Creative Director and author of *The Photoshop Show Starring Russell Brown*, includes a color reference that he uses to demonstrate how black

11.1

and white works. If you've ever had the opportunity to see Russell in action, you know how dynamic, passionate, and yes, crazy he is. (If you have never seen him in action, take this as a four-star must-see recommendation.)

Seeing Black and White (And Shades of Gray)

Several methods exist for converting an RGB image into a black-and-white one. Some methods are destructive—they throw away the color information. I discuss these methods even though I don't recommend them. The others work very well in conjunction with the practice of non-destructive Photoshop editing.

One of the most useful tests available in the darkroom to compare the degrees of exposure is the *ring around*. To conduct this test, create a series of prints varying in degrees of over- and underexposure. Process each print exactly the same, dry them, and then mount them around the "normal" print. The resulting ring around the normal print allows comparison of varying degrees of exposure. Contrast ring-around tests are also useful.

We are going to make an RGB to black-and-white conversion ring-around test to compare the results of each method. The image for this section is available in Chapter 11's folder on www.amesphoto.com/learning. The book code is **PW48255**.

First you create the files for the ring-around. This section shows most of the methods of converting color to black and white and what they do in the process. You use a photograph of Amanda, a model from the Click agency in Atlanta, for this section.

Step *1*: **Open For BW.tif in Photoshop CS2 by double-clicking it in Bridge.**

Step *2*: **Choose Image ⇨ Duplicate. Name the file** Grayscale **(11.2). Click OK.**

Step *3*: **Choose Image ⇨ Mode ⇨ Grayscale. When the Discard color information dialog box appears, click OK. Save the file as Grayscale.tif.**

11.2

Step 4: **Click the Channels tab.**

There is now only one channel: Gray. This is because all the color was removed during the conversion. You can't tone this file without first converting it back to RGB (11.3).

Step 5: **Duplicate For B&W.tif again. Name it** Desaturate.

Step 6: **Choose Image ⇨ Adjustments ⇨ Desaturate.**

Look in the document header. This file is still in RGB. Click the Channels tab for confirmation (11.4). Save the file and name it **Desaturate.tif**.

Step 7: **Look at the color circles in Desaturate.tif (11.5).**

The red, green, and blue circles have each been assigned the same pixel value. Each circle now shows the same tone of gray as the other two, including the overlapping complementary color areas.

11.3

11.4

11.5

Note

The Desaturate command, when used in multiple layers, affects the active layer only. You can achieve the same effect by choosing Image ➪ Adjustments ➪ Hue/Saturation or by using a Hue/Saturation adjustment layer and moving the Saturation slider to –100.

The rest of the steps use layers and are non-destructive. The first one is kind of off-the-wall. And it has some interesting properties.

Step *8*: **Duplicate For B&W.tif once again. Name it** Color Layer.

Step *9*: **Click the Create a New Layer icon at the bottom of the Layers palette or press ⌘/Ctrl+Option/Alt+ Shift+N.**

Step *10*: **Press D to set the default colors. Fill the layer with either black or white or any neutral tone.**

Step *11*: **Change the Blending Mode to Color.** The image changes to black and white (11.6).

11.6

The color Blending Mode applies the hue and saturation of the layer set to Color with the luminosity (grayscale tones) of the layer below it. In this example the color has no hue or saturation so only the grayscale information of the background layer shows. Let's look at how this can be useful for more than making color into black and white.

Step 12: **Duplicate Layer 1 by pressing ⌘/Ctrl+J.**

Step 13: **Choose a 150-pixel soft-edged brush. Set a shade of green as the foreground color. Paint green on the background of Layer 1 copy.**

The background of the image becomes green while retaining the gradations of the spotlight behind Amanda. You can reduce the intensity of green by lowering the opacity (11.7). This is useful in colorizing black-and-white photographs. Learn more about the color Blending Mode by creating copies of Layer 1 copy and finding the colors for Amanda's hair, skin, and eyes. Paint them in to colorize the black and white.

Step 14: **Discard Layer 1 copy or turn off its eye icon. Save the file as** Color Layer.psd. **Flatten the image and leave it open.**

You use it later in this section.

Step 15: **Make another duplicate of For B&W.tif. Name it** CM RGB 33.

Step 16: **Click the New Adjustment Layer icon at the bottom of the Layers palette and choose Channel Mixer. Enter 33% into each of the Source Channels fields. Select the Monochrome check box, and then click OK (11.8). Flatten the image and save the file.**

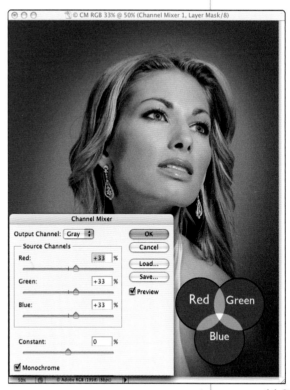

11.7   *11.8*

The next three versions of For B&W.tif illustrate the effect of each channel individually at 100%.

Step 17: **Make three duplicates of For B&W.tif. Name them** CM Red100%, CM Green100%, **and** CM Blue100%.

Step 18: **Add a Channel Mixer adjustment layer to CM Red100%. Then leave the Red channel at 100%. Select the Monochrome check box, and then click OK. Flatten and save the file.**

Step 19: **Activate CM Green100%. Add a new Channel Mixer layer. Enter** 0 **in the Red field and** 100 **in the Green field. Select the Monochrome check box, and then click OK. Flatten and save the file.**

Step *20*: **Activate CM Blue 100%. Add a new Channel Mixer adjustment layer. Enter** 0 **in the Red field and** 100 **in the Blue field. Select the Monochrome check box, and then click OK. Flatten and save the file.**

The three 100% versions represent the effect of black-and-white film being exposed through a red, green, or blue filter. Each color filter absorbs its color, leaving it white. This effect is demonstrated by each pure color of the filter turning completely white in the RGB circle according to which color is mixed at 100%. For example, the red circle is white when the Channel Mixer is set to 100% red (11.9).

Let's make two more duplicates to represent a realistic conversion to black and white.

Step *21*: **Make another duplicate of For B&W.tif. Name it** CM R 60 G 30 B 10.

Step *22*: **Add a Channel Mixer layer. Set the Red field to 60, the Green field to 30, and the Blue field to 10. Select the Monochrome check box and click OK (11.10). Flatten the file and save it.**

This conversion is very close to Kodak's Plus-X Pan black-and-white film. Now make one more conversion for the ring-around. This one is specific to the photograph of Amanda.

Step *23*: **Make one final copy of For B&W.tif. Name it** CM R 80 G 20.

Step *24*: **Add a new Channel Mixer layer to the file. Set the Red field to 80 and the Green to 20. Leave the Blue at 0. Select the Monochrome check box. Click OK. Flatten and save the file.**

11.9

Channel Mixer

Output Channel: Gray

Source Channels

Red: +60 %

Green: +30 %

Blue: +10 %

Constant: 0 %

☑ Monochrome

OK
Cancel
Load...
Save...
☑ Preview

11.10

Note

The guideline for using the Channel Mixer is to make certain that the channels add up to no more than 100%.

I have made a ring-around, well, let's call it a chart, of the effects. The document header indicates the effect (11.11). Arrange the documents you created on the screen in the same order. Let's do a row-by-row breakdown.

11.11

The top row shows differences among Grayscale, Desaturate, and the Channel Mixer (RGB 33%) methods. Take a close look at the RGB circles. The Grayscale image has a good distribution of colors. The circles show equal amounts of gray in the Desaturate and Channel Mixer (RGB 33%) images. They look flat.

The next row shows the 100% versions of red, green, and blue. The blue channel is least attractive for people. It also contains most of the noise in a digital photo or the grain in a photo shot on film and scanned. You can easily see that a combination of the red and green channels will yield a better black and white. Move on to the third row.

The neutral filled layer in the color Blending Mode does a respectable job of making color into black and white. The distribution is even, including the complementary colors. Compare it to the Channel Mixer: R 60, G 30, B 10. The additional amount of red and lower amount of blue open up the image. Now look at the last image in the row; the mix of red 80 and green 20 works very well for Caucasian skin.

The best part of Channel Mixer is that it allows each black-and-white conversion to be a custom fit. I love this. Think of it: Every color photograph has all the black-and-white filter possibilities you could ever want! Mixing channels is much more satisfying than mixing chemicals in the darkroom.

Okay. Let's put this information to work.

Flashback . . . to the '60s, '70s, and '80s when high-fashion, contrasting black-and-white photography was very en vogue. The skin tones were almost white if they were not blown-out completely. The images had mystical shadows. Black hair sported the most amazing detail. Eyes simply glowed. And it was all done without computers! How was this magic done?

Overexposure was the secret potion back in the day. Photographers added between a stop and a half to two and two-thirds stops of light to the diffused value. (See Chapter 3.) This meant that eyebrows and lips had to be applied significantly darker during makeup to record as a normal tone in the final photograph.

Fast-forward to the new millennium where overexposure still works really well on film though it's not so hot when capturing digitally. This section shows another example of simple postproduction wizardry. First you apply what you've just learned about turning color into black and white. Start with a full-color photograph, styled and art directed by L. J. Adams, of model Annie Shu from Elite Model Management/Atlanta (11.12).

Step *1*: **Open 2062-D-0325.tif by double-clicking it in Bridge.**
The retouching on this file is already done. When doing black-and-white conversions, you should first do the retouching on the color file.

Step *2*: **Do a quick scan of the channels by pressing ⌘/Ctrl+1 for Red, ⌘/Ctrl+2 for Green, and ⌘/Ctrl+3 for Blue (11.13).**
Once again the Red and Green channels have the better tones. Reviewing the channels is a good starting place when starting to convert photographs into black and white.

Step *3*: **Return to the composite, full-color view by pressing ⌘/Ctrl+~ (tilde).**
The skin tones are carried in the Red channel. Because Annie has naturally darker skin, we'll want to mix in more green. This step will be important, too, because we are going to open up the highlights later in this project.

Step *4*: **Create a new Channel Mixer adjustment layer. Enter 60 in the Red field and 40 in the Green field. Select the Monochrome check box. Click OK. Rename the layer** R 60 G 40.

11.12

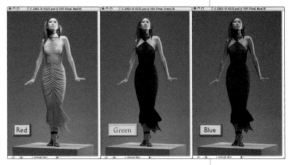

11.13

Step 5: **Make a new layer. Copy the visible layers to the new one by holding down the Option/Alt key and selecting Merge Visible from the Layer palette's fly-out menu. Name the layer** Base.

The result has good tonal range and contrast (11.14). I want to force attention to Annie's face. Moving the values of the tones in her gown lower would do just that. Now the temptation to use Curves or Levels is huge. There is another way.

Step 6: **Click the Background layer. Hide the Base and R 60 G 40 layers by clicking off their eye icons.**

Alternatively, hold down the Option/Alt key and click the eye icon of the Background layer.

11.14

Step 7: Make a new Channel Mixer adjustment layer. Enter 0 in the Red field and 100 in the Green one. Select the Monochrome check box. Click OK and name the layer G 100.

Step 8: Make a new layer. Name it BW 100%Green.

Step 9: Merge the Background and G 100 layers to BW 100%Green by holding down the Option/Alt key and choosing Merge Visible from the Layers palette fly-out menu or by pressing ⌘/Ctrl+Option/Alt+Shift+E.

Step 10: Drag BW 100%Green above Base. Click the eye icon on for Base.

The Layers palette looks like this (11.15).

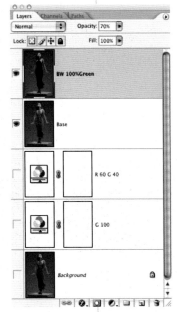

11.15

Now you have several ways that you could add the darker tones of the gown to the layer below. The tried-and-true and usually my personal favorite is drawing a path, making a selection, and then adding a layer mask. Another is to add a black layer mask and paint it in with white. Of course, there are the sloppy methods, such as using the Magic Wand (keep your fingers crossed—it helps) to select the gown, and so on. In this case there is an easier way.

Step 11: Double-click the BW 100%Green thumbnail in the Layers palette.

The Layer Style dialog box opens. Look in the Advanced Blending section for the Blend If drop-down menu. By default it is set to Gray. Perfect. The key to this step is in the This Layer slider.

Step 12: Click the Highlight slider. Drag it to the left until the highlight window reads 40.

The highlights on the gown from Base show through (11.16).

Step 13: Hold down the Option/Alt key. Drag the right half of the highlight slider until its window (the number right of 40) reads 195. Click OK.

So far the result of all of these steps is making the gown a non-reproducible, way too dark, gray tone. Wait, there's more.

11.16

Step *14*: **Select the Color Sampler tool from the toolbox. Hover the cursor over the gown around Annie's middle. Click to place Sampler #1.**

Note the readings in the Info palette (11.17). They are all 20. At best the gown is at the threshold of printing shadow areas with detail.

11.17

Step 15: **Lower the opacity of BW 100%Green to 70%.**
Note the shadows measured by the sampler now read 32. They will brighten up when you apply the fashion effect (11.18).

Step 16: **Click the eye icon of BW 100%Green on and off to see how the eye now naturally falls on Annie's face (11.19).**

Step 17: **Create a new layer above BW 100%Green. Name it** B&W. **Merge the visible layers to it (see Step 9).**

Step 18: **Open the Levels dialog box by choosing Image ⇨ Adjustments ⇨ Levels or by pressing ⌘/Ctrl+L. Hold down the Option/Alt key. Drag the highlight slider to the left.**
The document window goes black as the highlight slider starts to move. This is a good thing. Drag until white areas appear. Remember the area and then return the slider to its original position on the far right.

11.18

Step 19: **While watching the Info palette, move the cursor around the area until it is over the area with the highest value, probably around 232. Hold down the Shift key and click to place Sampler #2. Click Cancel to close the Levels dialog box.**

11.19

Step 20: **Make a new Curves adjustment layer. When the dialog box opens, click OK without making any changes. Name it** Curves 1. **Change the Blending Mode to Screen.**
The entire image brightens. Most important, Annie's face takes on that '60s almost-blown-out face and very open shadows look of overexposure. Note the Info palette. The shadows are way open at 59 (Sampler #1) and the brightest highlights are at 252 (Sampler #2) (11.20). All that's left is to focus the effect.

11.20

Step *21*: Choose the Elliptical Marquee tool. Draw a selection around the inside of the photograph's frame.

Step *22*: Choose Select ➪ Transform Selection. Drag the side handles of the bounding box toward the center point until the selection looks like this (11.21). Select the Commit check mark.

Step *23*: Drag the selection up until the lower half of the selection cuts through Annie's hands (11.22). Fine-tune its position with the arrow keys.

Step *24*: Invert the selection by pressing ⌘/Ctrl+Shift+I.

Step *25*: Fill the selection with black by choosing Edit ➪ Fill. In the Use menu choose Black (11.23). Press ⌘/Ctrl+D to deselect.

That hard edge is just not elegant. Let's fix it.

11.21

11.22

Step 26: Choose Filter ⇨ Blur ⇨ Gaussian Blur to open the Gaussian Blur dialog box. Enter 130.4 pixels in the Radius field. Click OK.

Step 27: Back off the Opacity of Curves 1 to 80%.

Step 28: Make a new layer above Curves 1. Merge the visible layers to it. Rename the layer Final. **Save your work.**

Step 29: Option/Alt+click the eye icon of the Final layer to hide the layers under it. Click the eye icon of the Base layer. Click the eye icon of Final on and off to see the before and after (11.24).

11.23

That's pretty much it. The Curves adjustment layer set to Screen has provided variable overexposure through the opacity and the layer mask. Annie's face and shoulders are now the highest tonal values. They are guaranteed to draw the viewer's eye. The tones of her gown make an arrow shape that points the eye toward her feet. The highlights once again bring the viewer to her face.

Note

The Filter Gallery enables you to apply multiple filters sequentially at the same time. Think of it as layers for filters. The dialog box is divided by default into three panes. On the left is the preview pane. The center pane houses the thumbnails of the available filters. The right-hand pane displays the options for each filter. Below that is the filter stack. The chosen filters are applied in the order they appear in the stack from the bottom up. Rearrange them for drastic changes in the effect. The Filter Gallery is worth hours of play. Play is the wellspring of creativity. Play well and prosper creatively!

11.24

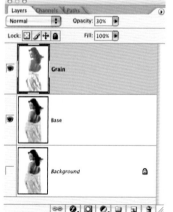

Having Fun with Black and White

The best part of working in black and white in Photoshop is that you don't have to spend hours and hours in the darkroom to play. There are no chemicals, no water, no dark . . . and yes, I do occasionally play DVDs or music videos while doing postproduction. One of the best things about Photoshop is that my clothes no longer have fixer stains nor do my hands carry chemical smells. Using Photoshop is so much better, and in this section I provide a series of fun little how-to's that include adding grain and toning photographs digitally.

ADDING GRAIN

Think about this. Film has grain. Digital does not have grain. When film was the only option, we talked incessantly about techniques for reducing the amount of grain in a photograph. Digital has no grain. So what are we talking about now? That's right. The topic on the table is how to add grain to digital files to (are you ready for this?) make them look more like film. Sheesh!

Step 1: Open 2062-F-0293.tif by double-clicking its thumbnail in Bridge.
This file has already been retouched and converted to black and white. It is an 8-bit file (11.25).

Step 2: Make a duplicate layer by pressing ⌘/Ctrl+J. Name it Base. Click the eye icon off for the Background layer.

Step 3: Duplicate the Base layer. Rename it Grain (11.26).

Step 4: Choose Filter ⇨ Filter Gallery. Click the disclosure triangle for the Artistic filters. Click (what else?) Film Grain. Set 15 in the Grain field. Set the Highlight to 15 and leave the Intensity field at 10. Click OK.

Step 5: Zoom in to 100% and scroll to Marie's face. Study the result of the Film Grain filter on the photograph (11.27).
It is scarily grainy. A natural response to too much of anything in Photoshop is to lower the opacity.

11.25

11.26

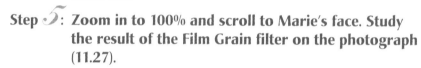

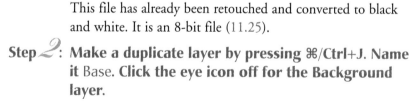

11.27

Step 6: **Enter** 50% **in the Opacity field with the Grain layer active (11.28).**

The result is more pleasing, appearing to be that of a photograph blown up from a negative shot on Kodak's Tri-X Pan film from a 35mm camera. Let's look at some modifications.

11.28

Step 7: **Duplicate Grain by pressing ⌘/Ctrl+J. Rename the layer** Grain Blurred.

Grain on film is not sharp edged. It is sharp when it is created digitally. Let's soften it some to make it look more filmlike.

Step 8: **Choose Filter ⇨ Blur ⇨ Gaussian Blur. Set the pixel radius to 1.0. Click OK. Compare the results (11.29).**

The image is softer overall due to the soft edges created by the blur. Of course, there's more. Let's explore finer grain.

11.29

Step 9: **Click the eye icon for Grain off. Lower the Opacity of Grain Blurred to 20% (11.30).**

This figure represents a fine grain film. There is one more subtle touch to add.

Step 10: **Click the eye icon for Grain on, select the layer, and lower its Opacity to 20%.**

Adding the sharp grain layer to the blurred one makes the structure appear subtly better. The grain effect you'll use on a printed piece will need tweaking depending on the paper you choose. Add the grain after you have sized the file for output (11.31).

TONING PHOTOGRAPHS DIGITALLY

Traditional methods for toning photographs often required offensive-smelling chemistry, especially if the desired result was the popular sepia-toned print. The process was time consuming, not totally repeatable, and hard on the nose. The odor was caused by sulfur and was reminiscent of rotten eggs. Lovely.

Toning images using tools in Photoshop has improved the results by making subtle changes quick, repeatable, and (whew) odor free.

11.30

11.31

Step *1*: **Double-click the thumbnail for 2062-P-203.psd in Bridge to open the photograph of Cara in Photoshop CS2.**
The Channel Mixer layer that converts the photograph to black and white is already in the layer stack.

Step *2*: **Make a new layer and merge the Background layer and Channel Mixer to it. Name it** B&W.

Step 3: B&W is highlighted. Create a new Hue/Saturation adjustment layer. Select the check box next to Colorize (the only function in Photoshop that actually does what it's named).

The default setting is a red tone (11.32).

Step 4: Drag the Hue slider to the right until 33 appears in the field.

It's that simple. Sepia! No fuss, no muss, and best of all, no smell (11.33)!

11.32

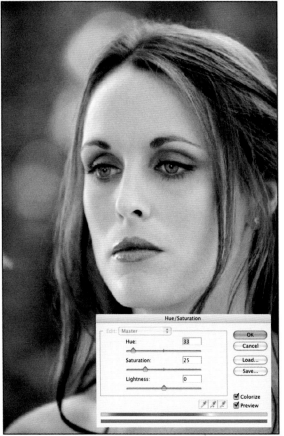

11.33

Hue controls the color, so let's explore the other sliders. We already know that moving the Saturation slider to 0 makes the image black and white. Because the base is already black and white, we won't go there.

Step 5: **Move the Saturation slider to the right until the field reads 100.**
Bright, huh? This is a great place to look for false, dare I say, "oversaturated" colors (11.34). Now for the Lightness slider—moving it all the way to 0 on the left makes the image black. Black without white isn't particularly useful. We'll go in the other direction.

Step 6: **Move the Lightness slider to the right and a reading of 80.**
When this slider reaches 100, the image is white (11.35). Save the file. This is a great way to make an image have the ghosted-back look for use behind type or as a background for a Web site.

Another method for toning uses a Curves adjustment layer in place of the Hue/Saturation adjustment layer. You can also use a Curves adjustment to fine-tune the colors and contrast of the Hue/Saturation layer effect. Experiment, play, enjoy!

In the next chapter, the subject is lingerie for a magazine editorial. We're shooting on location, so turn the page to join me, the crew, and our model Carrie Thomas in a high-rise condominium on Atlanta's famous Peachtree Street.

11.34

11.35

Chapter Twelve

Lingerie: A Day Being a Girl

The camera is a passport into worlds we might otherwise be denied travel.
Kevin Ames

Women fascinate me. Like many, many men, I love them, I like them, and I am an outsider in their world. Women do things that are totally understandable to other women and yet very mysterious to the men in their lives. My love of photographing women has offered a glimpse into their world. It isn't a secret one, especially to them. As a matter of surprise to me, when I asked about ironing in their underwear, every one of them said they did it, often. Why? "Because the outfit I want to wear is the one I'm ironing." Who knew?

Men don't think much about their underwear. Our choices are limited: boxers, trunks, briefs, or (does any man really wear them?) tighty-whiteys. Women on the other hand, love lingerie. Wearing it makes them feel good, sexy, desirable, cute, fun, happy, pretty, beautiful, and more. Shopping for it does, too. One model told me that she enjoyed walking down the street knowing how beautiful she looked in her underwear even though no one else did.

Many women also love quiet, alone time. Playing the piano, lounging on the sofa, putting on makeup, ironing, or dreamily watching the world through a window is somehow better in lingerie.

Over afternoon coffee, Linda Adams, a freelance art director/stylist, and I decided to produce a "day of life in lingerie" editorial. A lot of planning goes into the actual day of shooting. Our list includes location, hair and makeup, wardrobe, styling assistant, and photographic/digital assistant.

The location is a two-bedroom, fourth-floor condo overlooking world-famous Peachtree Street in Atlanta. Carrie Thomas from Elite Modeling Agency is the model. Janeen Loria does the makeup and hair. Cristle Grizzelle handles wardrobe. Linda picks the colors and styles to match each scene. Assistant Justin Larose and I set the lighting, camera angle, and settings. Like a movie, the editorial is not shot in sequence. The window light dictates the time each setup is photographed.

The lighting is kept simple. One flash head on a light stand, a 42-in. x 72-in. Chimera panel with reflector or a diffusion fabric, and a flag to keep flare off of the lens is the whole kit.

The entire shoot is done with the digital camera tethered to a Macintosh PowerBook G4 with an external 30GB OWC Mercury

On-The-Go FireWire drive. We use Photo Mechanic from camer-abits.com to copy the files onto the PowerBook and the external hard drive. Each scene is set, lit, metered, and photographed with a GretagMacbeth ColorChecker Gray Balance Card in the scene. The reference card is used to set the white balance and refine the diffused value on the camera. Adobe Bridge monitors the capture folder and generates previews on the fly. Using the reference card, I lock in the settings for each scene by saving new Camera Raw defaults in ACR3. Now Bridge enhances the shot as each frame is captured. This method saves lots of time when archiving at the end of the day.

While I shoot, Justin watches each image as it appears in Bridge on the PowerBook. He monitors the changing window light. Linda watches the take on the laptop, too, and steps in to smooth wrinkles or adjust a prop. The team behind the camera frees me to work with Carrie on pose and expression. Their feedback is important, too. It lets us all push the work farther than is prudent when shooting film.

The shoot continues through the day and finally wraps with everyone out the door by seven o'clock. We have made more than 800 photographs of eight scenes in ten hours. Linda and Cristle gather up the lingerie and accessories. Carrie changes into her street clothes. Janeen packs up her makeup. Justin and I load the gear into the car. Everybody says goodbye.

Back at the studio, we archive and proof the RAW files on the FireWire drive (see Chapter 4 for the complete workflow), divide them into 4GB-sized folders in the Finder (or Windows Explorer), and burn them to DVDs. We make a copy of each DVD and proof the archived discs by making JPGs from each file using

Bridge and the Image Processor in Photoshop CS2. We also generate a custom Web photo gallery in Photoshop and then post it to the Web. E-mails with links go out to the team who worked on the shoot and the magazine's photo editor. It is ten o'clock. Justin and I grab a quick meal and call it a night.

Having shot with film all my life, the speed the images are ready for review amazes me. I hope I never take this speed for granted. I know clients will as this process becomes commonplace. For better or not we live in a want-it-right-this-second world. In the morning over coffee at Aurora (my favorite Atlanta coffeehouse), I reviewed the take on my laptop and picked the photographs I liked for the editorial and to use in this chapter.

The projects in this chapter explore using some of the photographic techniques of Adobe Photoshop CS2 to solve issues that would have taken too much time to fix on location, such as overly shiny brass window handles, or a problem that is degrees bigger, such as when a manufacturer sends a bustier set that is a size too small for the model. This chapter also expands on how to create strategy maps for retouching and healing to layers.

To get started, download the files for Chapter 12 from www .amesphoto.com/learning. The code for the book is **PW48255**.

The Strategy Map

Step *1*: **Click the downloaded folder in Bridge.**
When the content pane populates, double-click 2062-M-0171.tif to open it. The file is in 16 bits per channel color.

Step 2: **Duplicate the Background layer by pressing ⌘/Ctrl+J or by choosing Layer ⇨ Duplicate Layer and click OK. Rename the layer** Retouch.

Step 3: **Create a new layer by pressing ⌘/Ctrl+Option/Alt+Shift+N or by choosing Layer ⇨ New ⇨ Layer and click OK. Name the layer** Strategy Map (**12.1**).

Step 4: **Press B+Shift+B to select the Pencil tool, and set the pixel size to** 4.

Step 5: **Open the Swatches palette and select RGB Green (12.2).**

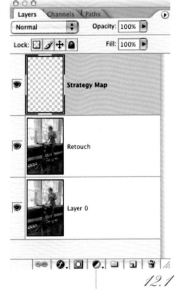

12.1

Step 6: **Zoom in to view actual pixels at 100% by pressing ⌘/Ctrl+Option/Alt+0 (zero) and then press the Home key.**

Examine the photograph tile by tile by pressing the Page Down key on the keyboard. ⌘/Ctrl+Page Up moves the view one tile to the right. ⌘/Ctrl+Page Down moves it one tile to the left. You have to hold down the Fn key, too, on Mac laptops. Windows laptops vary according to the manufacturer's whim. As you page through the image, circle in green the areas to be cleaned up. Refer to my version of the map and compare it with yours. They will be different. You and I see things differently. This is a good thing.

12.2

Step 7: **Save the file as** 2062–M–0171.psd.

Not all photographs require massive amounts of retouching. This one is typical of the tweaks that an image receives to get it ready for output.

Step 8: **Create a new layer above Retouch and name it** Healing.

Step 9: **Press J to select the Healing Brush, and on the Options bar select the Sample All Layers check box.**

TIF and PSD

Photoshop CS2's ability to work extensively in 16 bit allows the creation of the highest quality files. The 16-bit workflow offers potential problems to output vendors—service bureaus, prepress houses, and corporate clients who might not understand what 16 bit is and how it works with previous versions of Photoshop. Very few output devices can use 16-bit files. Graphics professionals will call the file corrupt when it won't output. Sometimes the problem is that a 16-bit file was delivered instead of one in 8 bit. Establishing a convention of what file type carries which bit depth is useful. In my workflow, I modify the 16-bit file generated either from Camera Raw or a camera manufacturer's converter in Photoshop CS2 using layers. Once the work is complete, I save it as a Photoshop document with the extension .psd.

The PSD file carries the original image data in the Background layer. The layered PSD files are always working files; PSDs are never delivered to clients. They are a work product; you might think of them as proprietary information that is your exclusive property. TIFs are always the *delivery* files that go to clients for output. Although TIFs *can* save layers, most of today's applications can't use them. A good practice is to *never save layered files as .tifs.*

Note: Some functions in Photoshop—mainly filters—do not work on 16-bit files. The workflow for these images is to finish the 16-bit editing and save

Step *10*: **Click the eye icon next to the Strategy Map layer to hide the layer. Starting at Carrie's neck, heal all the circled areas, working down her body. Use the Healing brush to remove the electrical cord from the floor. We'll burn down the window sill on the left later.**

Click the Strategy Map eye icon on periodically to make sure you are healing all the circled areas. Don't be concerned with the window hardware. That fix comes later. When you finish, press ⌘/Ctrl+S to save your work.

the file as a .psd. Choose Image ➪ Duplicate Image. This duplicate will be named the same as the original file with the addition of the word *copy* before the .psd extension (12.3). Convert this file to 8 bit. The word *copy* in the name of a PSD file is the cue that it is an 8 bit image.

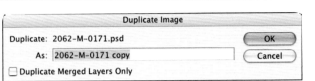

12.3

Look at this figure (12.4). The photograph on the left is 16 bit. Photoshop states the color space and the bit depth of the file in the header—in this case RGB/16. The document profile at the bottom shows both the color space and the bit depth. Additionally, by choosing Palette Options in the Info Palette, the document profile of the active window is displayed.

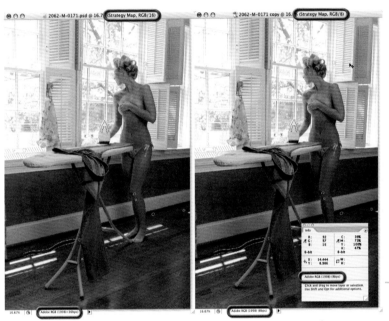

12.4

Restoring Shiny Hardware

The brass handle on the window and catch on the shutter are blown out in this photograph. It makes sense that reflective surfaces would do this especially when they are as strongly backlit as they are in this scene. Shooting a set of background brackets with the model out of the scene makes restoring the handles and shutter catch in the final image easy. It pretty much goes without saying that this only works when the camera is firmly mounted on a tripod. These techniques have a lot in common with those used in constructing Christina in Chapter 9. Capturing a background image just for its bits and pieces is a good practice. An image that is "underexposed" can provide exactly the right parts for the final image. All that matters is that the camera angle is very close.

Step *1*: **Open 2062-M-0064.tif.**
It has already been prepared for this step. This file is dimensionally the same size as 2062-M-0171.psd.

Step *2*: **Select the Lasso tool from the toolbar or press L to select it.**

Step *3*: **Locate the handle on 2062-M-0064 and draw a selection around it (12.5).**

Step *4*: **Select the Move tool from the toolbar or press V and click inside the selection.**
Hold down the Shift key and drag the selection onto 0179. It becomes a layer in 0179's stack. Rename it **Handle.**

Step *5*: **Drag the handle over the one by the iron in 0179.**
It does not exactly match.

Step *6*: **Press 5 on the keyboard to lower the Handle layer's Opacity to 50% and nudge it so the upper-left corner is positioned over the blown-out version (12.6).**

12.5

12.6

Step 7: **Press ⌘/Ctrl+T to select the Free Transform tool and drag the anchor point from the center of the bounding box to the corner where both handles align (12.7).**

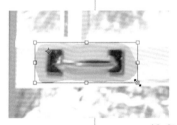

12.7

Step 8: **Hold down the Shift key, click the lower-right corner handle, and drag it diagonally away from the anchor point.**

The handle enlarges. Drag until it is slightly larger than the one it will replace. Adjust the rotation if necessary.

Step 9: **Click the check mark in the Options bar to accept the changes or press Return/Enter.**

Step 10: **Press 0 (zero) to return the Opacity of the Handle layer to 100%.**

Step 11: **Create a layer mask on the Handle layer by clicking the Add Layer Mask icon at the bottom of the Layers palette or by choosing Layer ⇨ Add Layer Mask ⇨ Reveal All.**

Step 12: **Press ⌘/Ctrl++ (plus sign) to zoom in to 200% and select a soft 20-pixel brush (12.8).**

Step 13: **Set the foreground color to black.**

D sets the default colors of black and white. X exchanges them if needed.

12.8

Step 14: **Paint over the white paint on the Handle layer.**

Leave a bit of the shadow under the handle itself. If you paint out the handle, press X to switch white to the foreground and paint it back in. Press X to go back to black. When you work on the inside edges of the handle, press the left bracket ([) key to reduce the brush size to 10 pixels (12.9).

12.9

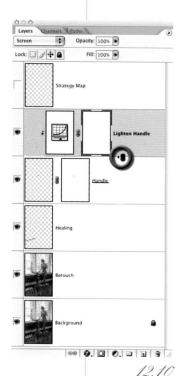

12.10

12.11

Step 15: Zoom out to the actual pixels view—100%.
The handle is now too dark. Changing the opacity of the Handle layer will only make it transparent. Here's how to lighten just the handle: Click the New Adjustment Layer icon at the bottom of the Layers palette and select Curves. When the Curves dialog box appears, click OK. Rename it **Lighten Handle**.

Step 16: Hold down the Option/Alt key and position the cursor between the Lighten Handle and Handle layers.
The nesting cursor appears.

Step 17: Click, and the Lighten Handle layer indents. A down-pointing arrow appears indicating that this layer is now grouped with Handle.
Handle is now underlined indicating it, too, is part of a group (12.10).

Step 18: Change the Blending Mode of Lighten Handle to Screen.
The handle is no longer burned out. It's brighter, and most important of all, it's believable (12.11)! Great photography and great Photoshop are all about the details!

Step 19: Return to Bridge and double-click 2062–M–0171darker.tif to open it.

Step 20: Select the Move tool from the toolbox. Press the Shift key and drag 2062–M–0171darker.psd onto 2062–M–0171.psd.
This step adds the darker version above Lighten Handle in the layer stack. Name the new layer **Darker**.

Note

{ I made the darker version of 2062–M–0171 by reducing the exposure and brightness in ACR3. The first project of Chapter 13 explains this technique in detail. }

Turn the Strategy Map layer on and turn off all the other layers except the Background layer. Turn the eye icon on the Final layer on and off. If every circle in the Strategy Map layer blinks, the work is complete. If areas outside the map blink, you did extra work. Congratulations! You are becoming just like me (now is a good time to be afraid . . . very afraid). Just kidding. Fix any that might have been missed.

Checking Work

Step 21: **Add a layer mask filled with black to Darker by pressing the Option/Alt key and clicking the Add Layer Mask icon at the bottom of the Layers palette (12.12).**

Step 22: **Select a 50-pixel brush with a soft edge at 100% opacity. Set white as the foreground color. Brush on Darker's layer mask and bring back the lower part of the window.**

Paint the sill back in as well. Change the brush opacity to 25%. Brush the blown-out mullion back in. When the brush is at a lower opacity, each new stroke builds up paint to a total of 25%.

Step 23: **Repeat Steps 2 through 12 on the other handle. Paint in the layer mask of Darker to reduce the shine on the pull above the clasp behind Carrie's head.**

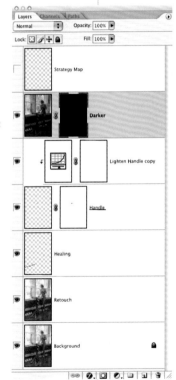

12.12

Squaring the Shot

One last thing about this photograph: It's a receding perspective caused by a low angle with the camera tilted up. Look at the windows behind Carrie. Their vertical lines are not perpendicular with the floor. That's the hard way to say, "The camera wasn't level when the photograph was made." It happens even when the camera is on a tripod as it was for all the images in this chapter. Oh well. Nobody's perfect. Especially me.

12.13

By now you have more than likely figured out that this kind of little thing can really bother me. If it doesn't make you crazy, skip this next section. On the other hand, if you want to follow along I'll show you how to quickly correct this faux pas.

Step 1: Press ⌘/Ctrl+R on the keyboard to show the rulers. Click in the vertical ruler and drag out a guide. Line it up with a mullion, one of the vertical dividers in the window pane. I have exaggerated the line by highlighting it in green.

Sure enough, the whole image is skewed clockwise (12.13).

Step 2: Make sure that the eye icon on Strategy Map is off and highlight the top Lighten Handle (you did fix the other handle, didn't you?) adjustment layer and make a new layer either by clicking the Create a New Layer icon at the bottom of the Layers palette or by choosing Layer ⇨ New ⇨ Layer. Rename the layer Final.

All the retouching is finished. And the work is finished except for this picky bit . . .

Step 3: **Hold down the Option/Alt key and select Merge Visible from the Layers palette fly-out menu (12.14).**
All the visible layers have been copied and merged together on the Final layer.

Step 4: **Select the Measure tool from the Eyedropper fly-out menu in the toolbar and then click and drag along the mullion in the window from Carrie's arm up to her eye.**
The Info palette reads 91.1° (12.15).

Step 5: **Choose Edit ➪ Transform ➪ Rotate.**
The measurement 1.1° is automatically entered in the Rotate field in the Options bar. The problem is that Transform doesn't know which direction to rotate so it defaults to clockwise. The preview does, too.

Step 6: **Enter a minus sign (–) in front of the 1.1° in the Rotate field.**
The preview corrects itself.

Step 7: **Select the Commit Transform check box or press Return/Enter.**
Take a look at the amount of rotation by Option/Alt+clicking on Final's eye icon. This hides all the layers except the active one. The transparent areas around the edge of the file show just how "off" 1.1° is. All's right with the world except for the transparency where Final was rotated (12.16).

Step 8: **Press ⌘/Ctrl+; (semicolon) to hide the guide.**
Final is highlighted and a brush icon appears next to the eye icon, indicating that any changes will be made to this layer.

Step 9: **Press C to select the Crop tool.**

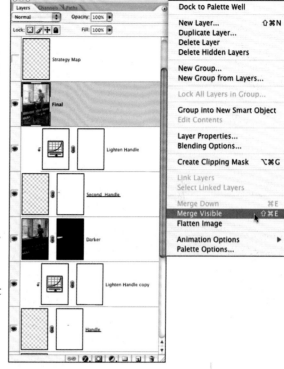

12.14

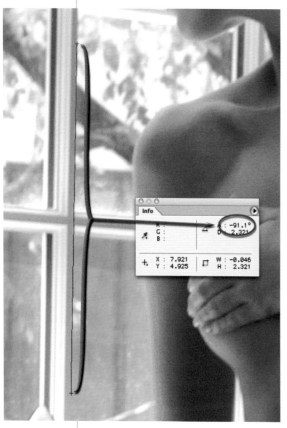

12.15

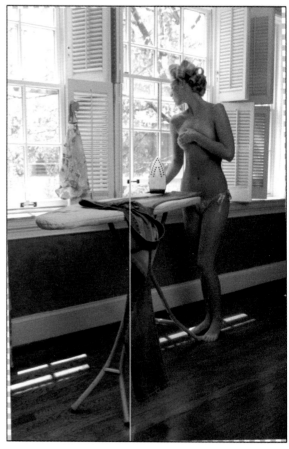

12.16

Where Did It Go?

Selecting the Hide button does exactly that. It hides the cropped area from view. The entire image is still there. Click the Move tool and highlight the Final layer. Drag it back and forth. Sure enough, there is the cropped transparency. Hide the Final layer and highlight only Layer 0. Drag it from side to side. The cropped data appears. Increase the canvas size to get all the cropped data back. Non-destructive Photoshop! Woo-hoo!

Photoshop CS2 has more 16–bit functionality than ever! The photographs in this entire chapter are retouched in 16 bit. This workflow ensures the highest quality file is available for output. If you are working in Photoshop CS, open 2062-M-0642.psd and convert it to 8 bits before continuing.

16-Bit Editing

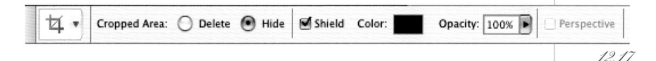

12.17

Step *10*: **Draw a cropping box around the image excluding the transparent areas. Select the Hide button in the Cropped Area section of the Options bar (12.17). Select the Commit Crop check box or press Return (Enter).**
The file looks cropped. All the information is still there.

Creating Midday Mood Lighting

I love this next shot—even though the light of midafternoon clashes a bit with the mood one might imagine for this ensemble of lingerie by La Perla. I want the day outside to be darker and the room secondary to Carrie, who is the center of attention. This technique drops the values of the light outside and coming through the window.

Step *1*: **Open 2062-M-0642.tif from the folder of images for this chapter.**
I included a retouching strategy map so you can practice using the Healing brush non-destructively. (See the previous section of this chapter.) Do all the retouching before you go on to Step 2.

Step *2*: **Click the Strategy Map eye icon to turn it off.**

Step *3*: **Create a new Curves adjustment layer and rename it** Window.

12.18

Step 4: Make black the foreground color and then fill the Window layer mask with black by pressing Option/Alt+Delete/Backspace (12.18).

Step 5: Change Window's Blending Mode to Multiply.

Step 6: Duplicate the Window layer by pressing ⌘/Ctrl+J, and rename it Sofa & Floor.

Step 7: Select the Brush tool and set it to 900 pixels with a soft edge and 100% Opacity.

Step 8: Highlight the Window layer and change the foreground color to white.

Paint from the upper-left corner to the right corner. The windows darken dramatically.

Step 9: Highlight the Sofa & Floor layer and change the Opacity of this layer to 50%.

Paint over the left side of the sofa and across the floor.

Step 10: Create a new layer and rename it Vignette.

Step 11: Draw an oblong circle around Carrie using the Elliptical Marquee tool.

Step 12: Choose Select ⇨ Transform Selection.

Rotate and/or size the circle until it looks like the one shown here (12.19). Select the Commit Transform check box or press Return/Enter (12.20).

12.19

12.20

Step 13: **Option/Alt+click the Add New Layer Mask icon to add a layer mask to Vignette.**

The layer mask is active. You can tell by the frame around Carrie and because the Layer Mask icon is displayed next to the eye icon. In the mask, the oval section is filled with black.

Step 14: **Click the layer thumbnail.**

The frame moves to it.

Step 15: **Make black the background color and fill Vignette with black by pressing ⌘/Ctrl+Delete/Backspace.**

Carrie is definitely the center of attention now. Worry not, there's more . . .

Step 16: **Select the Move tool (V) and press 5 on the keyboard to set Vignette's Opacity to 50%.**

Step 17: **Highlight the Layer Mask icon.**

Open the Gaussian Blur dialog box by choosing Filter ➪ Blur ➪ Gaussian Blur. Set the Radius to 200 pixels, and click OK.

Step 18: **The windows look artificial now. Get a 500-pixel soft brush and paint with 100% black over the shutters, windows, lampshade, wall above the table, tabletop, and molding.**

The layer mask is shown here (12.21).

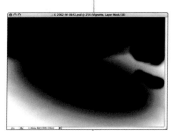

12.21

Step 19: **Highlight Vignette's thumbnail icon and choose Filter ➪ Noise ➪ Add Noise.**

In the Add Noise dialog box, set the amount to 3%, the distribution to Gaussian, and make sure the Monochromatic check box is selected.

Step 20: **Choose File ➪ Save As, select Photoshop from the Format drop-down menu, and name the file** 2062-M-0642.psd.

Step 21: **Choose Image ➪ Duplicate and click OK.**

Close 2062-M-0642.psd. Flatten the copy and then select the Crop tool and crop to taste.

12.22

12.24

12.23

Step 22: **Save the file as 2062-M-0642.tif and press ⌘/Ctrl+W to close it.**

Compare the Before (12.22), Final (12.23), and Final Cropped (12.24) versions of the image.

Beating the Wide-Angle Blues

Times occur when people have to be shot with wide-angle lenses. Usually those are the times when the subject really wants to shoot the photographer, or if you are the photographer, you want to shoot the art director for picking a location that has to be shot with a wide-angle lens. (One of the best parts of writing is getting really long, run-on sentences published in a book just to make your English teachers cringe! Ah ha! Not if you have an alert editor . . . and thankfully I do!) Shooting people this way makes them wide when they are in the foreground, as Carrie appears in this photograph (12.25). We both know she isn't from her appearances earlier in the chapter.

12.25

If the tiny, harshly lit location wasn't bad enough, the bustier/panty set was tiny, too, a full size *smaller* than Linda had specified. Carrie is small—though not that small. The bustier made her middle bulge. The leg holes squeezed the skin at the top of her thighs and tummy. So along with the regular retouching—healing blemishes, brightening the eyes, softening arm wrinkles, and removing hair frizzies—there is some body work to do as well.

Check out the strategy map for this project (12.26). There is a note to compress the image's width by 9%. The area around her middle needs shaping. The green lines indicate areas where the skin has been pushed out by the panties' being too small. Lines also mark wrinkles in the bustier and panties that must be smoothed.

There is serious work to be done, so let's get started. You already know how to do the healing work so I'll leave that up to you. Do the healing after the liquify step (Step 8).

12.26

Step 1: **Open 2062-M-0764.psd.**
This 16-bit file has already been color corrected and had the USM>Alias>© Action run. Study the Strategy Map layer, and then click its eye icon off.

Step 2: **Make a copy of the Background and name it** Compressed.

Step 3: **Select the Move tool, and then select Free Transform by pressing ⌘/Ctrl+T.**

Step 4: **Highlight the W field in the Options bar and enter** 91%.
The sides of the image compress toward the center.

Step 5: **Commit the transform and turn off the Background layer to avoid the confusion of seeing the slimmer file edges repeated.**
At first glance Carrie's head looks odd. Don't give it a second thought. In a minute or so it will look normal. If you don't believe me, show it to someone else. They'll comment on the outfit not the head compression.

Step 6: **Duplicate the Compressed layer (⌘/Ctrl+J) and rename it** Liquify.

To avoid even more confusion, highlight the Strategy Map layer, duplicate it, rename it **Strategy Map 91%**, and press ⌘/Ctrl+ Shift+T to run trans- form again. Strategy Map 91% now fits the Compressed layer. Click off the eye icon for both strategy maps.

	(W) Forward Warp Tool
	(R) Reconstruct Tool
	(C) Twirl Clockwise Tool
	(P) Pucker Tool
	(B) Bloat Tool
	(O) Push Left Tool
	(M) Mirror Tool
	(T) Turbulence Tool
	(F) Freeze Mask Tool
	(D) Thaw Mask Tool
	(H) Hand Tool
	(Z) Zoom Tool

12.27

Step 7: **Save the file.**

Step 8: **Choose Filter ➪ Liquify.**
The keyboard shortcut is ⌘/Ctrl+Shift+X.

LIQUIFY TO RESHAPE

The following steps show you how to use Liquify to fix the bustier-inspired bulges. This process is involved and covers quite a few steps. It will also help familiarize you with this powerful tool. Shown here is the Liquify toolbar (12.27). While working in the Liquify filter, some damage will happen in places. You'll repair these artifacts after you've applied the filter.

There is preparation to do within the Liquify filter to protect areas of the image that are adjacent to the ones to be moved about.

Step 9: **Click the Zoom tool in the Liquify filter's toolbar on the left edge of the dialog box and draw a box around the area shown here (12.28) to zoom in.**

Step 10: **Press F to activate the Freeze Mask tool.**
Select Green as the Mask color in the Options bar so that the protected areas stand out from the red bustier and panties. Mask the area to the right of Carrie's hip and side, including the elbow and upper arm.

Step 11: **Select the Push Left tool (O) and, starting at the hip on your right, stroke upwards using the left side of the brush to push the pixels to the left. Shape the skin back into an inward curve.**
This step takes three or four strokes. Be careful not to overdo it (12.29).

Step 12: **Do the left side.**
This time use a downward stroke starting above the rib cage and shaping down to the panty. Use long smooth strokes. Keep the + in the center of the brush from touching her skin (12.30).

Photoshop CS2 offers a tremendously improved 16-bit workflow. More and more tools are high-bit friendly in this release. Liquify now works in both 8 bit and 16 bit. As for the others, not to worry—Adobe has to leave something for us to look forward to. . . .

Now in 16 Bit . . .

12.28

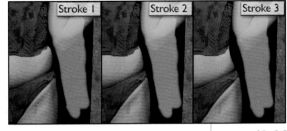

12.29

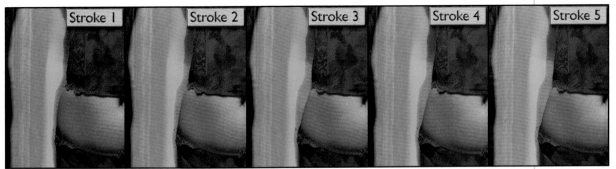

12.30

Freeze and Thaw Mask Tools

You can create, modify, and remove masks when working in the Liquify filter. The Freeze Mask tool paints a red mask that protects the area beneath it. The Thaw Mask tool removes the protection. Select the mask color via a drop-down menu in the View Options section of the control panel on the right side of the dialog box. You can hide the mask from view by clearing the Show Mask check box.

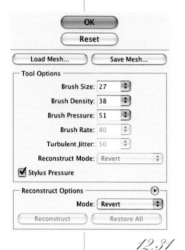

12.31

Step 13: Zoom in to 200%. Hold down the spacebar and drag the image over to the right.

Notice the distortions around her waist and arm above the elbow.

Step 14: Press R to select the Reconstruct tool, and set the options as shown here (12.31).

Brush along the green mask. Don't work to fix all the distortion, because you will bring back the old shape. Not good. You can get rid of the skin tone and reduce the wavy areas. If some of her skin reappears, press ⌘/Ctrl+Z (12.32). You can take care of the rest outside of the Liquify filter.

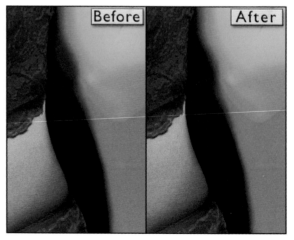

12.32

Step 15: **Click OK to commit the changes and click the Liquify layer's eye icon on and off to see how much that little bit of brushing helped.**

Now is the time to fix the Liquify-induced artifacts.

Step 16: **Zoom to 200% and scroll over the wall on the right side by Carrie's waist.**

Step 17: **Create a new layer above Liquify and name it** Healing.

Pick the Healing Brush and sample a nonwavy area. Heal close to her skin without affecting it.

Step 18: **Scroll over to the left.**

The Push Left tool wave pattern is very apparent on her arm. Before you can do the healing, you have some preparation work to do.

Step 19: **Using the Pen tool, outline down the bustier and around the line of the panty.**

If you aren't comfortable with the Pen tool, use the path named *left arm artifacts*. You probably need to modify it some to match the Liquify that you did. When the path is finished, go to the Paths palette, double-click the Work Path, and save it as **Path 1** (12.33).

Step 20: **⌘/Ctrl+click the path to make it into a selection and feather the selection 2 pixels.**

Now this next part is a little tricky and may be confusing. Hang in there with me. . . .

Step 21: **Go back to the Layers palette. Click the eye icon next to Liquify off, and heal from Compressed to Healing over the bulge.**

The effect will look like the bulge has been covered up. After you finish, deselect then click the Liquify eye icon on. The effect looks natural. The artifacts are gone. One of the advantages to non-destructive editing is that something is always left from previous steps to copy or heal from when recovering from Liquify's artifacts (12.34).

12.33

HEALING THE TUMMY LINE

The next concern is the indentation that the panty makes in her tummy. This would not be apparent if the bustier were not pushing her tummy down as well. What is that line, anyway? It's only a shadow. Remove the shadow and the image is back to flat abs-ville.

Step 22: **Draw a path all the way around the panty.**

If you don't want to draw your own, look in the Paths palette. It is named Panty (what else?). Make it into a selection. Check to make sure that none of the red panty is included in the path. If it is it will cause bleed with the healing brush.

12.34

Step 23: Choose Select ⇨ **Inverse or press ⌘/Ctrl+Shift+I to invert the selection.**
⌘/Ctrl+H will hide it.

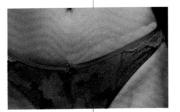

12.35

Step 24: **Sample the Healing brush on the light area above the shadow and heal along the panty line from one side to the other (12.35).**
Slick fix, huh?

Notice the skin creases along the leg holes. They, too, are caused by the panties being too small. Again this is a job for the Healing brush to cover the shadows.

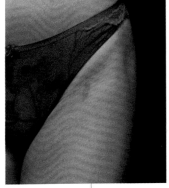

12.36

Step 25: **For the right leg, sample on the top of the thigh and heal the birthmark first (12.36).**
Then heal from the panty line away toward the hip. Don't heal the muscle dimple to the left edge of the right hip. It's pretty and Carrie works out to keep it.

The right leg is a little more work. The light in the room is harsh, causing texture and shadow to show readily. Carrie's weight is on the right leg. There are muscle shadows that would not show under softer light. (The elevator lobby was way too small with no room for anything more than a bare-bulb flash.)

Step 26: **Sample on the middle of her right thigh and heal the area above it completely (12.37).**
Lift the mouse button and view the work. Continue along the panty line. Remember this step is about healing the shadows. While you are at it, heal the razor bumps along the line as well (12.38). Deselect.

12.37

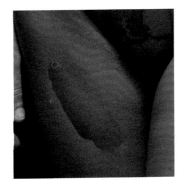

12.38

Wrinkles, wrinkles everywhere . . . it's time to heal the wrinkles. Yes, I use the Healing brush a lot. It whips the Clone Stamp tool hands down for this sort of task. Because you are close to the panty, heal the wrinkles along the right hip.

Step 27: **Sample just below the waistband in the area that has no pattern, and heal the wrinkles.**
Resampling as you work with wrinkles to prevent healing patterns from developing is a good idea.

Step 28: **Using the same techniques, heal the wrinkles on the bustier.**
This image is definitely looking better!

The right knee shows a lot of shadow and could do with some softening. Go ahead and put it on its own layer.

Step 29: **Create a new layer and name it** Heal Knee.
Sample the area just above the knee and heal the wrinkles. Sample the inside of the thigh and heal the shadow along the left of the knee. Repeat for the right shadow. Heal the skin just below the kneecap. When you have finished, the knee will be almost smooth and totally unbelievable.

Step 30: **Select the Move tool and press 5 on the keyboard to reduce the opacity of Heal Knee to 50%.**
Play with other opacities and see which one works best for you. The example shows before and after healing and 60% of Heal Knee showing (12.39).

Now heal the elbow creases on a new layer. We'll do her right arm together as a refresher.

Step 31: **Make a new layer by pressing ⌘/Ctrl+Shift+N. Name it** Elbow. **Choose the Healing brush and then pick a sample point including the edge of the bustier and heal back and forth along the wrinkle.**

Step 32: **Choose Edit ⇨ Fade or press ⌘/Ctrl+Shift+F and fade the healing to about 50%.**
Heal the wrinkle and bumps at the top of the arm joint, too (12.40).

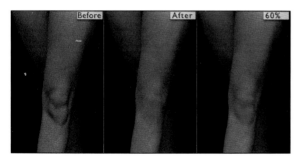

12.39

PRACTICING RETOUCHING TECHNIQUES

Finish healing the blemishes and lines that are shown on
the strategy map. Brighten the irises of the eyes (refer to
Chapter 8), fix the smudged lipstick, and tame the fly-
away hair. (Hint: Use the Clone Stamp tool when you are
working close to her face. Then heal any tonal inconsis-
tencies.) Some of these techniques might be hard to master without seeing them done.

The editorial that these images were from was very well
received. The editorial is available as a PDF in the folder
for this chapter if you want to see how they appeared in
print. The next chapter takes you on location to continue
the exploration of using Photoshop to control contrast
outdoors. I also show you how to take model Rachel
Keller to old ruins near Dublin, Ireland, digitally.
Placing a model in an existing location requires planning
at the camera as well as artfully applying the magic
provided by Photoshop CS2.

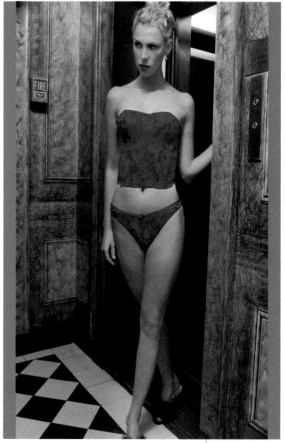

12.40

Chapter Thirteen

Indoors, Outdoors

Making photographs of women in the studio is relatively easy. It is a controlled-access environment. Outdoors is another matter entirely. The considerations range from security to weather. The light changes as the sun moves. (Okay, the earth rotates. You know what I mean.) There are insects and the curious who see a camera and wonder what's up, bugging the shoot in a whole other way. All of these factors can stress the photographer. Some of them stress the photography itself by having the potential to make the model feel uncomfortable. The key to making shoots work is this: If the model feels comfortable and at ease, the photographs will reflect those feelings. The converse is also true.

First and perhaps most important, models must be comfortable in their own skin. If they aren't, nothing can be done to make the photo shoot successful. The next comfort level is with the crew. In shooting women particularly, care has to be exercised in the choice of the crew. Respect in everything is key. Make sure another woman is in the crew, especially if the photographer is male. Remember the whole point is to come away with great photographs.

Controlling Contrast After the Shoot

Once again lingerie is the subject. The location for the shoot is the backyard of a home in midtown Atlanta. The elevated grounds are surrounded on one side by a stone fence and dense foliage on the other. The lush greenery breaks up the backgrounds and provides privacy. Lighting is natural. Cara is the model. This setup is on a deck; the background is a stone wall. Cara is seated in a metal chair draped with her robe (13.1). The warm, dappled light breaks through the leaves of the trees. Scattered patches of sunlight are overexposing areas in the photograph. The sun on Cara's face completely overexposes her face. It makes her squint, too. The same problem is happening on her leg. This is not pretty at all.

13.1

The solution lies in placing a Chimera 42 x 72-inch diffusion panel between the sun (origin of light) and Cara. You can see the panel's effect by the rectangular shadow cast on Cara (13.2). The larger source of light (the diffusion panel) is now soft and flattering. The diffused value is metered again. One f/stop of exposure is added at the camera to compensate for the density of the diffusion fabric. The additional exposure increases the brightness of the highlights outside of the area of soft light created by the panel by one stop as well. The overly bright highlights in the background compete with Cara for the viewer's attention. Reducing those highlights believably is the subject of this project.

The high-bit data contained in the RAW file is put to work to tone down the distracting highlights. The strategy map outlines the areas of concern (13.3). You can get the files for this section from www.amesphoto.com/learning. Click the cover of this book and enter the code **PW48255**. Download the folder for Chapter 13. It contains the RAW files 2062-R-014.dcr, 2062-R-073.dcr, and a .psd version with a strategy map.

13.2

Step 1: **Navigate to the folder you downloaded in Adobe Bridge. Double-click it to view thumbnails of the sample files. Click 2062-R-073.dcr to highlight it, then press ⌘/Ctrl+R to open the RAW file in ACR3.** The settings section shows that the image is displayed as shot. This is the out-of-the-camera untweaked file (13.4). Look at the histogram. There is a full range of exposure from shadows to highlights.

Step 2: **Place a color sampler (S) on the bright stone behind Cara.**
It reads R:255, G: 255, B:255. The highlights are blown out. If this was a JPEG, it would be game over. The high-bit-depth linear data contained in the RAW file means a lot more information exists than is shown in the preview.

Step 3: **Select the Show Workflow Options check box under the zoom controls. Set the dialog box to Space: Adobe RGB (1998), Size: 2008 by 3032, Depth: 8 Bits/ Channel, and Resolution: 300 pixels/inch. Click Open.**

13.3

13.4

Step 4: **Run the USM Alias © Action from the Postproduction Actions set.**
The function key assigned in Chapter 4 is F13 on the Mac and F12 on Windows,

Step 5: **Click the Return to Bridge icon in the menu bar. Press ⌘/Ctrl+R to open 2062-R-073.dcr again in ACR3.**
Photoshop CS2 will open multiple versions of RAW files without duplicating and renaming them as was the case with Photoshop 7 and CS.

Step 6: **Set the Color Sampler in the same place as in Step 2. Drag the Exposure slider to the left until the setting reads –1.30. Lower the Brightness to 27.**
Notice the readings in color Sampler #1—R: 228, G: 221, B: 211.

Step 7: **Move the Contrast slider to the left until it reads –25. Click Open.**
The highlights are much lower. So is the contrast. RAW makes lighting in postproduction easy.

Step 8: **Press V to select the Move tool. Hold down the Shift key, click the dark version, and drag it onto the first photograph opened in Step 3. Rename Layer 1** Dark Highlights.
The whole image on the screen is underexposed (13.5).

Step 9: **Hold down the Option/Alt key and click the Add Layer Mask icon at the bottom of the Layers palette.**
A new layer mask is filled with black. A layer mask filled with black is called a *hide all layers* mask. The properly exposed version complete with blown-out highlights is on the screen. Dark Highlights is active and its layer mask is selected (13.6).

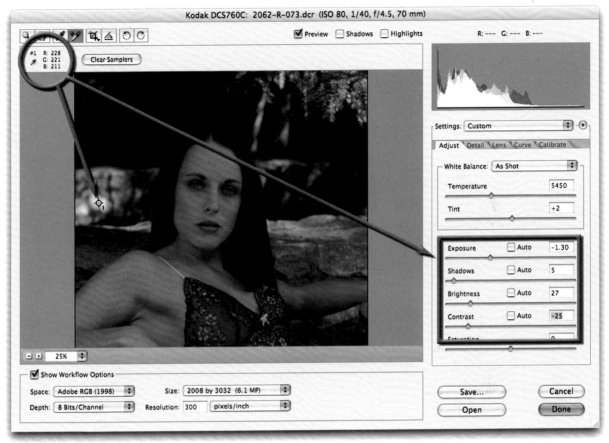

13.5

Step *10*: **Select the Brush tool. Set it 100 pixels in diameter with a hardness of 0% and an Opacity of 50%. Set the foreground color to white. Zoom to 100%.**

13.6

13.7

13.8

Step 11: Paint over the highlights.

As you paint, the layer mask reveals the darker highlights (13.7). Refer to the retouching strategy map for the areas to darken. Each time you lift the brush and paint over an area, another 50% of paint is added, darkening the highlights even more. Get a 200-pixel brush and darken the lower-left corner.

Step 12: Set the brush to 100% opacity. Paint over the bright evergreen trees in the upper-right and upper-left corners. After you finish, zoom out. Hold down the Option/Alt key and click the layer mask to see the paint.

The lighter areas reveal more of the Dark Highlights layer (13.8). This reduces the contrast of the background, bringing the eye forward in the image to Cara. Compare the darker background on the left to the original on the right (13.9).

Step 13: Make a new layer and rename it Retouch (13.10). **Hold down the Option/Alt key and choose Merge Visible from the Layers palette fly-out menu.**

If you use the shortcut ⌘/Ctrl+Option/Alt+Shift+E, you don't even have to make a new layer first. Photoshop CS2 does it for you. Cool and useful!

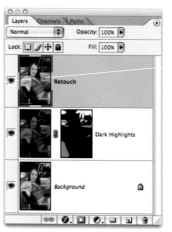

13.9

13.10

Cara is a natural beauty. And yes, her eyes are that bright naturally. My strategy for retouching her photograph is simple and subtle. Mainly it involves cleaning up some of the textures on her face and removing flyaway hairs. The body retouch is minimal. Make your own strategy and go for it!

Going Further

The RAW workflow offers postproduction options that are simply not available with camera-produced JPEGs or TIFs. The high bit depth versatility gives the digital photographer options that with film could only be accomplished on location by large crews equipped with extensive light modifiers. Often photographers had to settle. Times have changed—for the better. Check out the final version of Cara from this exercise (13.11). Fabulous!

Working In Studio for On Location

Occasionally the location, the photographer, and the model can't quite be in the same place at the same time. Now as much as we would all love to hang problems on the location, it is pretty much out of the question. Travel considerations, costs, and schedules all conspire against the success of the envisioned photograph.

Successful compositing has been a holy grail dangled as an unfulfilled fruit of digital imaging. The dream has been to take any location shot at any time of day (or night) and drop a person into it seamlessly. This is, of course, nothing more than whimsy, a fantasy or a pipe dream used to romance the promise—it isn't gonna happen any time soon. And more than likely it will never be as easy as they (remember "them"?) would like us to believe. That's not to say it's impossible. It's just not easy.

13.11

13.12

The problem is light. All the qualities have to match in order for a composite to be believed.

Shoot the location. Then look at the photograph closely. Careful study reveals the light, color, quality, and angle (check out the shadows). Go into the studio. Match what is happening in the photograph of the location. Then the composite can work.

This section covers the process of seeing the light in an image. The location is a ruin outside of Dublin, Ireland (13.12).

The sun is setting on the left side of the photograph. Open sky provides fill. The light to match is the warm directional sunlight coming from the left side.

The photographs of the model, Rachel Keller from the Elite modeling agency, were made specifically for insertion into this scene. A guide print of the photograph was on set to match the lighting. A Rosco #3407 warming gel was attached to a medium Chimera Super Pro lightbank. This light coming from the left provided the orange-ish late afternoon sun effect on Rachel. It was about 15 feet away. A large (4 x 6-foot) Chimera Super Pro lightbank was aimed from the right at 45 degrees from the lens and 45 degrees above to simulate fill light from an open sky. It can be argued that Rachel looks too well lit when compared to the building. I take lighting gear on location when shooting fashion to ensure the clothes and model look their best. Fashion shooting has an element of fantasy in it. In this case proper lighting on Rachel is part of my exercising artistic license to achieve the fantasy. A fan to move her hair and dress was blowing from the left as well. An iTunes play list by first assistant Justin "Top Forty" Larose flowed from the sound system, Rachel moved, and I made photographs. Twenty minutes and 120 shots later we reviewed the take. We had the shot. The challenge was determining which one to use.

Nine of the favorites for the composite are shown in the figure (13.13). My pick is 2062-I-0097.tif. Download it and Irish Ruins.tif from the Chapter 13 folder on www.amesphoto.com/learning. The book code is **PW48255**.

This project consists of four sections. The first two involve retouching Rachel and removing her from the studio background. The third section shows you how to prepare the location photograph. In the fourth section you blend the two together so that they appear seamless.

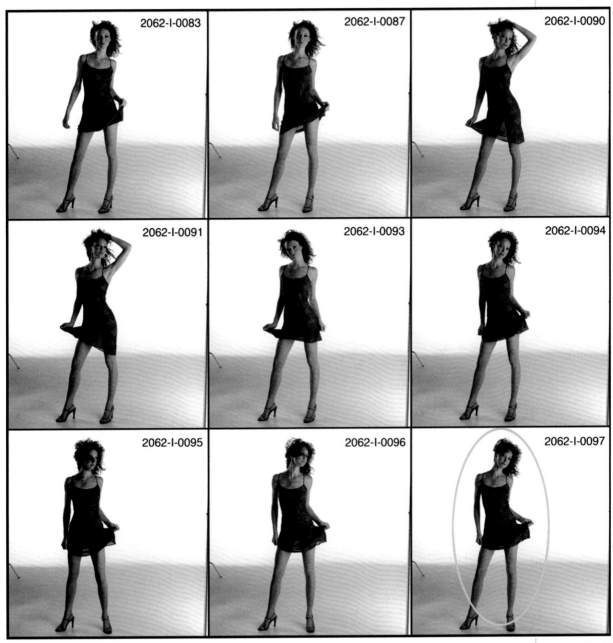

2062-I-0083

2062-I-0087

2062-I-0090

2062-I-0091

2062-I-0093

2062-I-0094

2062-I-0095

2062-I-0096

2062-I-0097

13.13

Retouching Rachel

Rachel has an Irish complexion. Her hair is naturally curly and red, her skin is pale with wonderful freckles. Some of them are large enough to draw the viewer away from her face. They have been circled on the retouching strategy map (13.14). Some lines need smoothing on her face and armpit. The skin on her legs needs some smoothing, too. Previous chapters cover all the retouching techniques used here. So the first section's step-by-step is to show the order of retouching Rachel.

Step 1: Navigate to Chapter 13's folder in Bridge. Double-click 2062-I-0097.tif to open it.

Step 2: Run the USM Alias © Action (press F13 in Mac, or F12 in Win). Press ⌘/Ctrl+J to duplicate the background layer, and rename it Retouch. **Heal the large blemishes on Rachel's face, arms, and shoulders.**

Step 3: Heal blemishes and lines on her legs and feet.

Heal Blemishes

Soften Lines

Soften Armpit

Dropout Background

Heal Leg Blemishes

Smooth Skin on Legs

13.14

Step 4: Heal the line at her armpit using one continuous stroke. Press ⌘/Ctrl+Shift+F to fade the healing about 50% to bring back part of the line.

Without the fade step, the retouched area is too perfect. The Fade Healing brush (or any Edit ➪ Fade command for that matter) set to 50% only works on the last brush stroke.

Step 5: Begin on Rachel's face. Heal the lines under her eyes.

There is a path named "eyes" to keep the Healing brush from bleeding eyeliner into the area under her eyes. You might want to use a separate layer named "under eyes" for this step. If you use one, make sure Sample All Layers is selected in the Healing Brush Options bar.

Step 6: Draw a path around the skin of Rachel's legs. Outline the skin between the straps of the shoes and around the ankle bracelet. Save your path by double-clicking Work Path in the Paths palette and clicking OK.

Of course, if you want to cut right to the next step, you can always use the path named Legs already drawn and most conveniently located in the Paths palette.

Healing Under Eyes

Let's face it. The Healing brush rules for eliminating lines everywhere except under eyes with mascara on the lower lashes. The Healing brush reaches outside the brushed area shown on the screen and blends the sampled data to that under the just-healed area. When a large tonal or color difference exists, that difference is included in the calculation. A dark or colored blend results. Large, dark "poor, poor, pitiful me" crying–all–night eyes appear (13.15). And they aren't pretty. Here's the fix: Zoom in to at least 200%. Draw a selection around the area to be healed; for the best precision, use the Pen tool. There's a path for this part of the exercise, too. ⌘/Ctrl+click on Eyes in the Paths palette. Do not feather. Here's the trick. Change the Blending Mode of the Healing brush to Darken. Sample an area of clear skin, and then heal under Rachel's eye (13.16). The brush only heals areas that are darker than the sampled area. Heal the under-eye lines. Tah-dah! No bags (13.17)!

13.15

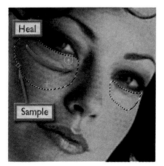

13.16

13.17

13.18

Step 7: ⌘/Ctrl+click the just-created path (or Legs) in the Paths palette to make it into a selection (13.18). Click the Layer tab to return to the Layers palette.

Step 8: Press ⌘/Ctrl+Option/Alt+D and feather the selection 0.7 pixels. Click OK.

Step 9: Make the selection into its own layer by pressing ⌘/Ctrl+J. Rename it Legs.

Step 10: ⌘/Ctrl+click on the new Legs layer to activate the selection again. Choose Select ➪ Modify ➪ Contract. Enter 5 in the pixels field in the Contract Selection dialog box. Click OK.

Of Days and Fashions Past

Fashion changes. Well, duh. That is its nature after all. One of these [r]evolutions is bare-legged women in dresses. There was a time before Photoshop that this was not acceptable. Pantyhose were the order of the day. Stockings made the shape of the leg, covered blemishes on the skin, and made the legs in photographs perfect.

Women in today's world are far more active. They are involved in sports, careers, and family pursuits that can and do inflict bruises, scratches, and other "unsightly" marks on their legs. Hose have been relegated to formal dress-up events.

Smooth flawless legs are still desirable, especially in photographs where they can be observed more closely than in real life. Photoshop offers the ability to smooth the skin without reverting to those "oh-so-last-millennium" hose, tights, or (aaarrrggghhh) leggings.

Step *11*: **Click the Lock Transparency icon (13.19).**

Step *12*: **Press Q to enter Quick Mask mode. Choose Filter ⇨ Blur ⇨ Gaussian Blur. Enter 3 pixels. Click OK.**
The blur extends almost to the edge of the skin (13.20). Press Q and return to Normal mode. The marching ants reappear.

Step *13*: **Invert the selection by pressing ⌘/Ctrl+Shift+I.**
This selection extends into the skin 5 pixels from the edge over a 3-pixel feather.

Step *14*: **Choose Filter ⇨ Blur ⇨ Gaussian Blur and apply a 1.5-pixel blur to the selected area (13.21).**

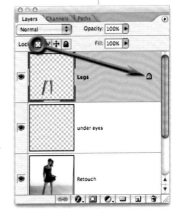

13.19

13.20

Blurred skin

13.21

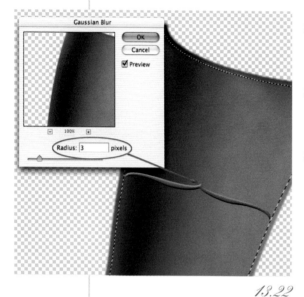

13.22

Step *15*: **Invert the selection again. Blur the skin on the inside of the leg 3 pixels (13.22).**

Step *16*: **Deselect by pressing ⌘/Ctrl+D.** The transparency is still locked on the Legs layer.

Step *17*: **Choose Filter ⇨ Noise ⇨ Add Noise. Enter** 1.15% **in the Amount field. Choose Gaussian and select Monochrome. Click OK.**
Rachel's legs and feet look smoother without being plastic. Noise added to the blurred skin helps it retain some of the skin's natural texture (13.23).

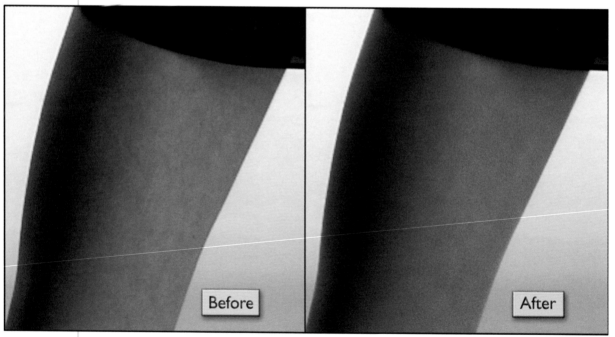

13.23

No, not the late great Kurt Cobain's grunge band–great printed output without banding or posterization. And there's the fact that skin looks like skin, not plastic! Remember it's "About a Girl . . ." after all–and making her look right.

Blur + Noise = Nirvana

Step 18: Merge the visible layers to a new one. Hold down the entire left side of the keyboard–okay, just ⌘/Ctrl+Option/Alt+Shift+E–to make it so.

Step 19: Rename the new layer Rachel and save the file as 2062-0097.psd. Keep it open to use in the next section.

CREATING A LAYER OF HER OWN

This next section floats Rachel and that ab fab red hair onto her own layer. Then she will be ready for a (digital) journey to Ireland.

13.24

Step 1: Go to the Paths palette and select New Path from the fly-out menu. Draw a path around Rachel's body. As the path reaches her head, draw it inside her hair (13.24).
The path is shown in green for clarity. As always, should you choose not to make your own path, one is provided in the Paths palette. It is named Rachel.

Step 2: Make the path into a selection. Feather it .7 pixels.

Step 3: Go to the Layers palette and press ⌘/Ctrl+J to make the selection into a layer.
Name the layer **Rachel's head** (13.25).

Step 4: **Select the Elliptical Marquee tool. Drag a selection around Rachel's neck, face, and hair. Highlight the Rachel layer (13.26).**

Step 5: **Press ⌘/Ctrl+J to make the selection into a layer. Name the layer** Hair. **Click the Hair layer and drag it above Rachel's head.**

Step 6: **Click off the eye icon on the Rachel layer and all of the layers below it to hide those layers.**

Rachel appears against a transparent background (gray and white checkerboard) with a white ring around her head (13.27).

13.25

13.26

Step 7: **Hair is selected. Add the layer Rachel's head to the selection by ⌘/Ctrl+clicking it.**
Both layers are highlighted.

Step 8: **Open Irish Ruins.tif.**

Step 9: **Select the Move tool (V). Click 2062-I0097.psd. Click either of the highlighted layers and drag them onto Irish Ruins.tif. (13.28).**
Irish Ruins.tif's layer stack now includes the linked layers Hair and Rachel's head. Rachel still has a white halo around her head.

13.27

The next steps are similar to bringing back Adair's hair in Chapter 8. The difference is that Rachel's hair has to blend with the colors of the background instead of 255 white. This technique works as long as the halo around the hair is brighter than the background.

Step 10: **Irish Ruins.tif is active. Drag the selected layers until it looks like this (13.29). Double-click Hair to open the Layer Style dialog box.**
At the bottom are the Blend If sliders. Drag the highlight slider for "This layer:" slowly to the left. The halo begins to disappear. Keep dragging until it is gone. Stop while you can still see what looks like white fringe around the hair against the wall of the ruins.

13.28

13.29

Step *11*: **Hold down the Option/Alt key. Click the right half of the slider and drag it back to the right.**
Some of the hair comes back. You want the numbers to read somewhere around 100 for the left half and 255 for the right. Click OK (13.30).

Step *12*: **Hide the Background layer. Copy the two visible layers to a new one by pressing ⌘/Ctrl+Option/Alt+ Shift+E. Name this layer** Rachel Medium Shot. **Hide Rachel's Head and Hair.**

13.30

Step *13*: **Show the Background layer. Choose Layers ⇨ Matting ⇨ Remove White Matte.**
Rachel's hair now looks natural against the ruins (13.31).

Placing someone in a scene when they are way forward (think close to the camera) is easy. A lot of telltales that give away the compositing are missing. Cast shadows and depth of field (or in this case lack of it) are clues. People look at photographs and know when they aren't right even though they can't quite say why.

CREATING SHALLOW DEPTH OF FIELD

The work on Rachel is complete for this version. Some of the disconnects mentioned earlier are in this photograph. Rachel is sharper and more detailed than the background image, but the background image is still too sharp. A photograph made late in the day would be shot with the lens aperture (f/stop) set almost wide open to allow a faster shutter speed and help freeze the model's hair. The large aperture would produce quite a shallow depth of field. Rachel would be sharp and the ruins would be out of focus. A tool added to Photoshop CS, the Lens Blur filter, is perfect for finishing this photograph. Even better, the version of this filter in Photoshop CS2 works in 16 bit.

Step *1*: **Duplicate the Background layer by highlighting it and pressing ⌘/Ctrl+J. Rename it** Depth of Field.
Non-destructive editing always works on a copy of the Background layer.

Step *2*: **Click the Channels tab. Click the Create New Channel icon at the bottom of the palette.**
The new channel is named Alpha 1. It is used to create the depth of field effect in Step 5.

Step *3*: **Set the default colors by pressing D on the keyboard. Press X to make black the foreground color.**

Step *4*: **Select the Gradient tool (G). Click the Foreground to Background icon in the Options bar (13.32).**

Step 5: Click the RGB composite eye icon to show the image. Hide Alpha 1 by clicking its eye icon. Shift+click at the bottom of the image, and then drag up to the first daylight coming through the wall of the ruins (13.33). Alpha 1 is used to tell Lens Blur where the focus is sharp and the areas in the distance for it to go soft. Black in Alpha 1 will be sharp and white will be out of focus. The grays in the channel transition from sharp to soft.

Step 6: Choose Filter ⇨ Blur ⇨ Lens Blur. When the really humongous Lens Blur dialog box opens, choose Alpha 1 as the Source in the Depth Map menu. Drag the Blur Focal Distance slider to the right until it reads 20. Set the Shape to Hexagon with a Radius of 35 (13.34).

This setting controls the amount of blur. Each time a setting is changed, the preview redraws. I've worked out the numbers for this image. Play with them when you are using this tool on your photographs.

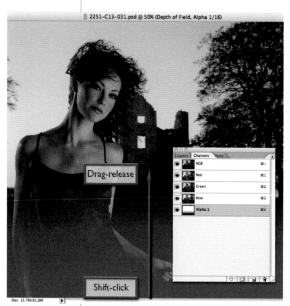

13.33

Note

One result of blurring an image is the highlights become grayer. In the Lens Blur dialog box, the Specular Highlights section gives them a boost. The Threshold slider controls the point where all pixels above the setting are treated as specular (mirror) highlights of the origin and/or the source of light. Brightness increases the highlights. The ruins have no specular highlights because the sun is below the horizon, so these settings are left at 0.

Lens Blur (50%)

13.34

Step 7: **Leave the Blade Curvature and Rotation at 0. Same with the Specular Highlight settings. Set the Noise to 3, the Distribution to Uniform, and select Monochrome. Click OK.**

Lens Blur pretty much closes the believability deal for this version of Rachel and the ruins (13.35). Let's record the visible layers and then move on to another version all in the same file.

13.35

Note

{ Lens Blur is a blurring filter. (I know you know that.) Any time a digital image is blurred, add noise (usually about 3%) to prevent banding or posterization. }

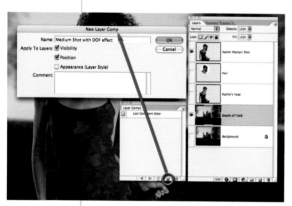

13.36

Step 8: **The Depth of Field and Rachel Medium Shot layers are visible. Click the Layer Comps tab in the Palette Well in Photoshop's menu bar. Click the New Layer Comp icon at the bottom to record their position and visibility. Name this one** Medium Shot with DOF effect **and click OK (13.36).**

Rachel Full-Length Feature

Placing a model in front of a scene is fairly easy. I'll push the difficulty up a step by placing Rachel into the field of grass with the ruins in the background.

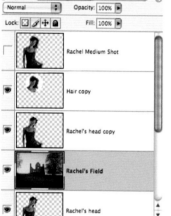

13.37

Step 1: **Set up the layer stack as follows so that it looks like this (13.37):**

Hide Depth of Field and Rachel Medium Shot.

Show the Background, Rachel's head, and Hair layers. Duplicate the Background layer by highlighting it and pressing ⌘/Ctrl+J.

Rename the layer **Rachel's Field**.

Select both Rachel's head and Hair by clicking the first one and ⌘/Ctrl+clicking the second.

Hold down the Option/Alt key and drag the layers up the layer stack until you see a solid black line.

Bicubic (Better) and More . . .

Both Photoshop CS and CS2 sport one improved and two new interpolation modes for enlarging or reducing image size. Bicubic (Better) is the improved overall interpolation algorithm. It's great for general reducing and enlarging using 110% steps. Bicubic Smoother is for enlarging. Bicubic Sharper is designed for reducing large files that might be used on the Web, for instance. These settings are global. They affect Free Transform, Crop, and Image Size. Image Size has an override drop-down menu that defaults to the preference setting after each use.

Release the mouse. Rachel's head copy and Hair copy appear in the layer stack.

Drag Rachel's Field up the stack until it is under Rachel's head copy and Hair copy.

Step 2: **Select Rachel's head copy and Hair copy. Press ⌘/Ctrl+T to open Free Tranform. Click the link icon in the Options bar between the W and H entry windows to lock the proportions together. Highlight the W window and enter** 40%. **Position Rachel until your screen looks like this (13.38). Select the Commit check box.**

Step 3: **Merge the two selected layers (Rachel's head copy and Hair copy) into one by pressing ⌘/Ctrl+E. Rename the merged layer** Rachel in the Field. **Remove the white fringe from her hair by choosing Layer ⇨ Matting ⇨ Remove White Matte.**

Two issues remain: the overall sharpness of the background and the grass at her feet. Let's fix the focus first. (Once again it's time for Lens Blur with a twist.)

13.38

Tip

A 16-bit transform results in much higher quality image interpolation for both up- and downsizing. The use of the appropriate Bicubic sampling method in the General Preferences dialog box improves the quality of the transform, too. Open the General Preferences dialog box by pressing ⌘/Ctrl+Option/Alt+K. Select General from the top menu. Set the Image Interpolation to Bicubic Smoother for enlarging an image or Bicubic Sharper for reducing it, whichever you do more frequently. Click OK. Transform and Image Size now default to this preference. (This option is not available in versions of Photoshop older than CS.)

Step 4: ⌘/Ctrl+click the layer thumbnail of Rachel in the Field to load the pixels as a selection.

This feature is new in Photoshop CS2. In CS, ⌘/Ctrl+clicking anywhere in the layer would load the selection. That no longer works in CS2.

Step 5: Click the Channels tab and then click the Create New Channel icon. The new channel is white. Rachel's outline is shown by the selection. Choose Edit ⇨ Fill, and then fill the selection with black.

Rachel's outline appears in black on the channel.

Step 6: Click the RGB composite eye icon to view the photograph and Alpha channel 2.

If Rachel doesn't appear in red, double-click Alpha 2 and choose Selected Areas for the indicated color and an Opacity of 100% (13.39).

Step 7: Make the foreground color black. Get a 0% hardness 125-pixel brush. Align the bottom edge of the brush with the bottom-left edge of the frame and click. Release the mouse and line up the brush the same way on the far right edge.

Step 8: Hold down the Shift key and click.

A soft straight line in red is drawn edge to edge through Rachel's feet (13.40).

13.39

Holding down the Shift key after clicking with a tool that uses a brush (Clone Stamp, Brush, Pencil, Healing brush, and so on) constrains the brush to a straight line connecting the first click and the Shift+click.

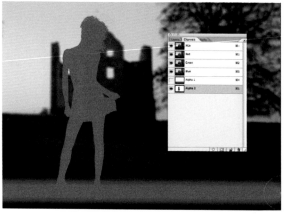

13.40

The new Alpha channel tells the Lens Blur filter what areas of the background are to be sharp or blurred and how much blur to apply. Black areas of the Alpha channel (0) will be sharp. White areas (255) will be the most blurred. Areas of transition shown on the Alpha channel as grays are blurred according to the value of the gray. Dark grays are sharper. Light grays are softer.

Depth Map

Step 9: **Hide Alpha 2 and click the RGB composite in the Channels palette to select it and the other color channels. Click the Layers tab.**

Step 10: **Select Rachel's Field. Choose Filter ⇨ Blur ⇨ Lens Blur. Choose Alpha 2 as the Depth Map. Set the Blur Focal Distance to 0 and the Radius to 20.**
Because Rachel is farther back in the scene, the amount of the background that is out-of-focus is less.

Step 11: **Click OK.**
Alpha 2 is position specific. After you apply the blur to Rachel's Field, Rachel can't be moved.

That takes care of softening up the background. Now there is the problem of a field of really thick grass. . . .

UNDER FOOT: HIGH HEELS AND TALL GRASS

Look at Rachel's feet. Only a photographer could ask a model to walk a field of tall grass in high heels. Anyway, the grass would naturally cover part of her feet.

Step 1: **Highlight the layer Rachel's Field and then select the Lasso tool (L). Draw a selection of grass from the area to the right of where Rachel is standing (13.41). Jump the selection to a new layer by pressing ⌘/Ctrl+J. Name the new layer Grass. Drag the layer above Rachel in the Field.**

Note
Depth of field is the area in focus in front of and behind the point of focus. In this case Rachel is the focal point. The distribution of depth of focus is one-third in front and two-thirds behind the sharp subject.

Note
Positioning is very important. Once Rachel is in position, you can't move her without undoing the Lens Blur filter. Then you have to redo Alpha 2 before you can Lens Blur Rachel's Field again. This is because the depth mask used to create the apparent depth of field is specific to Rachel and where she stands in the photograph.

13.41

13.42

Step 2: Select the Move tool (V) and drag Grass over Rachel's feet. Add a layer mask to Grass. Paint with black with a medium-soft (50% hardness) brush on the mask to reveal Rachel's shoes sinking into the lush, thick grass (13.42).

Step 3: Press ⌘/Ctrl+Shift+N to create a new layer; name it Grass Blades.

Step 4: Select the Clone Stamp tool and make sure that Sample All Layers is selected in the Options bar. Click the Brushes tab in the palette well. Choose the Grass brush (13.43).

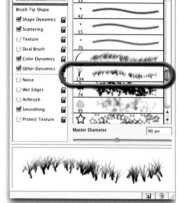

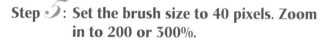

13.43

Step 5: Set the brush size to 40 pixels. Zoom in to 200 or 300%.

Step 6: Sample the grass and clone blades of grass along the edges of Rachel's shoes and feet (13.44).

Break up the lines with this technique on both shoes and the heel of the left one. Now Rachel is grounded (pun intended) and believable by this tiny detail.

The phrase, "the devil is in the details," really says it all when it comes to making composites believable. The results from the last six steps are almost complete. I'll refine them a bit more with a drop shadow of all things.

Step 7: Click the Layer Styles icon (the white f in a black circle) at the bottom of the palette. Choose Drop Shadow.

The Layer Styles dialog box appears.

Step 8: Fill in the options as follows: Opacity: 55, Angle: −135, Distance: 0, Spread: 0, and Size: 1. Click the preview on and off to see the admittedly subtle difference. Click OK.

This drop shadow adds a small amount of dimension to the painted-in grass. I admit this is totally picky. And it is one of those finishing touches that make all the difference when someone looks closely at the work (13.45).

13.44

13.45

These techniques allow truly cool flexibility in placing models in new locations. The key to its success is paying attention to the details of light, shadow, where the feet meet the ground, and of course, depth of field. The Lens Blur filter is a great new 16-bit tool that makes composites even more believable by bringing depth of field control into post production.

Locations with models who are actually there are lots of fun to shoot. Using Photoshop enhances colors, occasionally changes them, and of course, touches up things that can't be handled due to budget at the time of the shoot. The next chapter gives you a look into the "glamorous" world of shooting swimwear on location and how enhancement in Adobe Photoshop CS2 not only saves the day (literally) but also adds that "little something" that makes the final photographs jump.

Chapter Fourteen

On the Beach: Swimwear

Nature has no mercy at all. Nature says,
"I'm going to snow. If you have on a bikini and no snowshoes,
that's tough. I am going to snow anyway."
Maya Angelou

Use the Google search engine to find information on "sunshine state," and you get 45.9 million listings, most of them for Florida. The official Internet site of the Florida legislature is *Sunshine Online*. Construction companies consult *callsunshine.com* before digging up Florida's streets. So you would think that photographing swimsuits in Miami for a magazine editorial in the *sunshine* would be a no-brainer. Maya is right. Nature has *no* mercy.

Right after I checked out the fabulous locations at the Sonesta Resort Key Biscayne with the magazine's publicist, Deborah Roker, the sunshine went away. Not only was the sunshine gone, it was replaced by a downpour of rain that lasted all afternoon then on through the night. The next morning dawn broke to overcast skies, a brisk chilly breeze, and the threat of more precipitation. Elite models Tia Hinton and Adelina Guerrero arrived at the hotel to be fitted with the latest swimwear by stylist Liz Lyons Powers. Assistant Justin Larose and I moved the camera, PowerBook, and lights to the beach to prepare the first setup. About an hour later the overcast sky brightened a bit. The lights were ready. Tia and Adelina arrived and we started to shoot.

A dozen frames later the rain came. Justin and I quickly broke down the gear and moved it inside as the sprinkles turned into a downpour. It was ten in the morning. Welcome to my world—professional photography and the *sunshine* state. My father the fruit rancher maintained that anyone who counts on the weather for a living is crazy. Point taken.

By noon there was no sign of a break in the rain. Matthias Kammerer, the resort's general manager, graciously granted us permission to start shooting inside in the hotel's lobby (14.1). The fountain in the lobby was created by the same artist who designed the fountain at the pool. I realized that with some clever lighting and postproduction in Adobe Photoshop CS2, this location would enable us to get shooting and provide visual continuity while we quietly prayed to the weather goddess for her elusive sunshine. Always have a Plan B.

14.1

Faking Sunlight

The sunshine, if any had come our way, would have been diffused a bit by the clouds. I wanted my guess of what the light might be later to match what we were doing inside. The lighting in the lobby consisted of one head and a reflector pointed into a 42-in. x 72-in. Chimera light panel covered with translucent fabric.

We were able to work through four setups in the lobby. Guests, front desk staff, bellmen, and the concierge all enjoyed watching the beautiful women posing in the latest swimwear.

14.2

Justin archived the RAW files to CDs that evening and built out a Web Photo Gallery for review. Back in Atlanta, I reviewed the take and jotted down file numbers of shots I liked (14.2). The shape of Tia's body, her lowered chin, and smile is the winner for this suit by Luli Fama. Download the folder for Chapter 14 from www.amesphoto.com/learning to begin this exercise. The code is **PW48255.**

Step *1*: **Open 2062-Q-0201.dcr by double-clicking it in Adobe Bridge.**
The exposure and color balance setting have already been set for you. Rotate the file to vertical and set the bit depth to 16 Bits/Channel. Click Open. The retouching strategy map (14.3) outlines the work to be done in this project. The file 2062-Q-0201Map.psd included in the folder has the strategy layer for you to reference.

Step *2*: **Duplicate the Background layer by pressing ⌘/Ctrl+J. Rename it** Retouch.

Add Sky to Background

Strap Twisted

Smooth Skin

Fix White String Ends

14.3

Healing Lines that Cross a Shadow

To heal lines that cross a shadow, sample in the middle of the shadow (14.4) and then align the Healing brush in the center of the shadow. Heal into the shadow (14.5) and then into the highlight. The sample of the shadow is seamlessly healed along with the line.

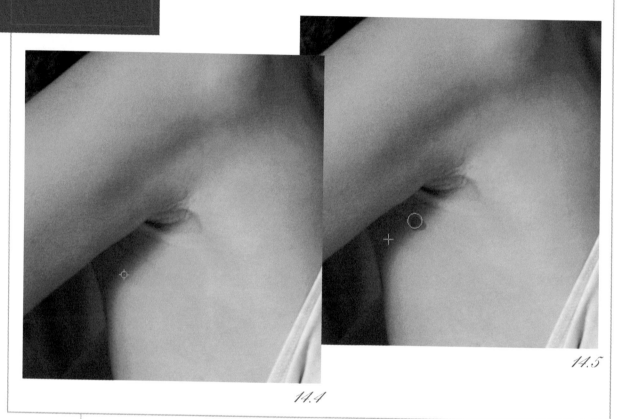

14.4

14.5

Note

All the work in Step 3 has been shown in detail in previous chapters. Please refer to them for detailed step-by-step instructions.

Step 3: Do the retouching outlined on the strategy map to remove blemishes and soften the lines on Tia's neck and face. Heal any blemishes on her body that draw attention. Brighten her eyes.

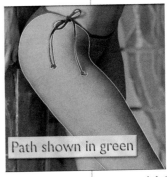

14.6

Look closely at the skin on Tia's hip below her bikini line. There is texture that could use smoothing.

Step 4: Use the Pen tool to draw a path around her hip excluding the bikini, strings, and shadows. Only outline the front leg (14.6). Save your path.

Step 5: ⌘/Ctrl+click on Path 1 to make it into a selection. You can also drag Path 1 to the Load Path as Selection icon (14.7).

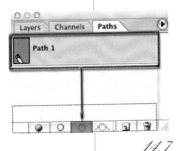

14.7

Step 6: Press ⌘/Ctrl+Option/Alt+D to open the Feather Selection dialog box; feather the selection 0.3 pixels.

Step 7: Return to the Layers tab. Press ⌘/Ctrl+J to make the selection into its own layer. Name it Leg.

Step 8: Click the Lock Transparent Pixels icon located under the blending modes drop-down menu in the Layers palette.
A padlock icon appears on the right edge of the Leg layer (14.8).

Step 9: Choose Filter ➪ Blur ➪ Gaussian Blur. Enter 2 pixels and click OK.

14.8

Step 10: Hold down the ⌘/Ctrl key and click the Leg layer thumbnail to load its pixels as a selection.

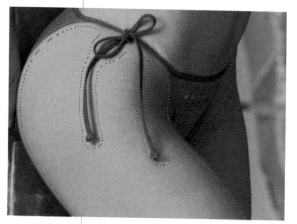

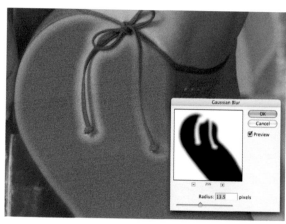

14.9

14.10

Step 11: Choose Select ⇨ Modify ⇨ Contract, enter 10 pixels, and click OK (14.9).

Step 12: Enter Quick Mask mode by pressing Q. Open the Gaussian Blur dialog box. Enter 13.5 pixels and click OK (14.10). Press Q once more to exit Quick Mask mode.

Step 13: Open the Gaussian Blur dialog box again. Blur the Leg layer 5.1 pixels. Press ⌘/Ctrl+D to deselect.

Achieving Realistic Texture

Compared to the rest of Tia's skin, the leg altered in the preceding section looks plastic and fake. Follow these steps to add some noise and use a couple of blending modes to make it look real:

Step 14: Choose Filter ⇨ Noise ⇨ Add Noise.
Once again, use 3% for the amount. This time, change the Distribution to Uniform. Select the Monochromatic check box (14.11). Click OK.

Step 15: Choose Edit ⇨ Fade ⇨ Add Noise or press ⌘/Ctrl+Shift+F to open the Fade dialog box. Set the Opacity to 75% and the Mode to Luminosity.
The result is better, but it's still too smooth. Any hint of the underlying texture is gone.

Step 16: Duplicate the Leg layer by pressing ⌘/Ctrl+J. Rename Leg Copy to Leg Darken. **Rename Leg to** Leg Lighten.

Step 17: Change the Blending Mode of the Leg Lighten layer to Lighten and the Leg Darken layer to Darken.

Step 18: Set the Opacity of Leg Lighten to 60% and Leg Darken to 50% (14.12). **Save the file as** 2062-Q-0201.psd.

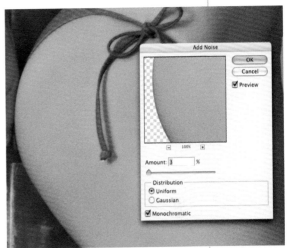

14.11

The combination of the two layers alternately lightens and darkens the textures. The Leg Lighten layer lightens the pixels underneath it while the Leg Darken layer does the same thing for the darker pixels. Lowering the opacity of the layers reveals varying amounts of the underlying texture. Compare the results of the skin on Tia's front leg to that on her side above the bikini. They are very similar. This enhancement is realistic.

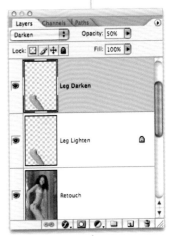

14.12

Performing Touchups

The retouching portion is almost complete. The next step is to get rid of the white fabric that is showing on the ends of the strings and straighten out the twist on the strap on her top.

Step 19: Highlight the Retouch layer. Select the Magic Wand tool from the toolbox and set up the Options bar as shown here.

Step 20: Zoom into 200%. Click the Magic Wand on the white end of the knotted string. Feather the selection 0.3 pixels (14.13).

Step 21: Select the Clone Stamp tool from the toolbox and sample on the wide part of the string. Using a 10-pixel brush, clone the sampled area over the selected white end.

The selection constrains any overcloning. Press ⌘/Ctrl+H to hide the marching ants and check your work (14.14). Repeat for the other two string ends.

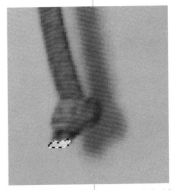

14.13

[357]

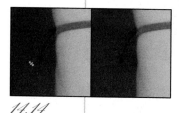

14.14

Note

If the Magic Wand selects an area outside the white, reduce the tolerance. Press Enter and type a lower tolerance number. Press Enter again.

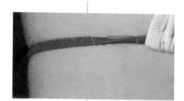

14.15

14.16

14.17

Finally, fix the twist in the strap on the top:

Step 22: **Draw a path around the strap where it would be if it was not twisted (14.15).**
Save the path as **Path 2** or use Path 2 from 2062-Q-0201Map.

Step 23: **⌘/Ctrl+click on Path 2 to load it as a selection (14.16). Feather the selection 1 pixel.**

Step 24: **Return to Layers. Use the Clone Stamp tool to sample the strap to the left of the selection by Option/Alt+clicking. Clone over the selected area.**
The selection constrains the cloning to the strap (14.17). Press ⌘/Ctrl+D to deselect.

Step 25: **Make a new layer above Leg Darken. Hold down the Option/Alt key and choose Merge Visible from the Layer palette's fly-out menu. Rename the layer** Tia. **Hide all the other layers by holding down Option/Alt and clicking the eye icon on the Tia layer.**

That wraps up the retouching and enhancements to Tia. The next section shows you how to take this shot-in-the-lobby photograph into the great sunshine-filled outdoors.

Getting Our Sun-Filled Shot

One of the expectations that editors have of their photographers is that they will get the shot—one way or another. Ideally everything works out on the day of the shoot. And just when did anything ever happen exactly as planned? While I would love to tell you that adding the beach behind Tia was always part of my plan, the truth is the idea didn't happen in Florida. I figured it out while reviewing the Web photo gallery back in the studio. If it had occurred to me during the photography, I would have put a white background behind Tia to make her hair easier to work with. Oh well. The point is that with good skills behind the camera and in front of the computer, the photographer in you can make the image happen.

The three things that make this shot come together are knocking out the background, dealing with Tia's hair, and matching the focus of the replacement scene with the pillars of the fountain. We'll start with the background.

It's Pen tool time again! I can feel your excitement.

Step 1: Use the Pen tool to draw a path around the pillars, ceiling, inside of Tia's hair, and the opening behind her (14.18). (Hint: The pillars are out of focus. Cutting the path into the out-of-focus areas is a good thing.) Save the path as Path 3.
As always, a premade path is available, in this case in 2062-Q-0201Map.psd. Use the technique from the previous section to move the path into place. I encourage you to make your own paths. The Pen tool is so versatile and useful; it is the single most powerful selection tool in Photoshop.

14.18

I know you're eager to open up the background for the sky and ocean scene. Before moving on to that, we need a copy of the hair we are about to remove for later steps.

Step 2: Click off of Path 3 to deselect it and return to Layers. Use the Elliptical Marquee tool to draw a circle around Tia's head, including all of her head and part of the background (14.19).

Step 3: Press ⌘/Ctrl+J to make the selection into a separate layer. Rename it Hair. **Click the eye icon off on the Hair layer.**

Step 4: Click the Tia layer to activate it.

Step 5: Click the Paths palette. ⌘/Ctrl+click Path 3 to turn it into a selection.

14.19

14.20

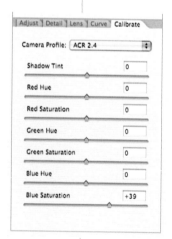

14.21

Step 6: Go back to the Layers palette, hold down the Option/Alt key, and click the Add Layer Mask icon at the bottom of the Layers palette.

The background walls and part of Tia's hair disappear to transparency. They are hidden by the layer mask (14.20).

Step 7: Open 2062-Q-0903.dcr in Camera Raw by double-clicking it in File Browser.

We'll only use the sky and ocean as the background. The image was chosen because Elizabeth is standing to one side, offering a good portion of the background to work with.

Step 8: At the bottom of the Camera Raw dialog box, use these settings: Space: Adobe RGB (1998), Size: 3032 by 2008, Depth: 16 Bits/Channel, and Resolution: 300 pixels/inch. Prepare the Adjust tab as follows: White Balance: As Shot, Temperature: 5450, Tint: +2, Exposure: +0.40, Shadows: 14, Brightness: 50, Contrast: +27, and Saturation: 0. Rotate the image 90 degrees counterclockwise.

One more adjustment in the Camera Raw dialog box will enhance the sky and ocean.

Step 9: Click the Calibrate tab. Increase the Blue Saturation to +39. Click Open (14.21).

Step 10: Select the Move tool (V). Hold down the Shift key and drag 2062-Q-0903.dcr (the file just created from Camera Raw) on top of 2062-Q-0201.psd. Close 2062-Q-0903.dcr without saving.

The photograph of Elizabeth is now covering Tia.

Step 11: Enter Free Transform mode by pressing ⌘/Ctrl+T.

Step 12: Ctrl+click (right-click) inside the photograph to bring up the Free Transform context menu. Choose Flip Horizontal (14.22). Select the Commit Transform check box.

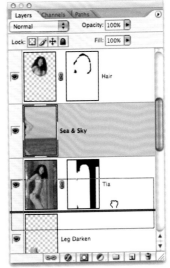

14.22

14.23

Step 13: **Rename Layer 1 to** Sea & Sky. **Click in the thumbnail and drag it just below the Tia layer (14.23).**
Elizabeth is now peeking out behind Tia (14.24).

Step 14: **Select the Move tool from the toolbox. Hold down the Shift key and drag Elizabeth behind the red column on the left.**

Step 15: **Enter Free Transform mode again. Enter** 175% **in the W: field and** 111% **in the H field.**
Notice that Elizabeth's leg shows behind Tia's (14.25).

14.24

14.25

14.26

Step 16: Solve this problem by entering 468.3 pixels in the X field and 1682.8 pixels in the Y field. Select the Commit Transform check box to accept the changes.
The transformation has been done in 16 bit, meaning there will be no loss of image quality in the final file.

Step 17: Choose Image ➪ Duplicate. Rename the file 2062-Q-0201 8-bit.psd.

Step 18: Choose Image ➪ Mode ➪ 8 Bits/Channel. Press ⌘/Ctrl+S to save this file. Click Save in the Save dialog box.
All the 16-bit work is finished (14.26).

Step 19: Save and close 2062-Q-0201.psd.
This keeps all the 16-bit work intact for future use. (Such as when the editor changes her/his mind! Note: I said *when*, not if!)

Fixing Tia's Hair

Tia has one of the worst cases of helmet hair going on. This section deals with extracting her hair from the background on the Hair layer.

Step 1: Select the Hair layer. Option/Alt+click on the eye icon on the Hair layer.
This hides all the other layers. Another way of pulling hair off of a background is by using the Extract filter.

Step 2: Choose Filter ➪ Extract to open the Extract dialog box.

Step 3: Select the Zoom tool from the menu bar on the left of the dialog box. Zoom in until you can see detail in Tia's hair (14.27).

Step 4: Select the Highlighter tool (B). Paint green, the default color, over all the hair that extends into the background. Hold down the spacebar, and click and drag to scroll to a new section. Highlight all around the edges of Tia's hair (14.28). At the bottom of the image, close the circle with green highlight.

14.27

14.28

Step 5: **Select the Fill tool (G) and click inside the highlighted area.**
It fills with blue. Click Preview (14.29).

Step 6: **Click Display in the Preview section of the dialog box. Choose Other from the drop-down menu and choose a shade of blue (14.30). Click OK.**
Review the extraction. It won't look perfect. That's alright. Click OK.

Step 7: **Click the eye icons of the Tia and Sea & Sky layers to reveal them. Click the layer mask thumbnail on Tia to make the layer and the layer mask active.**

14.29

14.30

14.31

14.32

Step 8: Select the Brush tool with a 70-pixel soft-edged brush. Set black as the foreground color. Paint the brown background away where it showed through the layer mask (14.31).

After you modify the layer mask, the result will look like this (14.32). Tia's hair on the right side looks great. On the left it's kind of shabby. The next part of the process enhances the Hair layer. And you won't believe how simple the fix is!

Step 9: Highlight the Hair layer. Duplicate it by pressing ⌘/Ctrl+J.

Done. Yep. It's that simple! Now we'll finesse it a little bit.

Step 10: Merge the Hair copy layer down into the Hair layer by pressing ⌘/Ctrl+E. Add a layer mask to the Hair layer.

Step 11: Paint with black using a 30-pixel 25% hard-edged brush to hide the hair that looks too unreal.

Step 12: Make a new layer and rename it Hair Retouch.

Step 13: Select the Clone Stamp tool. Select the Sample All Layers check box in the Options bar. Option/Alt+click in a thick area of Tia's hair. With a 9-pixel soft-edged brush, fill in the areas that look thin.

Match the color selection areas with the areas being covered as closely as you can. Don't worry about subtle color differences.

Step 14: Get the Healing brush. Select the Sample All Layers check box in the Options bar. Heal any areas that are mismatched in color and texture (14.33).

Now if you are like me, and are really picky about how the hair looks, well, get over it. You and I are the only ones who know exactly what the original photograph looks like. And I'm not telling. No one will know if you keep quiet, too.

Seriously, it only has to look believable, not perfect. This is one of the secrets of working in Photoshop. Hair never looks the same as the original. Some loss of detail always occurs. Following is a set of six quick bonus steps for you if this is truly driving you crazy.

14.33

Step 1: **Highlight the Hair layer. Draw a selection around Tia's hair on the right (14.34).**

Step 2: **Make the selection into its own layer by pressing ⌘/Ctrl+J. Rename the layer** Frizzies.

Step 3: **Open Free Transform (⌘/Ctrl+T) and drag the bounding box to Tia's left side. Rotate the layer by placing the cursor just outside one of the corner handles until the rotate cursor appears. Drag the handle counterclockwise until the hair frizzies are facing out (14.35). Select the Commit Transform check box.**

14.35

14.34

14.36

14.37

Step **4**: Drag the Frizzies layer above the Hair Retouch layer.

Step **5**: Select the Move tool. Drag the frizzies into place.

Step **6**: Add a layer mask to the Frizzies layer and use a black soft-edged brush to blend the sharp edges into Tia's hair (14.36).
Done!

Blurring the Background

The only task left to do is make the background a little more out of focus. The edges of the pillars are too distinct. Look at the original photograph. They are quite soft. The sharpness is a side effect of the layer mask on the Tia layer. We'll handle that first.

Usually the solution is simple. Blur the layer mask on the Tia layer and the pillars will show most of their original softness. In this project, a couple of areas must remain sharp. And there is spillover from another layer. Look at the space between Tia's arms (14.37). Some of the wall from the Hair layer is showing. It comes from making the copy of Tia's Hair too large initially. This kind of thing happens, and here's how to deal with it:

Step **1**: Click the Layer Mask icon in the Hair layer to highlight the layer. With a black brush, paint out the background until only sky shows behind Tia's arm (14.38).

Next you set up the layer needed to bring back some of the sharpness in Tia's arm.

Step 2: Activate the Tia layer and copy it by pressing ⌘/Ctrl+J.
It is automatically named Tia copy.

Step 3: Ctrl+click (right-click) in the Layer Mask icon of the Tia copy layer to show the context menu. Choose Apply Layer Mask (14.39).

Step 4: Holding down the Option/Alt key, click the Add Layer Mask icon.
A black layer mask is added to the Tia copy layer. The next step is to blur the layer mask to bring back the softness of the original.

Step 5: Highlight the Tia layer and click the layer mask. Choose Filter ⇨ Blur ⇨ Gaussian Blur, set a 5.1 pixel radius in the Gaussian Blur dialog box, and click OK.

Step 6: Activate the Tia copy layer by clicking its Layer Mask icon. Zoom in to 100% and scroll to the sky revealed behind Tia's arms.

Step 7: Select the Brush tool from the toolbox. Make the brush 30 pixels in size and soft edged. Set the foreground color to white. Paint over Tia's arms using the soft edge of the brush to blend the out-of-focus pillar into the sharpness of her arm.

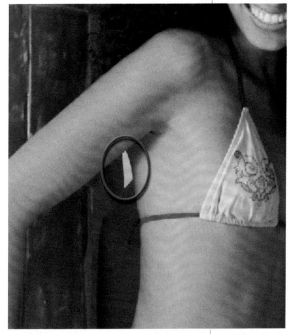

14.38

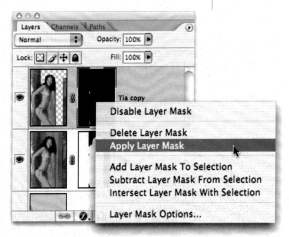

14.39

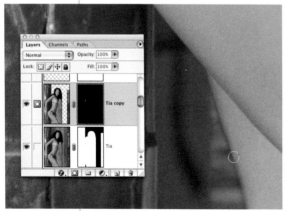

Step *8*: Scroll down to her leg. Paint along the edge of her leg and bring back the sharpness (14.40).

Varying the Depth of Field

There is simply too much foreground-to-horizon detail in the ocean. In a photograph such as the one of Tia, the ocean would continue to get softer as it falls off towards the horizon line. The sky is fine. After all, what is sharp about a sky? This is a job for the Lens Blur filter, which enables you to vary the depth of field.

14.40

As always, some setup is required before you apply the filter for the effect.

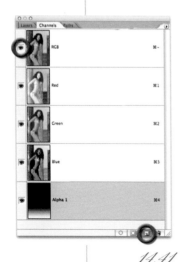

14.41

Step *1*: Click the Gradient tool icon in the toolbox (G). Press D to set the default colors and set black as the foreground color.

Step *2*: Click the Channels tab. Click the Create New Channel icon. Click the RGB channel eye icon to show the image (14.41).

Step *3*: Click at the horizon line, hold down the Shift key, and drag the gradient from the horizon line to the bottom of the frame. It appears in shades of red (14.42).

The Shift key constrains the gradient to being parallel to the horizon. Hide the Alpha 1 channel by clicking its eye icon off. Click the RGB channel.

Step *4*: Return to the Layers palette and click Sea & Sky. Choose Filter ⇨ Blur ⇨ Lens Blur to open the Lens Blur dialog box.

The preview reveals the previous transforms to the layer.

14.42

Step 5: Set the Depth Map source to Alpha 1, the channel with the gradient on it. Set the Blur Focal Distance to 255. In the Iris section choose Hexagon (6) as the Shape. Set the Radius to 86. In the Noise section set the Amount at 3 and the Distribution to Gaussian, and select the Monochromatic check box. Click OK.

Step 6: Make a new layer named Final and merge the visible layers to it by pressing ⌘/Ctrl+Option/Alt+ Shift+E (14.43). Save the file as 2062-Q-0201 8-bit.psd.

14.43

That's it. We have successfully moved a photograph made in the lobby of a hotel out into the sunshine. Now I admit that while making sunshine with Photoshop is not nearly as much fun as actually shooting outside, it has its place. The editor never saw the original and is convinced that she actually saw this scene when she did a media tour of the property a week after the shoot.

A PDF of the editorial as it appeared in *Jezebel* magazine is available on www.amesphoto.com/learning. Click the "Chapter 14" or the "Learn More" link. This project is also featured on my CD, *Studio to Location* from Software Cinema.

Some of the other suits from the indoor shoot are shown here (14.44, 14.45). They, too, went through the process of making sunshine for publication (14.46, 14.47).

14.44

14.45

14.46

14.47

Shooting Later That Same Day

By two o'clock, the rain finally stopped. The sky finally cleared, bringing Florida's claim to fame to center stage. After a quick lunch, we moved to the pool. Don't worry about the models swimming right after eating—I was the one in the water for this series. As you can see from the shot of me in the pool with the camera, the sun was falling with that wonderful late afternoon directional quality that carries so much magic (14.48). It meant, too, that the wall behind the models would be in the shade, lit by the open sky behind me. The sun is coming from the left. A reflector fabric on a 42-in. x 72-in. panel by Chimera Lighting is bouncing the sun onto the girls, opening up the shadows by lowering the contrast (14.49). The sunlight is hitting Tia and Adelina directly. The highlights on the side of Tia's face and on Adelina's suit and torso are burned out completely. The readings in these areas are 255 across the board. The contrast of the situation is too high to capture either with digital or on film. Cutting the exposure would have killed any detail in the shadows.

We controlled the highlights by placing another panel with diffusion fabric to soften the sun coming from the right. The diffusion panel reduces the amount of direct sun so much that the bounce panel on the left side becomes the primary source of light (14.50).

This series of poolside photographs shows the light as it was without manipulation other than the normal Levels or Curves adjustment. When the weather cooperates, not all photographs have to have the huge interventions that the sky replacement project entailed. This page from the editorial shows both the front and rear views of the suit (14.51). The water in the lower right-hand corner of the image provides an ideal space for type.

Photograph courtesy of Bruce, the dentist from Ohio.

14.48

14.49

14.50

As the sun moved lower towards the western horizon, which is artificially high due to surrounding high-rise buildings, we moved our location to the beach. Elite model Elizabeth Suttle had arrived to be fitted during the session at the pool. Justin and I shot Elizabeth in a black diva one-piece suit (14.52) while Tia and Adelina changed into new suits by Huit (14.53). Rotating models this way allowed us to shoot six outfits before sunset. We completed all twelve suits in a single day of shooting. Despite the rain, we completed the shoot a half day early.

14.51

14.52

14.53

Free Transforming Without Loss: Introducing Smart Objects

Smart Objects are brand new to Photoshop CS2. They embed a copy of all of the data in them into the Photoshop document allowing a new level of non-destructive editing. Smart Objects do add size to a file. The flexibility as you'll see in the next exercise is well worth the increase in file size.

Step 1: **Open the file, Transforming Smart Objects.psd by double-clicking it in Bridge.**

The layer stack shows two identical layers, Pixels and Smart Object, side by side (14.54).

14.54

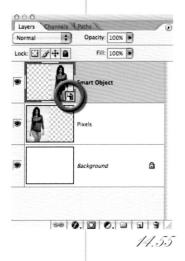

14.55

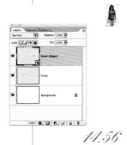

14.56

Step 2: **Click the layer labeled Smart Object to highlight it. Choose Group into New Smart Object from the Layer palette's fly-out menu.**

Notice the thumbnail now has a Smart Object icon in its corner (14.55).

Step 3: **Click Pixels in the layer stack to make it active. Press ⌘/Ctrl+T to enter Free Transform. Click the link icon in the Options bar.**

This constrains the proportions of the width and height entry windows.

Step 4: **Enter 10% in the W field. Pixels shrink in the frame. Select the Commit check box to complete the transformation. Click ⌘/Ctrl+D to deselect.**

Step 5: **Click Smart Object to highlight it. Press ⌘/Ctrl+T to enter Free Transform. Once again click the link icon and enter 10% in the Width field and select the Commit check box.**

Both layers are now 10% of their original size (14.56).

Step 6: **Highlight the Pixels layer. Open Free Transform (⌘/Ctrl+T), click the link icon, and enter 1000% in the Width box. (Yep, that's a BIG move!) Select the Commit check box.**

The result is (no surprise at all) really, really soft.

Step 7: **Click Smart Object to highlight it. Again open Free Transform.**

Notice that a Smart Object retains the size of the previous transformation, in this case 10%. Photoshop actually stores a copy of the original layer and refers to it when making changes to a Smart Object.

Step 8: **Click the link icon, enter 100% in the Width box, and commit the transform.**

Woo-hoo! Smart Object is as sharp as ever (14.57).

Smart Objects can dramatically increase the size of a Photoshop file, which might have been a concern in days gone by. Today, storage both on hard drives and discs is cheap. Use Smart Objects liberally! They are another level of unlimited undos forever!

14.57

Shooting at Sunset

With the sun (which has finally dipped below the horizon) behind the camera, we have maybe 15 minutes of shooting left. Here, Adelina sports a Dolce & Gabbana bikini and a mesh top from Lulu K (14.58). This image was made with available light; there was no fill flash. Here is a simple method for brightening the foreground. Again, the high-bit depth capture of RAW files proves most useful.

Step *1*: **Press ⌘/Ctrl+R in Bridge to open 2062-Q-1233.dcr in the ACR3 dialog box. Rotate the file if necessary.** This version is the background. The settings are designed to enhance the colors of the ocean and the sunset.

14.58

Step 2: **Reduce the exposure setting to –0.50 and increase the shadows to 15.** Leave Contrast and Saturation at their defaults (14.59).

Step 3: **Click the Calibrate tab. Set the Shadow tint to +10, the Red Saturation to +23, the Blue Hue to +19, and the Blue Saturation to +40. Click Open.** The Calibration tab allows you to apply color changes to the linear data of a RAW file. These changes are more robust than those made downstream using the Hue/Saturation adjustment. Any modifications that you can make in Camera Raw will yield a superior result to edits made in 8 or 16 bit.

Step 4: **Save the file as** 2062-Q-1233.psd. **Leave it open in Photoshop.** The foreground looks good. The sky is still a little blown out. Next you use ACR3 to enhance the sunset right from the layer stack.

Step 5: **Choose File ⇨ Place from Photoshop's menu bar. Navigate to 2062-Q-1233.dcr and click Place.** The photograph opens in ACR3.

Step 6: **Bring the Exposure slider down to –150. Lower the Brightness slider to 6 and bump up the Contrast slider to +67. Click Open to place the file in the layer stack as a Smart Object (14.60). It appears in Free Transform mode. Select the Commit check box to finish the placement. Name the layer** Sky and ocean. The sky looks great, but the rest of the image is just too dark.

Step 7: **Add a layer mask to the Smart Object layer (Sky and ocean). Select the Gradient tool from the toolbar. Set white as the foreground color and black as the background color. Set up its Options bar as shown here (14.61).**

Note

Photoshop CS2 has a new command in the File menu—Place. The Place command allows you to add a RAW file to the layer stack as a Smart Object (also new to CS2). You can edit Smart Objects infinitely without any loss of image quality. See "Free Transforming Without Loss: Introducing Smart Objects" earlier in this chapter for more information.

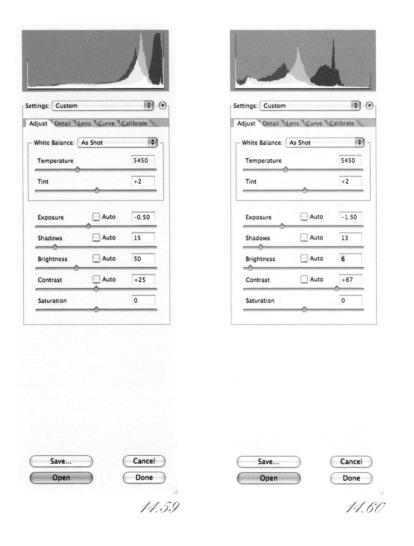

14.59   14.60

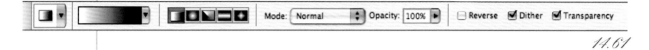

14.61

14.62

Step 8: Draw a gradient onto the layer mask. Click at the top of the frame, press and hold down the Shift key, and drag to the level of Adelina's eyes (14.62).

When you release the mouse button, the gradient fills the layer mask, blending the sunset into the photograph.

Step 9: Click the layer thumbnail of the Smart Object (Sky and ocean) to make it active. Choose File ⇨ Place again and select 2062-Q-1233.dcr again to add it to the layer stack. Name this Smart Object Adelina.

The file opens in ACR3. You would think you could just duplicate the Smart Object in the layer stack and edit the duplicate with different settings. It doesn't work that way. You have to place a new version of the RAW file to have separately editable RAW files in a layer stack or duplicate a placed RAW file by choosing Layers ⇨ Smart Objects ⇨ New Smart Object Via Copy.

Step 10: Bump the Exposure slider up to +1.50. Move the Shadows slider to 9. Move the Brightness and Contrast sliders back to their default settings. Click Open to place the file into the layer stack as a Smart Object. Again select the Commit check box in Free Transform to complete placing it.

The next steps create a mask so only the brighter Adelina on this layer appears in the final version. The efficient way to make a mask is to find one in Channels that's close to what you want, and then modify it to serve instead of starting from scratch. In this case I am looking for the most contrast between Adelina and the ocean.

Step 11: Click the Channels tab grouped with the Layers palette. Press ⌘/Ctrl+1 to view only the red channel.

Look at the green (⌘/Ctrl+2) and the blue (⌘/Ctrl+3) channels. The green channel has the most contrast. Drag it to the New Channel icon at the bottom of the palette. Green copy appears at the bottom. It is highlighted and ready to edit. If you see red, hide the RGB composite channel by clicking its eye icon.

Step *12*: **Press ⌘/Ctrl+L to open the Levels dialog box. Enter** 68, 0.78, **and** 226 **in the Input Levels entry windows to make the ocean brighter and Adelina darker. Click OK (14.63).**

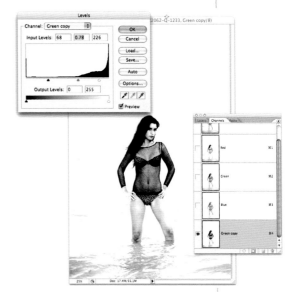

Green copy is what's known as an alpha channel. It will be used to make a selection. Alpha channels work like layer masks. White in an alpha channel reveals what's selected, and black conceals it. The effect I'm going for is to brighten Adelina and nothing else. Adelina is dark in Green copy. The water and sky are lighter, almost white. Using this alpha channel as the basis for combining the lighter Smart Object with the underlying layers, the water would be white and Adelina dark—exactly the opposite of what I want to happen. I want the dark areas (Adelina) to be white and the light areas of the ocean and sky to be black.

14.63

Step *13*: **Choose Image ⇨ Adjustments ⇨ Invert (or press ⌘/Ctrl+I).**
The area's values are now reversed in Green copy.

Step *14*: **Use the Pen tool to draw a path around Adelina. Click the Paths tab. Double-click Work Path to access the Save Path dialog box. Click OK to accept Path 1. Notice that I have completely avoided outlining her hair. For clarity, the path is stroked in green (14.64).**
If you are drawing your own path in this exercise, first of all, congratulations! Second, don't draw it to modify Adelina's shape. You can do that on your own later. If you don't want to draw your own path, open 2062-Q-1233 with path.psd.

Step *15*: **⌘/Ctrl+click on Path 1 in the Paths palette to load it as a selection. Open the Feather Selection dialog box by pressing ⌘/Ctrl+Option/Alt+D. Enter .9 pixels. Click OK (14.65).**

14.64

14.65

14.66

Step 16: Fill the selection with white. Set white as the foreground color, and then press Option+Alt+Delete (Backspace). Zoom in to 200%. Deselect (⌘/Ctrl+D). Get a small brush at 50% hardness and paint white over Adelina's face (14.66).

Step 17: Change the brush's Blending Mode to Overlay. Set the foreground color to black. Reduce the viewing size to 100%.

This Blending Mode protects the white when you're painting with black and vice versa.

Step 18: Enlarge the brush and paint black over the gray areas in the ocean using the brush in the Overlay mode.

When you paint out the reflection where Adelina's legs enter the water, don't worry about painting black into them. The Overlay mode protects the white of her legs (14.67).

Step 19: Press ⌘/Ctrl+~ (tilde) to make the RGB composite channel.

If your keyboard doesn't have the tilde key, click the eye icon for the RGB channel to reveal the channel. The image turns pink.

Step 20: Hide Green copy by clicking its eye icon off. The pink disappears.

The composite channel and the red, green, and blue channels are highlighted.

Step 21: ⌘/Ctrl+click on Green Copy to load it as a selection. Click the Layers tab.

The selection shown by the marching ants surrounds Adelina (14.68).

Step 22: Option/Alt+click the Add Layer Mask icon at the bottom of the Layers palette.

Bang! Adelina jumps off of the background and is way too bright (14.69). The traditional way to compensate for this overlit version is to lower the opacity of the 2062-Q-1233 Adelina layer to around 50%. This layer is really a copy of the original RAW file.

14.67

14.68

14.69

Note

If your Macintosh is running under OSX Panther (version 10.3) or Tiger (version 10.4), the keyboard shortcut for Feather Selection has been reserved for the operating system. It is the shortcut to hide/reveal the Dock. You can get it back by opening Keyboard & Mouse in System Preferences in the Dock. Click the Keyboard Shortcut chicklet. Clear the Automatically Hide and Show the Dock check box.

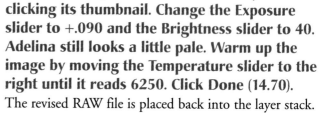

The Department of Redundancy Department

As we reach the end of the last project in the book, I'm sure you've noticed that a lot of the techniques are similar to the point of being redundant. Actually the differences, while slight, offer great finesse over the final result. Choosing the best method to apply in a given situation works only when you have seen many differing ways of doing the same job. Hair has been moved from one background to another at least four distinct ways in the projects in this book alone. Redundancy with differences is a good thing.

Step 23: **Open the Smart Object Adelina in ACR3 by double-clicking its thumbnail. Change the Exposure slider to +.090 and the Brightness slider to 40. Adelina still looks a little pale. Warm up the image by moving the Temperature slider to the right until it reads 6250. Click Done (14.70).** The revised RAW file is placed back into the layer stack.

A day of photography on location is challenging, hectic, and as you have seen, richly rewarding. We all had a great time making these images. The magazine was pleased with the work and ran the editorial just as this book was coming off the press. A location shoot produces more than photographs; it makes memories for all involved. Here is one of my favorites.

The award for Who-Had-The-Most-Fun-On-The-Shoot goes to my assistant, Justin Larose (14.71). Look at that grin. Can you blame him? He's the one in the middle of Tia, Adelina, and Elizabeth! Justin has moved on since this shoot. He has assisted in New York and now shoots full time for Turner Broadcasting.

Well, that's about it. We've worked through many different projects together. Following this chapter is an appendix and, frankly, it's important. It is a list of the people who made the photographs possible: the models, makeup artists, assistants, and stylists. Take a moment to read

14.70

these credits. Without these people and their contributions, this book would not have happened. (If you're curious, the appendix also includes a list of the gear used to make the photographs: the cameras, lenses, lighting equipment, computers, monitors, color management tools, and such.)

Let me know what worked for you in the book. More importantly, tell me what didn't. My e-mail address is kevin@amesphoto.com. I look forward to hearing from you.

Last and most certainly not close to least, thanks for buying this book and for spending your valuable time working with the most popular subject in the history of photography (women) and learning about Photoshop, photography's most fascinating tool.

14.71

Resources

Photoshop CS2: The Art of Photographing Women was written on an Apple Macintosh G-5 Dual 2GHz with Microsoft Word for Mac. The photographs and illustrations were produced on Apple Macintosh G-4 and G-5 computers using Adobe Photoshop CS2. Colors were proofed on a Fuji Pictrography 4500 and in PDF format. The book was produced electronically in Indianapolis, Indiana, with QuarkXpress 6.5 on Apple Macintosh G-5s. The typeface families used are Adobe Garamond, Christiana, and Courier.

Professional Assistance

A photo shoot includes a lot of people. Talent agents help with casting the models. The models work hard to help bring concepts to life. Stylists pull clothes and props, then dress the models and prepare the set as well. Hair and makeup artists bring out the natural beauty that the camera records. Assistants make sure everything is at the photographer's fingertips without being asked. These are the professionals who have made the photographs in *Photoshop CS2: The Art of Photographing Women* happen. If you are working on location in the South, I recommend them.

THE MODELS

LeAnn Campbell, Picture This/Jamestown, TN

Amanda Daniels, Click Models of Atlanta

Heather Donaldson

Tiffany Dupont, Elite/Atlanta and CED Talent/Los Angeles

Marie Friemann

Adelina Guerrero, Elite/Miami

Jennifer Hendrickson, Elite/Atlanta

Tia Hinton, Elite/Atlanta

Adair Howell, Elite/Atlanta

Rachel Keller, Elite/Atlanta

Joanna Lamb, Elite/Atlanta

Amy Lucas, Houghton Talent

Mary Beth Montgomery, Elite/Atlanta

Virgina Morse, NEXT Model Management/Los Angeles

Cara Orten

Christina Parfene, Elite/Atlanta

Laura Phillips, Elite/Atlanta

Mindy Samus

Annie Shu, Elite/Atlanta

Elizabeth Shuttle, Elite/Miami

Carrie Thomas, Elite/Atlanta

Ava Ward, Click Models of Atlanta

Valerie White, Click Models of Atlanta

HAIR AND MAKEUP

Fawn Green for M.A.C., Click Models of Atlanta

Brian Keller, Click Models of Atlanta/Carter Barnes

Janeen Loria, CREWS (www.crewsinc.net or www.moodymakeup.com)

Tracey L. Miller-Smith (www.lightscameralipstick.com)

Paige Schneider, CREWS (www.crewsinc.net)

Nicole Sohn, CREWS (www.crewsinc.net)

Tony & Guy, Atlanta

STYLISTS

L. J. Adams, CREWS (www.crewsinc.net; linda@dlancystreet.com)

Christa Levet, CREWS (www.crewsinc.net)

Jamiya Williams

STYLING ASSISTANTS

Cristle Grizzelle

LaTara Jester

Lakisha Minter

Jamiya Williams

PHOTOGRAPHIC ASSISTANT

Justin Larose (404-808-2381)

CLOTHING AND PROPS

In Atlanta: Almanac, Atlanta Beach, Bano Italian Design, Bob Ellis, Intimacy, Jeffery, L'Asia, Luna, The PropMistress

In New York: Sanyo

RESOURCES

Click Models of Atlanta, Inc., 79 Poplar Street, Suite B, Atlanta, GA 30303; 404-688-9700

CREWS, Shirlene Brooks; 877-504-6880; shrilene@crewsinc.net; www.crewsinc.net

Cunningham, Escot, Dipene Talent Agency, 10635 Santa Monica Blvd., Suite 135, Los Angeles, CA 90025; 310-475-7573; www.cedtalent.com (contact Leslie Cascales at lcascales@cedtalent.com)

Elite Atlanta, 1701 Peachtree Street NW, Suite 210, Atlanta, GA 30309; 404-872-7444 (contact Lois Thigpen at loisthigpen@eliteatlanta.com)

Houghton Talent, 919 Collier Road NW, Atlanta, GA 30318; 404-603-9454 (contact Mystie Buice at mystie@houghtontalent.com)

National Association of Photoshop Professionals, 333 Douglas Road East, Oldsmar, FL 34677; 813-433-5000; www.photoshopuser.com

Photo Barn, 4400 Business Park Court, Lilburn, GA 30047; 770-921-9500; www.photobarn.com

Professional Photographers of America, 229 Peachtree Street NE, Suite 2200, Atlanta, GA 30303; 404-522-8600; www.ppa.com

Professional Photographic Resources, 667 Eleventh Street, Atlanta, GA 30318; 404-885-1885; www.ppratlanta.com

Showcase Photographics, 2323 Cheshire Bridge Road, Atlanta, GA 30324; 404-325-7676; www.showcaseinc.com

Gear

There is a tradition in photography books that the equipment used to make the photographs be listed with each image along with the exposure information. Those using Adobe Photoshop CS2 can find the exposure information in Bridge under the Metadata tab for each of the sample files you downloaded from www .amesphoto.com/learning. Alternatively, choose ⌘/Ctrl+K in Bridge and select Exposure and Focal Length in the Additional Lines of Thumbnail Metadata in the General pane. The cameras, lenses, supports, and lighting equipment used in creating the photographs that appear in *Photoshop CS2: The Art of Photographing Women* are listed here:

CAMERAS, CAMERA SUPPORTS, AND LENSES

Canon 1Ds, Canon 1Ds Mark II with 24-70mm f/2.8 L USM, 70-200mm f/2.8 L USM IS Canon EF lenses (www.canoneos.com)

Foveon Studio Camera with 17-35mm f/2.8, 28-70mm f/2.8 Canon EF lenses (www.foveon.com)

Kodak/Nikon F-5 DCS-760C and Kodak Nikon SLRn with 17-35mm f/2.8D, 28-70mm f/2.8D, and 80-200mm f/2.8D AFS Nikkor lenses (www.kodak.com)

Leaf DCBII mounted on a Fuji GX680II with 80mm and 135mm Fujinon lenses (www.leafamerica.com and www.fujifilm.com)

Sigma SD9 and SD10 cameras with 15-30mm f/3.5-4.5, 20-40mm f/2.8, Sigma DG and 70-200 mm f/2.8 Sigma APO and 180mm f/2.8 Sigma Macro APO lenses (www.sigmaphoto.com)

CAMERA SUPPORTS

Foba Studio Stand (www.sinarbron.com)

Gitzo Studex 1320 and Studex 1509 tripods (www.bogenphoto.com)

LIGHTING STUDIO

Matthews Studio Equipment: C Light Stands, Grip Heads, Grip Arms, Mafer and Matthellini Clamps, Flags, Scrims, and Cookies (www.msegrip.com)

Norman: 2000D, P4000, PH4000 power packs, LH2000 and LH2400 flash heads with reflectors including 22-in. (beauty dish) with grid spot, 16-in. and 10-in. (www.photo-control.com)

Pocket Wizard Plus and MultiMax Studio and Location (www.pocketwizard.com)

Chimera Super Pro II medium and large soft boxes, large strip light with fabric grids, 72-in. x 42-in. light panels with diffusion, white reflective and black fabric panels (www.chimeralighting.com)

LIGHTING LOCATION

Chimera: Super Pro II medium soft boxes, 72-in. x 42-in. light panels with diffusion, white reflective and black fabric panels

Comet CS2400T, CX244, and CL1250 power packs (www.dynalite.com)

Comet CAX Slide, CB-25H, CL-24II flash heads

Lowel Light: Omni Stands, KS Stands, Full Pole

Matthews Studio Equipment: C Light Stands, Grip Heads, Grip Arms, Mafer and Mathellini Clamps

LIGHTING RESOURCES

Chimera Lighting (www.chimeralighting.com)

Comet Electronic Flash (www.dynalite.com)

Lowel-Light Manufacturing (www.lowel.com)

Matthews Studio Equipment (www.msegrip.com)

Norman Electronic Flash (www.photo-control.com)

DIGITAL IMAGING

Apple Macintosh Computers (www.apple.com)

G-5 Dual 2 GHz processor with 4.5GB RAM

G-4 Dual 1.42 GHz processor with 2GB RAM

G-4 PowerBook 1.67 GHz processor with 2GB RAM

LaCie Biggest 800 Terabyte RAIDS (www.lacie.com)

MacBook Pro 2.16 GHz Core Dual processor with 2GB RAM

Other World Computing FireWire 400, 800, and On The Go external drives (www.macsales.com)

SOFTWARE

Adobe Photoshop CS2 (www.adobe.com)

iView Media Pro (www.iview-multimedia.com)

Portfolilo 8.0 (www.extensis.com)

MONITORS

Apple Cinema Displays, 20-in. and 23-in. (www.apple.com)

Barco Reference Calibrator

Radius Press View

GRAPHICS TABLETS

Wacom Cintiq 18

Wacom Intuos3 6 x 8 & 6 x 11 (www.wacom.com)

PRINTERS

Epson 900, 1270, 4800 and 7600 (Ultrachrome Inkset) (www.epson.com)

Fuji Pictrography 3000 (www.fujifilm.com)

HP Designjet 130nr (www.hp.com)

COLOR MANAGEMENT

A to Z Color Consulting (www.atozcolor.com/prod.html)

GretagMacbeth Eye One Publish (www.i1color.com)

X-Rite Pulse (www.xrite.com)

WEB SITE PROGRAMMING

Dynamic Page (www.dynamicpage.com)

SOUNDTRACK

It takes an awful lot of music to write a book. I convert my CDs to MP3 format and play them back with Apple's iTunes, as well as spend way too much money at the iTunes Music Store. Music helps with inspiration on shoots, and the rhythms make the typing faster. The bands and artists whose music contributed to the writing of this book, in no particular order, are

Modest Mouse, Snow Patrol, Beck, Bush, Nora Jones, Sublime, Poe, Alanis Morissette, Alien Ant Farm, Bowling for Soup, Fountains of Wayne, Garbage, Gwen Stefani, Audioslave, The Ataris, The Chevelles, Weezer, Foo Fighters, Blink 182, Nirvana, The Killers, The Knack, The Beatles, Pink Floyd, Led Zeppelin, Franz Ferdinand, Elvis, Three Doors Down, Train, The 5, 6, 7, & 8s, 311, Jimmy Eat World, Jean Michael Jarre, Tenacious D, Keith Jarrett, R.E.M., U2, The Rolling Stones, Steppenwolf, Joan Jett, Pat Benatar, Placebo, The Police, Portishead, Morphine, Cocteau Twins, Red Hot Chili Peppers, Rickie Lee Jones, Sister Hazel, Bare Naked Ladies, Collective Soul, Guster, Smashing Pumpkins, Pearl Jam, Zwan, Yes, Styx, Queen, No Doubt, Cake, Cardigans, Garbage, Chicago, Chumbawamba, Coldplay, Counting Crows, Sheryl Crowe, David Bowie, Dire Straits, Mark Knopfler, Dirty Vegas, Eminem, Cream, Fuel, Filter, Gorillaz, The Laura Glyda Band, The RZA, Heart, Hole, James, The James Gang, Jane's Addiction, The Violent Femmes, John Mayer, Angie Aparo, The Lemonheads, Live, Massive Attack, Madonna, Natalie Imbruglia, Prodigy, Radiohead, Tal Bachman, Stone Temple Pilots, The Thorns, Van Morrison, Wyclef Jean, Pink, and Warren Zevon. We miss you Warren.

Appendix B

Photoshop CS2 Shortcuts and Tools

Many shortcut keys are available in Adobe Photoshop CS2. So many that if you want to set up your own shortcut keys using the command, Edit ➪ Keyboard Shortcuts, you'll find there are not a lot of keys left to use. The point is that you don't have to know them all. Here are the ones I use all the time and ones you might, too.

The shortcuts are listed with the Mac OS commands first and then the commands for Windows (after the slash). For example, the command for Feather is ⌘+Option+D on the Mac and Ctrl+Alt+D in Windows. The Shortcut is written here as ⌘/Ctrl+Option/Alt+D. (By the way, the letters are uppercase for clarity. Don't use uppercase or the caps lock key for any of Photoshop CS2's shortcuts.)

You might think that because I put the Mac commands first I prefer Mac over Windows. The reality is I did it alphabetically by manufacturer. Apple comes before Microsoft.

Menu Shortcuts

Save File	⌘/Ctrl+S
Save File As	⌘/Ctrl+Shift+S
Close File	⌘/Ctrl+W
Close All Open Files	⌘/Ctrl+Option/Alt+W
Levels	⌘/Ctrl+L
Repeat Previous Levels Settings	⌘/Ctrl+Option/Alt+L
Curves	⌘/Ctrl+M
Repeat Previous Curves Settings	⌘/Ctrl+Option/Alt+M
Invert	⌘/Ctrl+I
New Document	⌘/Ctrl+N

Layers

New Layer with New Layer dialog box	⌘/Ctrl+Shift+N
New Layer	⌘/Ctrl+Option/Alt+Shift+N
Merge Down	⌘/Ctrl+E
Merge Visible Layers	⌘/Ctrl+Shift+E
Merge Visible Layers to a New Layer	⌘/Ctrl+Option/Alt+Shift+E
Copy a Selection to a New Layer	⌘/Ctrl+J
Cut a Selection and Paste to a New Layer	⌘/Ctrl+Shift+J
Cycle Forward Through Blending Modes (in the Move tool)	Shift key++ (plus sign)
Cycle Backward Through Blending Modes (in the Move tool)	Shift key+- (minus sign)
Layer Opacity (in the Move tool)	Press keyboard numeral 1 for 10%, 2 for 20%, 3 for 30%, and so on. Press 0 for 100%. Press two keys in rapid succession for in-between numbers (for example, 24 = 24%).

Selections

Select All	⌘/Ctrl+A
Deselect	⌘/Ctrl+D
Feather Selection	⌘/Ctrl+Option/Alt+D*
Inverse Selection	⌘/Ctrl+Shift+I
Hide Selection	⌘/Ctrl+H
Luminosity Selection from RGB Composite	⌘/Ctrl+Option/Alt+~ (tilde key)
Luminosity Selection from Red Channel	⌘/Ctrl+Option/Alt+1
Luminosity Selection from Green Channel	⌘/Ctrl+Option/Alt+2
Luminosity Selection from Blue Channel	⌘/Ctrl+Option/Alt+3

Tools

V	Move tool
M	Marquee tools
L	Lasso tools
W	Magic Wand
C	Crop tool
J	Healing, Patch, and Color Replacement tools
B	Brush and Pencil tools
S	Clone and Pattern Stamp tools
G	Gradient and Paint Bucket tools
A	Path and Direct Selection tools
P	Pen tool and Freeform Pen tool
T	Type tool
U	Shape tools
I	Eye Dropper, Color Sampler, and Measure tools

Tools

Q	Quick Mask mode
F	-Full Screen with Menu Bar (gray background), Full Screen (black background), Standard (Document window)
Brush Size	[(next size smaller),] (next size larger)
Brush Edge Softer	Shift+[(softens the brush 25% per stroke)
Brush Edge Harder	Shift+] (hardens the brush 25% per stroke)

I have not listed all the tools in the toolbox as shortcuts because there are some destructive tools that I never use. (For example, I never use the Eraser tool.) Also, knowing every single keyboard shortcut is not necessary. On the other hand, if you want to prove that you have no life whatsoever, learn the keyboard shortcuts for the blending modes. Here are some of the common ones. Choose the Move tool. Hold down Shift+Option/Alt. Type M for multiply, S for screen, O for overlay, C for color, N for normal. After that their shortcuts are truly intuitive (kidding): G for lighten, K for darken, and E for difference. You can figure out the rest if you'd like. And in spite of this admitted knowledge, I do in fact have a life . . . sort of.

In addition, there is a cool way to customize tool selection. Photoshop's default requires holding down the Shift key and pressing the tool's letter to cycle through the nested options (for example, L+Shift+L cycles from the Lasso tool to the Polygonal Lasso tool). If you go to the General Preferences pane by pressing ⌘/Ctrl+K, and clear the Use Shift Key for Tool Switch checkbox, pressing the letter M and then M again moves between the Rectangular and Elliptical Marquee tools. This is a huge timesaver.

*Macintosh Users—The command for feather is reserved by the system to hide and show the Dock. You can turn this off in System Preferences ➪ Keyboard & Mouse ➪ Keyboard Shortcuts ➪ Dock, Expose, and Dashboard and clear Automatically hide and show the Dock. You might also want to disable ⌘+Option+~ (the shortcut for loading luminosity as a selection in Photoshop) by clearing Move Focus to the window drawer and ⌘+~ (select the RGB composite channel) by clearing Move focus to next window in active application. Surprisingly, this last one still works in applications other than Photoshop when it is cleared. Go figure.

Index

Index

Index

Download the Project Files

All of the files used in *Photoshop CS2: The Art of Photographing Women* are available as free downloads from www.amesphoto.com/learning. The book code is **PW48255**. Other tips, techniques, ideas, extras, and new projects will be posted from time to time making your investment in this book even more valuable. Be sure to add learning@amesphoto.com to your address book so your registration link doesn't become lost in spamworld. E-mail me at learning@amesphoto.com to ask questions or make comments and observations about the book. I look forward to hearing from you.